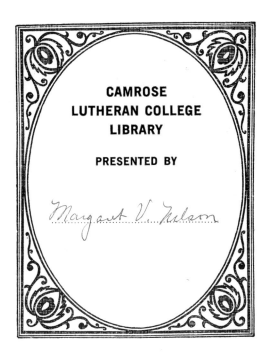

THE NEW AMERICAN POETRY

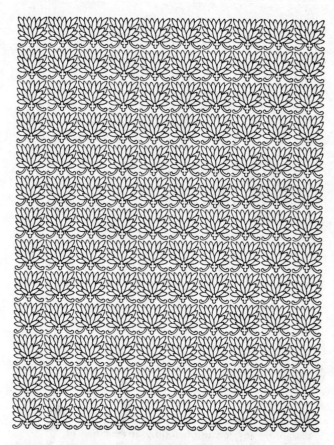

THE NEW AMERICAN POETRY

EDITED BY DONALD M. ALLEN

GROVE PRESS, INC. · NEW YORK
EVERGREEN BOOKS LTD. · LONDON

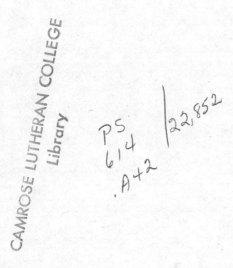

ACKNOWLEDGMENTS AND PERMISSIONS

The editor is indebted to the following poets and their publishers for permission to reprint copyrighted work:

HELEN ADAM: "I Love My Love," by permission of *Extansis*.

BROTHER ANTONINUS: "Advent," by permission of *Timbrel & Choir;* "A Canticle to the Waterbirds" and "The South Coast," from *The Crooked Lines of God* © 1959 by University of Detroit Press, with the author's permission.

JOHN ASHBERY: "A Boy" and "The Instruction Manual," from *Some Trees* © 1956 by Yale University Press, with their permission; "How Much Longer Will I Be Able To Inhabit the Divine Sepulcher . . . ," by permission of *Big Table*.

PAUL BLACKBURN: "The Continuity" by permission of *The Black Mountain Review;* "The Assistance," from *The Dissolving Fabric,* with the permission of The Divers Press; "Night Song for Two Mystics," by permission of *Chicago Review;* and "Sirventes," by permission of *Evergreen Review*.

ROBIN BLASER: "Poem by the Charles River," by permission of *Measure*.

EBBE BORREGAARD: "Some Stories of the Beauty Wapiti," from *The Wapitis,* with the permission of The White Rabbit Press.

RAY BREMSER: "Poem of Holy Madness, Part IV," by permission of *Exodus*.

JAMES BROUGHTON: "Feathers or Lead?" by permission of *Measure*.

PAUL CARROLL: "Father," by permission of *Big Table*.

GREGORY CORSO: "Birthplace Revisited," "Zizi's Lament," "Uccello," and "But I Do Not Need Kindness," from *Gasoline* © 1958 by Gregory Corso, with the permission of City Lights Books; "Poets Hitchhiking on the Highway," "Paranoia in Crete," "A Dreamed Realization," "From Another Room," "Notes After Blacking Out," and "Marriage," from *The Happy Birthday of Death* © 1960 by Gregory Corso, with the permission of New Directions.

ROBERT CREELEY: "The Innocence," from *Le Fou* © 1952 by *Golden Goose,* with the author's permission; "The Kind of Act of," from *The Kind of Act of,* with the permission of The Divers Press; "The Immoral Proposition," from *The Immoral Proposition,* with the permission of Jonathan Williams; "A Counterpoint," "The Warning," and "The Whip," from *All That Is Lovely in Men* © 1955 by Robert Creeley and Dan Rice, with the permission of Jonathan Williams; "A Marriage," from *If You* © 1956 by Robert Creeley, with the author's permission; "If You," "Just Friends," "Ballad of the Despairing Husband," "The Three Ladies," "The Door," and "The Way," from *A Form of Women* © 1959 by Robert Creeley, with the permission of Jargon Books and Corinth Books, Inc.; "The Awakening," by permission of

The editor dedicates his
book to his mother and to
the memory of his father

PREFACE

In the years since the war American poetry has entered upon a singularly rich period. It is a period that has seen published many of the finest achievements of the older generation: William Carlos Williams' *Paterson, The Desert Music and Other Poems,* and *Journey to Love;* Ezra Pound's *The Pisan Cantos, Section: Rock-Drill,* and *Thrones;* H.D.'s later work culminating in her long poem *Helen in Egypt;* and the recent verse of E. E. Cummings, Marianne Moore, and the late Wallace Stevens. A wide variety of poets of the second generation, who emerged in the thirties and forties, have achieved their maturity in this period: Elizabeth Bishop, Edwin Denby, Robert Lowell, Kenneth Rexroth, and Louis Zukofsky, to name only a few very diverse talents. And we can now see that a strong third generation, long awaited but only slowly recognized, has at last emerged.

These new younger poets have written a large body of work, but most of what has been published so far has appeared only in a few little magazines, as broadsheets, pamphlets, and limited editions, or circulated in manuscript; a larger amount of it has reached its growing audience through poetry readings. As it has emerged in Berkeley and San Francisco, Boston, Black Mountain, and New York City, it has shown one common characteristic: a total rejection of all those qualities typical of academic verse. Following the practice and precepts of Ezra Pound and William Carlos Williams, it has built on their achievements and gone on to evolve new conceptions of the poem. These poets have already created their own tradition, their own press, and their public. They are our avant-garde, the true continuers of the modern movement in American poetry. Through their work many are closely allied to modern jazz and abstract expressionist painting, today recognized throughout the world to be America's greatest achievements in contemporary culture. This anthology makes the same claim for the new American poetry, now becoming the dominant movement in the second phase of our twentieth-century literature and already exerting strong influence abroad.

In order to give the reader some sense of the history of the period and the primary alignment of the writers, I have adopted the unusual device of dividing the poets into five large groups, though these divisions are somewhat arbitrary and cannot be taken as rigid categories. Within each of the five sections the poets are ranked by year of birth, and their poems by year of composition as a means of showing the range and variety and sequence of development in an individual writer's work.

The first group includes those poets who were originally closely identified with the two important magazines of the period, *Origin* and *Black Mountain Review,* which first published their mature work. Charles Olson, Robert Duncan, and Robert Creeley were on the staff of Black Mountain College in the early fifties, and Edward Dorn, Joel Oppenheimer, and Jonathan Williams studied there. Paul Blackburn, Paul Carroll, Larry Eigner, and Denise Levertov published work in both magazines but had no connection with the college.

While both publication and instruction at Black Mountain College align Robert Duncan with the first group, he actually emerged in 1947-1949 as a leading poet of the second group, the San Francisco Renaissance, where he was originally associated with Brother Antoninus, Robin Blaser, Jack Spicer and others in Berkeley, and with James Broughton and Madeline Gleason in San Francisco. Helen Adam, chiefly through her superb readings, has helped establish the ballad made new as an important trend in the poetry of the Bay Area; and Lawrence Ferlinghetti, through his readings with jazz bands and his recordings, has recreated a popular oral poetry we have not had since Vachel Lindsay. Bruce Boyd, Kirby Doyle, Richard Duerden, and Philip Lamantia are all natives of the San Francisco area, while Ebbe Borregaard came from Long Island and Lew Welch from the Northwest.

The Beat Generation, the third group, was originally associated with New York, but they first attracted national attention in San Francisco in 1956 when Allen Ginsberg, Jack Kerouac, and Gregory Corso joined Gary Snyder, Philip Whalen, and others in public readings. Three significant publications of 1956-1957 aligned their work with that of many writers of the first, second and fifth groups: *Ark II / Moby I, Black Mountain Review* No. 7, and the "San Francisco Scene" issue of *Evergreen Review.*

John Ashbery, Kenneth Koch, and Frank O'Hara, of the fourth group, the New York Poets, first met at Harvard where they were associated with the Poets' Theatre. They migrated to New York in the early fifties where they met Edward Field, Barbara Guest, and James Schuyler, and worked with the Living Theatre and the Artists' Theatre.

The fifth group has no geographical definition; it includes younger poets who have been associated with and in some cases influenced by the leading writers of the preceding groups, but who have evolved their own original styles and new conceptions of poetry. Philip Whalen and Gary Snyder grew up in the Northwest and became close friends at Reed College, before moving to San Francisco. Both Stuart Perkoff and Michael McClure came to the West Coast from the Midwest, Perkoff to settle in Venice West and McClure in San Francisco, where Ron Loewinsohn and David Meltzer have also moved in recent years. John Wieners studied at Black Mountain College and founded *Measure* in his home town of Boston. Edward Marshall, another New England poet, was first published in *Black Mountain Review;* he makes his home in New York. Gilbert Sorrentino lives in Brooklyn where he edits *Neon,* and LeRoi Jones in New York where he edits *Yūgen.*

Occasionally arbitrary and for the most part more historical than actual, these groups can be justified finally only as a means to give the reader some sense of milieu and to make the anthology more a readable book and less still another collection of "anthology pieces." The statements on poetics, the biographical notes and the bibliography are aids to a more exact understanding of literary history.

Charles Olson's "Projective Verse" essay and his letter to Elaine Feinstein present the dominant new double concept: "composition by field" and the poet's "stance toward reality"; and Robert Creeley's two essays give further definition in this area. Robert Duncan and Denise Levertov define positions which differ sharply from Lawrence Ferlinghetti's or Allen Ginsberg's. James Schuyler describes the ambiance of the New York poets, and Philip Whalen, Gary Snyder, Michael McClure, John Wieners, and LeRoi Jones send back reports from the fronts on which they are engaged. These statements are interim reports by the poets; they lead directly back to the poems, to the actual work of the period, waiting to be read and studied for what it alone can reveal.

The preparation of this anthology presented a series of formidable problems. As I have said, only a fraction of the work has been published, and that for the most part in fugitive pamphlets and little magazines. The field is almost completely uncharted; there is, not very surprisingly, very little first-rate criticism of any of the new poetry, and that little has been written by the poets themselves. Consequently, I have had to go directly to the poets for manuscripts and counsel, and I am heavily indebted to each of them for invaluable aid. Charles Olson, Robert Creeley, Frank O'Hara, and Allen Ginsberg have given me throughout the solid support and encouragement without which I should not have been able to complete this project. I owe almost as large a debt to Robin Blaser, LeRoi Jones and James Schuyler for much needed and deeply appreciated advice and assistance.

D. M. A.

CONTENTS

The New American Poetry: 1945-1960

Contents

Contents

Contents

Contents

Contents

I

CHARLES OLSON

THE KINGFISHERS

1

What does not change / is the will to change

He woke, fully clothed, in his bed. He
remembered only one thing, the birds, how
when he came in, he had gone around the rooms
and got them back in their cage, the green one first,
she with the bad leg, and then the blue,
the one they had hoped was a male

Otherwise? Yes, Fernand, who had talked lispingly of Albers & Angkor Vat.
He had left the party without a word. How he got up, got into his coat,
I do not know. When I saw him, he was at the door, but it did not matter,
he was already sliding along the wall of the night, losing himself
in some crack of the ruins. That it should have been he who said, "The kingfishe
who cares
for their feathers
now?"

His last words had been, "The pool is slime." Suddenly everyone,
ceasing their talk, sat in a row around him, watched
they did not so much hear, or pay attention, they
wondered, looked at each other, smirked, but listened,
he repeated and repeated, could not go beyond his thought
"The pool   the kingfishers' feathers were wealth   why
did the export stop?"

It was then he left

2

I thought of the E on the stone, and of what Mao said
la lumiere"
                    but the kingfisher

2

de l'aurore"
>   but the kingfisher flew west
est devant nous!
>   he got the color of his breast
>   from the heat of the setting sun!

The features are, the feebleness of the feet (syndactylism of the 3rd & 4th digit)
the bill, serrated, sometimes a pronounced beak, the wings
where the color is, short and round, the tail
inconspicuous.

But not these things are the factors. Not the birds.
The legends are
legends. Dead, hung up indoors, the kingfisher
will not indicate a favoring wind,
or avert the thunderbolt. Nor, by its nesting,
still the waters, with the new year, for seven days.
It is true, it does nest with the opening year, but not on the waters.
It nests at the end of a tunnel bored by itself in a bank. There,
six or eight white and translucent eggs are laid, on fishbones
not on bare clay, on bones thrown up in pellets by the birds.

>   On these rejectamenta
as they accumulate they form a cup-shaped structure) the young are born.
And, as they are fed and grow, this nest of excrement and decayed fish become
>   a dripping, fetid mass

Mao concluded:
>   nous devons
>   nous lever
>   et agir!

3
When the attentions change / the jungle
leaps in
>   even the stones are split
>   they rive

Or,
enter
that other conqueror we more naturally recognize
he so resembles ourselves

But the E
cut so rudely on that oldest stone
sounded otherwise,
was differently heard

as, in another time, were treasures used:

(and, later, much later, a fine ear thought
a scarlet coat)

> "of green feathers   feet, beaks and eyes
> of gold
>
> "animals likewise,
> resembling snails
>
> "a large wheel, gold, with figures of unknown four-foots,
> and worked with tufts of leaves, weight
> 3800 ounces
>
> "last, two birds, of thread and featherwork, the quills
> gold, the feet
> gold, the two birds perched on two reeds
> gold, the reeds arising from two embroidered mounds,
> one yellow, the other
> white.
> > "And from each reed hung
> > seven feathered tassels.

In this instance, the priests
(in dark cotton robes, and dirty,
their dishevelled hair matted with blood, and flowing wildly
over their shoulders)
rush in among the people, calling on them
to protect their gods

And all now is war
where so lately there was peace,
and the sweet brotherhood, the use
of tilled fields.

4

Not one death but many,
not accumulation but change, the feed-back proves, the feed-back is
the law

> Into the same river no man steps twice
> When fire dies air dies
> No one remains, nor is, one

Around an appearance, one common model, we grow up
many. Else how is it,
if we remain the same,
we take pleasure now
in what we did not take pleasure before? love
contrary objects? admire and/or find fault? use
other words, feel other passions, have
nor figure, appearance, disposition, tissue
the same?

> To be in different states without a change
> is not a possibility

We can be precise. The factors are
in the animal and/or the machine the factors are
communication and/or control, both involve
the message. And what is the message? The message is
a discrete or continuous sequence of measurable events distributed in time

is the birth of air, is
the birth of water, is
a state between
the origin and
the end, between
birth and the beginning of
another fetid nest

is change, presents
no more than itself

And the too strong grasping of it,
when it is pressed together and condensed,
loses it

This very thing you are

II

>   They buried their dead in a sitting posture
>   serpent   cane   razor   ray of the sun

>   And she sprinkled water on the head of the child, crying
>   "Cioa-coatl! Cioa-coatl!"
>   with her face to the west

>   Where the bones are found, in each personal heap
>   with what each enjoyed, there is always
>   the Mongolian louse

The light is in the east. Yes. And we must rise, act. Yet
in the west, despite the apparent darkness (the whiteness
which covers all), if you look, if you can bear, if you can, long enough

>   as long as it was necessary for him, my guide
>   to look into the yellow of that longest-lasting rose

so you must, and, in that whiteness, into that face, with what candor, look

and, considering the dryness of the place
        the long absence of an adequate race

>   (of the two who first came, each a conquistador, one healed, the oth
>   tore the eastern idols down, toppled
>   the temple walls, which, says the excuser
>   were black from human gore)

hear
hear, where the dry blood talks
        where the old appetite walks

>   la piu saporita et migliore
>   che si possa truovar al mondo

where it hides, look
in the eye how it runs
in the flesh / chalk

                              but under these petals
                              in the emptiness
                              regard the light, contemplate
                              the flower

whence it arose

                         with what violence benevolence is bought
                         what cost in gesture justice brings
                         what wrongs domestic rights involve
                         what stalks
                         this silence

                         what pudor pejorocracy affronts
                         how awe, night-rest and neighborhood can rot
                         what breeds where dirtiness is law
                         what crawls
                         below

                                        III

I am no Greek, hath not th'advantage.
And of course, no Roman:
he can take no risk that matters,
the risk of beauty least of all.

But I have my kin, if for no other reason than
(as he said, next of kin) I commit myself, and,
given my freedom, I'd be a cad
if I didn't. Which is most true.

It works out this way, despite the disadvantage.
I offer, in explanation, a quote:
si j'ai du goût, ce n'est guères
que pour la terre et les pierres

Despite the discrepancy (an ocean   courage   age)
this is also true: if I have any taste
it is only because I have interested myself
in what was slain in the sun

          I pose you your question:

shall you uncover honey / where maggots are?

    I hunt among stones

1949

I, MAXIMUS OF GLOUCESTER, TO YOU

By ear, he sd.

But that which matters, that which insists, that which will last
where shall you find it, my people, how, where shall you listen
when all is become billboards, when all, even silence, is
when even the gulls,
my roofs,
when even you, when sound itself

        Where, Portygee Hill, she sang
        and over the water, at Tarr's
        (the water glowed, the light west,
        black, gold, the tide
        outward at evening

        The fixed bells rang, their voices
        came like boats over the oil-slicks,
        like milkweed hulls

        And a man slumped,
        attentionless,
        against pink shingles

            (sea city

    2
one loves only form,
and form only comes
into existence when
the thing is born

        born of yourself, born
        of hay and cotton struts

of street-pickings, wharves, weeds
you carry in, my bird

of a bone of a fish
of a straw, or will
of a color, of a bell
of yourself, torn

(o bird
o kylix, o
Antony of Padua
sweep low, bless
the roofs,
the gentle steep ones
on whose ridge-poles the gulls sit,
from which they depart

And the flake-racks
of my city

3

ove is form, and cannot be without
mportant substance (the weight, say, 50 carats, each one of us, perforce,
ur own goldsmith's scale (feather to feather added,
nd what is mineral, what is curling hair, what string
ou carry in your nervous beak, these
nake bulk, these, in the end, are
um

(o my lady of good voyage
in whose arm,
in whose left arm rests no boy
but a carefully carved wood, a painted
schooner
a delicate mast, a bow-sprit

for forwarding

4

e underpart is, though stemmed, uncertain
, as sex is, as moneys are, facts
be dealt with as the sea is, the demand

that they be played by, that they only can be, that they must
be played by, said he coldly,
the ear

But love is not easy,
and how shall you know,
New England, now
that pejorocracy is here, now
that street-cars, o Oregon, twitter
in the afternoon, offend
a gold-black loin?

how shall you strike,
swordfisherman, the blue-red back
when, last night, your aim
was mu-sick, mu-sick, mu-sick
and not the cribbage game?

>   (o Gloucesterman,
>   weave your birds and fingers
>   new, your roof-tops
>   clean shat on, racks
>   sunned on
>
>   American, braid
>   with others like you, such
>   extricable surface
>   as faun and oral satyr lesbos vase
>   o kill kill kill kill kill
>   those
>   who advertise you
>   out

>   5

in, the bow-sprit, bird, beak
in, the act is in, goes in, the form
what holds, what you make, what is
the object, strut, strut

what you are, what you must be, what you can
right now hereinafter erect

Off-shore, by islands in the blood, I, Maximus, tell y
(as I see it, over the waters, from this place
where I am, where I hear, where I can still hear

from where I carry you a feather
as though, sharply, I picked up,
in the first of morning delivered you,
a jewel, it flashing
more than a wing, than any old romantic thing
than memory, than place, than any thing other than

that which you also carry, than that which is
(call it a nest) around the bend of, call it
the next
second

1950

THE SONGS OF MAXIMUS

SONG 1

colored pictures
of all things to eat: dirty
postcards
And words, words, words
all over everything
No eyes or ears left
to do their own doings (all

invaded, appropriated, outraged, all senses

including the mind, that worker on what is

And that other sense
made to give even the most wretched, or any of us, wretched,
that consolation (greased
lulled
even the street-cars

song

SONG 2

       all
wrong
       And I am asked — ask myself (I, too, covered
with the gurry of it) where
shall we go from here, what can we do
when even the public conveyances
sing?
       how can we go anywhere,
even cross-town
           how get out of anywhere (the bodies
all buried
in shallow graves?

SONG 3

       This morning of the small snow
I count the blessings, the leak in the faucet
which makes of the sink time, the drop
of the water on water as sweet
as the Seth Thomas
in the old kitchen
my father stood in his drawers to wind (always
he forgot the 30th day, as I don't want to remember
the rent
       a house these days
so much somebody else's,
especially,
Congoleum's

       Or the plumbing,
that it doesn't work, this I like, have even used paper clips
as well as string to hold the ball up   And flush it
with my hand
       But that the car doesn't, that no moving things moves
without that song I'd void my ear of, the musickracket
of all ownership . . .

                    Holes
in my shoes, that's all right, my fly
gaping, me out
at the elbows, the blessing
                    that difficulties are once more

            "In the midst of plenty, walk
            as close to
            bare
                    In the face of sweetness,
            piss
                    In the time of goodness,
            go side, go
            smashing, beat them, go as
            (as near as you can

            tear

            In the land of plenty, have
            nothing to do with it
                            take the way of
            the lowest,
            including your legs, go
            contrary, go

            sing

SONG 4

I know a house made of mud & wattles,
I know a dress just sewed
                    (saw the wind
blow its cotton
against her body
from the ankle
            so!
it was Nike

        And her feet: such bones
I could have had the tears
that lovely pedant had

who couldn't unwrap it himself, had to ask them to, on the schooner's deck

and he looked,
the first human eyes to look again
at the start of human motion (just last week
300,000,000 years ago
                    She
was going fast
across the square, the water
this time of year, that
scarce

And the fish

SONG 5

I have seen faces of want,
and have not wanted the FAO: Appleseed
's gone back to
what any of us
New England

SONG 6

you sing, you

who also

wants

                                                        1951

MAXIMUS, TO HIMSELF

I have had to learn the simplest things
last. Which made for difficulties.
Even at sea I was slow, to get the hand out, or to cross
a wet deck.
              The sea was not, finally, my trade.
But even my trade, at it, I stood estranged

from that which was most familiar. Was delayed,
and not content with the man's argument
that such postponement
is now the nature of
obedience,

>   that we are all late
>   in a slow time,
>   that we grow up many
>   And the single
>   is not easily
>   known

It could be, though the sharpness (the *achiote*)
I note in others,
makes more sense
than my own distances. The agilities

>   they show daily
>   who do the world's
>   businesses
>   And who do nature's
>   as I have no sense
>   I have done either

I have made dialogues,
have discussed ancient texts,
have thrown what light I could, offered
what pleasures
doceat allows

>   But the known?
This, I have had to be given,
a life, love, and from one man
the world.

>   Tokens.
>   But sitting here
>   I look out as a wind
>   and water man, testing
>   And missing
>   some proof

I know the quarters
of the weather, where it comes from,
where it goes. But the stem of me,
this I took from their welcome,
or their rejection, of me

> And my arrogance
> was neither diminished
> nor increased,
> by the communication

2
It is undone business
I speak of, this morning,
with the sea
stretching out
from my feet

1953

THE DEATH OF EUROPE

(a funeral poem for Rainer M. Gerhardt)

Rainer,
the man who was about to celebrate his 52nd birthday
the day I learned of your death at 28, said:
"I lie out on Dionysius' tongue"!

the sort of language you talked, and I did,
correctingly —
        as I heard this other German wrongly,
from his accent, and because I was thinking of you,
talking of how much you gave us all hearing
in Germany (as I watch a salamander on the end of a dead pine branch
snagging flies), what I heard this man almost twice your age say was,
"I lie out on a dinosaur's tongue"!

for my sense, still, is that,
despite your sophistication
and your immense labors . . .

It will take some telling. It has to do with what WCW
(of all that you published in *fragmente,* to see Bill's
R R BUMS in futura!

                              it has to do with how far back are
Americans,
as well as,
Germans

                              "walk on spongey feet
                              if you would cross

                              carry purslane
                              if you get into her bed

                              guard the changes
                              when you scratch your ear

       I
It is this business
that you should die!
Who shot up,
out of the ruins,
and hung there,
in the sky,
the first of Europe
I could have words with:

as Holderlin on Patmos you
trying to hold bay leaves
on a cinder block!

                              Now I can only console you,
                              sing of willows,
                              and dead branches,
                              worry the meanness
                              that you do not live,
                              wear the ashes
                              of loss

                              Neither of us
                         carrying a stick
                         any more

Creeley told me
how you lived

    II
I have urged anyone
back (as Williams asked
that Sam Houston
be recognized
              as I said,
Rainer, plant
your ash

      "I drive a stake into the ground, isn't it silly,"
I said out loud in the night, "to drive a stake into the ground?"

How primitive
does one have to get? Or,

as you and I were both open
to the charge: how large

can a quote

get, he

said, eyeing me

with a blue

eye

                         Were your eyes

                         brown, Rainer?

                         Rainer,

                         who is in the ground,

                         what did you look like?

Did you die of your head bursting

like a land-mine?

Did you walk

on your own unplanted self?

III

It is not hell you came into,
or came out of. It is not moly
any of us are given. It is merely
that we are possessed of
the irascible. We are blind
not from the darkness
but by creation we are
moles. We are let out
sightless, and thus miss
what we are given, what woman
is, what your two sons
looking out of a picture at me,
sitting on some small hillside —

they have brown eyes, surely.

Rainer, the thyrsus
is down

I can no longer
put anything
into your hands

It does no good
for me to wish
to arm you

I can only carry laurel,
and some red flowers,
mere memorials, not cut
with my own knife an oar
for you, last poet
of a civilization

                              You are nowhere
                              but in the ground

    IV
What breaks my heart
is that your grandfather
did not do better, that our grandmothers
(I think we agreed)
did not tell us
the proper tales

so that we are as raw
as our inventions, have not the teeth
to bite off Grandfather's
paws

(O, Rainer,
you should have ridden your bike
across the Atlantic instead of your mind,
that bothered itself too much
with how we were hanging on
to the horse's tail, fared, fared
we who had Sam Houston, not
Ulysses

                              I can only cry: Those
                              who gave you not enough
                              caused you to settle for
                              too little
                                        The ground
                              is now the sky

    V
But even Bill
is not protected,
no swift messenger
puts pussley
even in his hand,
open,

as it is, no one says how
to eat
at the hairy table

         (as your scalp
also lifted,
         as your ears
did not stay

silk

                O my collapsed brother,
                the body
                does bring us
                down
                      The images
                have to be
                contradicted
                          The metamorphoses
                are to be
                undone

                The stick,
                and the ear

                are to be no more than

                they are: the cedar

                and the lebanon

                of this impossible

                life.

                I give you no visit

                to your mother.

                What you have left us

                is what you did

                It is enough

It is what we

praise

I take back

the stick.

I open my hand

to throw dirt

into your grave

I praise you

who watched the riding

on the horse's back

It was your glory to know

that we must mount

O that the Earth

had to be given to you

this way!

O Rainer, rest

in the false

peace

Let us who live

try

                                                        1954

A NEWLY DISCOVERED 'HOMERIC' HYMN

(for Jane Harrison, if she were alive)

Hail and beware the dead who will talk life until you are blue
in the face. And you will not understand what is wrong,

they will not be blue, they will have tears in their eyes,
they will seem to you so much more full of life
than the rest of us, and they will ask so much, not of you no
but of life, they will cry, isn't it this way, if it isn't
I don't care for it, and you will feel the blackmail, you will not know
what to answer, it will all have become one mass

Hail and beware them, for they come from where you have not been,
they come from where you cannot have come, they come into life
by a different gate. They come from a place which is not easily known,
it is known only to those who have died. They carry seeds
you must not touch, you must not touch the pot they taste of,
no one must touch the pot, no one must, in their season.

Hail and beware them, in their season. Take care. Prepare
to receive them, they carry what the living cannot do without,
but take the proper precautions, do the prescribed things, let
down the thread from the right shoulder. And from the forehead.
And listen to what they say, listen to the talk, hear
every word of it — they are drunk from the pot, they speak
like no living man may speak, they have the seeds in their mouth —
listen, and beware

Hail them solely that they have the seeds in their mouth, they
are drunk, you cannot do without a drunkenness, seeds can't,
they must be soaked in the contents of the pot, they must be all one mass.
But you who live cannot know what else the seeds must be. Hail
and beware the earth, where the dead come from. Life
is not of the earth. The dead are of the earth. Hail and beware
the earth, where the pot is buried.

Greet the dead in the dead man's time. He is drunk of the pot.
He speaks like spring does. He will deceive you. You are meant
to be deceived. You must observe the drunkenness. You are not to
drink. But you must hear, and see. You must beware.

Hail them, and fall off. Fall off! The drink is not yours,
it is not yours! You do not come
from the same place, you do not suffer as the dead do,
they do not suffer, they need, because they have drunk of the pot,

hey need. Do not drink of the pot, do not touch it. Do not touch
hem.

       Beware the dead. And hail them. They teach you drunkenness.
You have your own place to drink. Hail and beware them, when they come.

                                                    1955

THE LORDLY AND ISOLATE SATYRS

The lordly and isolate Satyrs — look at them come in
on the left side of the beach
like a motorcycle club! And the handsomest of them,
the one who has a woman, driving that snazzy
convertible
            Wow, did you ever see even in a museum
such a collection of boddisatvahs, the way
they come up to their stop, each of them
as though it was a rudder
the way they have to sit above it
and come to a stop on it, the monumental solidity
of themselves, the Easter Island
they make of the beach, the Red-headed Men

                     These are the Androgynes,
the Fathers behind the father, the Great Halves

Or as that one was, inside his pants, the Yiddish poet
a vegetarian. Or another — all in his mouth — a snarl
of the Sources. Or the one I loved most, who once,
once only, let go the pain, the night he got drunk,
and I put him to bed, and he said, Bad blood.

        Or the one who cracks and doesn't know
that what he thinks are a thousand questions are suddenly
a thousand lumps thrown up where the cloaca
again has burst: one looks into the face and exactly as suddenly
it isn't the large eyes and nose but the ridiculously small mouth
which you are looking down as one end of

                                                    — as the Snarled Man
is a monocyte.

          Hail the ambiguous Fathers, and look closely
at them, they are the unadmitted, the club of Themselves,
weary riders, but who sit upon the landscape as the Great
Stønes. And only have fun among themselves. They are
the lonely ones

          Hail them, and watch out. The rest of us,
on the beach as we had previously known it, did not know
there was this left side. As they came riding in from the sea
— we did not notice them until they were already creating
the beach we had not known was there — but we assume
they came in from the sea. We assume that. We don't know.

          In any case the whole sea was now a hemisphere,
and our eyes like half a fly's, we saw twice as much. Every-
thing opened, even if the newcomers just sat, didn't,
for an instant, pay us any attention. We were as we had been,
in that respect. We were as usual, the children were being fed pop
and potato chips, and everyone was sprawled as people are
on a beach. Something had happened but the change
wasn't at all evident. A few drops of rain
would have made more of a disturbance.

          There we were. They, in occupation of the whole view
in front of us and off to the left where we were not used to look.
And we, watching them pant from their exertions, and talk to each other,
the one in the convertible the only one who seemed to be circulating.
And he was dressed in magnificent clothes, and the woman with him
a dazzling blond, the new dye making her hair a delicious
streaked ash. She was as distant as the others. She sat in her flesh too.

          These are our counterparts, the unknown ones.

They are here. We do not look upon them as invaders. Dimensionally

they are larger than we — all but the woman. But we are not suddenly

small. We are as we are. We don't even move, on the beach.

It is a stasis. Across nothing at all we stare at them.
We can see what they are. They don't notice us. They have merely
and suddenly moved in. They occupy our view. They are between us
and the ocean. And they have given us a whole new half of beach.

As of this moment, there is nothing else to report.
It is Easter Island transplanted to us. With the sun, and a warm
summer day, and sails out on the harbor they're here, the Con-
temporaries. They have come in.

Except for the stirring of the leader, they are still
catching their breath. They are almost like scooters the way
they sit there, up a little, on their thing. It is as though
the extra effort of it tired them the most. Yet that just there
was where their weight and separateness — their immensities —
lay. Why they seem like boddisatvahs. The only thing one noticed
is the way their face breaks when they call across to each other.
Or actually speak quite quietly, not wasting breath. But the face
loses all containment, they are fifteen year old boys at the moment
they speak to each other. They are not gods. They are not even stone.
They are doubles. They are only Source. When they act like us
they go to pieces. One notices then that their skin
is only creased like red-neck farmers. And that they are all
freckled. The red-headed people have the hardest time
to possess themselves. Is it because they were over-
fired? Or why — even to their beautiful women — do the red ones
have only that half of the weight?

We look at them, and begin to know. We begin to see
who they are. We see why they are satyrs, and why one half
of the beach was unknown to us. And now that it is known,
now that the beach goes all the way to the headland we thought
we were huddling ourselves up against, it turns out it is the
same. It is beach. The Visitors — Resters — who, by being there,
made manifest what we had not known — that the beach fronted wholly
to the sea — have only done that, completed the beach.

The difference is
we are more on it. The beauty of the white of the sun's light, the

blue the water is, and the sky, the movement on the painted lands-
cape, the boy-town the scene was, is now pierced with angels and
with fire. And winter's ice shall be as brilliant in its time as
life truly is, as Nature is only the offerer, and it is we
who look to see what the beauty is.

> These visitors, now stirring
to advance, to go on wherever they do go restlessly never completing
their tour, going off on their motorcycles, each alone except for
the handsome one, isolate huge creatures wearing down nothing as
they go, their huge third leg like carborundum, only the vault
of their being taking rest, the awkward boddhas

> We stay. And watch them
gather themselves up. We have no feeling except love. They are not
ours. They are of another name. These are what the gods are. They
look like us. They are only in all parts larger. But the size is
only different. The difference is, they are not here, they are not
on this beach in this sun which, tomorrow, when we come to swim,
will be another summer day. They can't talk to us. We have no desire
to stop them any more than, as they made their camp, only possibly
the woman in the convertible one might have wanted to be familiar
with. The Leader was too much as they.

> They go. And the day

> *1956*

AS THE DEAD PREY UPON US

As the dead prey upon us,
they are the dead in ourselves,
awake, my sleeping ones, I cry out to you,
disentangle the nets of being!

I pushed my car, it had been sitting so long unused.
I thought the tires looked as though they only needed air.
But suddenly the huge underbody was above me,
> and the rear tires

were masses of rubber and thread variously clinging together

as were the dead souls in the living room, gathered
about my mother, some of them taking care to pass
beneath the beam of the movie projector, some record
playing on the victrola, and all of them
desperate with the tawdriness of their life in hell

I turned to the young man on my right and asked, "How is it,
there?" And he begged me protestingly don't ask, we are poor
poor. And the whole room was suddenly posters
                                        and presentations
of brake linings and other automotive accessories, cardboard
displays, the dead roaming from one to another
as bored back in life as they are in hell, poor and doomed
to mere equipments

                    my mother, as alive as ever she was, asleep
when I entered the house, as I often found her, in a rocker
under the lamp, and awakening, as I came up to her,
                                        as she ever had

I found out she returns to the house once a week, and with her
the throng of the unknown young, who center on her
                                        as much in death
as other like suited and dressed people did in life

O the dead!

                    And the Indian woman and I
                    enabled the blue deer
                    to walk

                    and when it got to the kitchen,
                    out of our sight,
                    it talked
                    Negro talk.

                    It was like walking a jackass,
                    and its talk
                    was the pressing gabber of gammers,
                    of old women

We helped walk it around the room
because it was seeking socks
or shoes for its hooves
now that it was acquiring

human possibilities

In the five hindrances men and angels
stay caught in the net, in the immense nets
which spread out across each plane of being, the multiple nets
which hamper at each step of the ladders as the angels
and the demons
and men
go up and down

Walk the jackass
Hear the victrola
Let the automobile
be tucked into a corner of the white fence
when it is a white chair. Purity

is only an instant of being. The trammels

recur

In the five hindrances, perfection
is hidden

I shall get to the place
10 minutes late.

It will be 20 minutes
of 9. And I don't know,

without the car,

how I shall get there

O peace, my mother, I do not know how differently
                                        I could have done
what I did or did not do.

That you are back each week
That you fall asleep with your face to the right

That you are as present there when I come in
as you were when you were alive

That you are as solid, and your flesh
is as I knew it, that you have the company
I am used to your having

but oh that you all find it such a cheapness!

o peace, mother, for the mammothness
of the comings and goings of the ladders of life

The nets we are entangled in. Awake,
my soul, let the power into the last wrinkle
of being, let none of the threads and rubber of the tires
be left upon the earth. Let even your mother
go. Let there be only paradise

The desperateness is, that the instant
which is also paradise (paradise
is happiness) dissolves
into the next instant, and power
flows to meet the next occurrence

Is it any wonder
my mother comes back?
Do not that throng
rightly seek the room
where they might expect
happiness? They did not complain
of life, they obviously wanted
to see the movie, each other, merely to pass
among each other there,
where the real is, even to the display cards,
to be out of hell

The poverty
of hell

O souls, in life and in death,
awake, even as you sleep, even in sleep
know what wind

even under the rearend of the ugly automobile
lifts it away, clears the sodden weights of goods,
equipment, entertainment, the foods the Indian woman,
the filthy blue deer, the 4 by 3 foot 'Viewbook,'
the heaviness of the old house, the stuffed inner room,
lifts the sodden nets

> and they disappear as ghosts do,
> as spider webs, nothing
> before the hand of man

> The vent! You must have the vent,
> or you shall die, which means
> never to die, the ghastliness

> of going, and forever
> coming back, returning
> to the instants which were not lived

> O mother, this I could not have done,
> I could not have lived what you didn't,
> I am myself netted in my own being

> I want to die. I want to make that instant, too,
> perfect

> O my soul, slip
> the cog

II

The death in life (death itself)
is endless. Eternity
is a false cause

The knot is otherwise, each topological corner
presents itself, and no sword
cuts it, each knot is itself its fire

Each knot of which the nets are made
is for the hands to untake
the knot's making, and touch alone
can turn the knot into its own flame

             (o mother, if you had once touched me

             o mother, if I had once touched you)

The car did not burn. Its underside
was not presented to me
a grotesque corpse. The old man

merely removed it as I looked up at it.
He carefully put it in a corner of the picket fence
like — was it my mother's white dog?

or a child's chair

             The woman,
             playing on the grass,
             with her son (the woman next door)

             was angry with me whatever it was
             slipped across the playpen or whatever
             she had out there on the grass

             And I was quite flip in reply that
             anyone who used plastic
             had to expect things to skid

             and to break, that I couldn't worry
             that her son might have been hurt
             by whatever it was I sent skidding

             down on them.

             It was just then I went into my house
             and to my utter astonishment
             found my mother sitting there

             as she always had sat, as must she always
             forever sit there her head lolling
             into sleep? Awake, awake my mother

             what wind will lift you too
             forever from the tawdriness,
             make you rich as all those souls

             crave crave crave

to be rich?

And right they are. We must have
what we want. We cannot afford
not to. We have only one course:

the nets which entangle us are flames

O souls, burn
alive, burn now

that you may forever
have peace, have

what you crave

O souls,
go into everything,
let not one knot pass
through your fingers

Let not any they tell you
you must sleep as the knots come
through your authentic hands

What passes
is what is, what shall be, what has
been, what hell and heaven is
is earth to be rent, to shoot you
through the screen of flame which each knot
hides as all knots are a wall ready
to be shot open by you

The nets of being
are only eternal if you sleep as your hands
ought to be busy. Method, method
I too call on you to come
to the aid of all men, to women most
who know most, to woman to tell
men to awake. Awake, men,
awake

I ask my mother
to sleep. I ask her
to stay in the chair.
My chair
is in the corner of the fence.
She sits by the fireplace made of paving stones. The blue deer
need not trouble either of us.

And if she sits in happiness the souls
who trouble her and me
will also rest. The automobile

has been hauled away.

                                                              1956

VARIATIONS DONE FOR GERALD VAN DE WIELE

I. LE BONHEUR

dogwood flakes
what is green

the petals
from the apple
blow on the road

mourning doves
mark the sway
of the afternoon, bees
dig the plum blossoms

the morning
stands up straight, the night
is blue from the full of the April moon

iris and lilac, birds
birds, yellow flowers
white flowers, the Diesel
does not let up dragging
the plow

                as the whippoorwill,
the night's tractor, grinds

his song

         and no other birds but us
are as busy (O saisons, o chateaux!

Délires!

        What soul
is without fault?

Nobody studies
happiness

Every time the cock crows
I salute him

I have no longer any excuse
for envy. My life

has been given its orders: the seasons
seize

the soul and the body, and make mock
of any dispersed effort. The hour of death

is the only trespass

II. THE CHARGE

dog wood flakes
the green

the petals from the apple-trees
fall for the feet to walk on

the birds are so many they are
loud, in the afternoon

they distract, as so many bees do
suddenly all over the place

With spring one knows today to see
that in the morning each thing

is separate but by noon
they have melted into each other

and by night only crazy things
like the full moon and the whippoorwill

and us, are busy. We are busy
if we can get by that whiskered bird,

that nightjar, and get across, the moon
is our conversation, she will say

what soul
isn't in default?

can you afford not to make
the magical study

which happiness is? do you hear
the cock when he crows? do you know the charge,

that you shall have no envy, that your life
has its orders, that the seasons

seize you too, that no body and soul are one
if they are not wrought

in this retort? that other wise efforts
are efforts? And that the hour of your flight

will be the hour of your death?

III. SPRING

The dogwood
lights up the day.

The April moon
flakes the night.

Birds, suddenly,
are a multitude

The flowers are ravined
by bees, the fruit blossoms

are thrown to the ground, the wind
the rain forces everything. Noise —

even the night is drummed
by whippoorwills, and we get

as busy, we plow, we move,
we break out, we love. The secret

which got lost neither hides
nor reveals itself, it shows forth

tokens. And we rush
to catch up. The body

whips the soul. In its great desire
it demands the elixir

In the roar of spring,
transmutations. Envy

drags herself off. The fault of the body and the soul
— that they are not one —

the matutinal cock clangs
and singleness: we salute you

season of no bungling

1956

THE DISTANCES

So the distances are Galatea

and one does fall in love and desires
mastery

old Zeus — young Augustus

Love knows no distance, no place

is that far away or heat changes
into signals, and control

old Zeus — young Augustus

Death is a loving matter, then, a horror
                              we cannot bide, and avoid
by greedy life

          we think all living things are precious
          — Pygmalions

                        a German inventor in Key West
who had a Cuban girl, and kept her, after her death
in his bed
                        after her family retrieved her

he stole the body again from the vault

Torso on torso in either direction,
                young Augustus
                     out via nothing where messages
are

       or in, down La Cluny's steps to the old man sitting
a god throned on torsoes,

            old Zeus

Sons go there hopefully as though there was a secret, the object
to undo distance?
                    They huddle there, at the bottom
of the shaft, against one young bum

                 or two loving cheeks,

       Augustus?

You can teach the young nothing
                 all of them go away, Aphrodite
tricks it out,

          old Zeus — young Augustus

Charles Olson

You have love, and no object

                        or you have all pressed to your nose
which is too close,

        old Zeus hiding in your chin your young
        Galatea

the girl who makes you weep, and you keep the corpse live by all
your arts

        whose cheek do you stroke when you stroke the stone face
        of young Augustus, made for bed in a military camp,
        o Caesar?

O love who places all where each is, as they are, for every moment,
yield

        to this man

                that the impossible distance
be healed,

        that young Augustus
        and old Zeus

be enclosed

        "I wake you,
stone. Love this man."

                              17 October 1959

ROBERT DUNCAN

THE SONG OF THE BORDERGUARD

The man with his lion under the shed of wars
sheds his belief as if he shed tears.
The sound of words waits —
a barbarian host at the borderline of sense.

The enamord guards desert their posts
harkening to the lion-smell of a poem
that rings in their ears.

    — Dreams, a certain guard said,
    were never designd so
    to re-arrange an empire.

    Along about six o'clock I take out my guitar
    and sing to a lion
    who sleeps like a line of poetry
    in the shed of wars.

The man shedding his belief
knows that the lion is not asleep,
does not dream, is never asleep,
is a wide-awake poem
waiting like a lover for the disrobing of the guard;
the beautiful boundaries of the empire
naked, rapt round in the smell of a lion.

(The barbarians have passd over the significant phrase)

    — When I was asleep,
        a certain guard says,
    a man shed his clothes as if he shed tears
        and appeard as a lonely lion
    waiting for a song under the shed-roof of wars.

40

I sang the song that he waited to hear,
I, the Prize-Winner, the Poet Acclaimd.

Dear, dear, dear, dear, I sang,
believe, believe, believe, believe.
The shed of wars is splendid as the sky,
houses our waiting like a pure song
housing in its words the lion-smell
        of the beloved disrobed.

I sang: believe, believe, believe.

            I the guard because of my guitar
believe. I am the certain guard,
certain of the Beloved, certain of the Lion,
certain of the Empire. I with my guitar.
Dear, dear, dear, dear, I sing.
I, the Prize-Winner, the Poet on Guard.

The borderlines of sense in the morning light
are naked as a line of poetry in a war.

1951

AN OWL IS AN ONLY BIRD OF POETRY

a vale for James Broughton

A cross leaves marks the tree we fancy.
        Regular art rules.
        Under hand beauty demands
the secret howl to cross the table
        on bloody stumps
            were wings added later to mar
the 17th century flying style.

INCLUDE A PRAYER
include lions rise or as sentences raised,
include fore gone conclusions in a maze,
include my blind in designing your window,
include my window in raising your blind,
include a long time in my forever yours,

include April and July in all your years,
include the lions eye that sheds the lambs tears,
include the lambs eye or as paragraphs rest,
include the bird that belongs to each beast,

include:

include the breasts and Mary's face,
include the horns of the cow in Grace,
include the words in pasture are kind,
include the scream when he starts to pray,
include the sun at the opening of day,
include the night in what you find,

Small lions are kittens and love to purr.

include the fathering Night and Day,
include the orders descending thru words,
include the elegances of no rhyme,
include the roar of a lion in triumph,
include break orderly converse to address divine disorders
    abruptly,
include the tree upon which our life hangs,
include the metaphor in which from that tree Christ is crucified,
include all martyrs in the sense of fun,
include chairs and tables as comfortable things,
include the bird in the angel with wings,

FIGURE 1
    The vowels are physical
    corridors of the imagination
    emitting passionately
    breaths of flame. In a poem
    the vowels appear like
    the flutterings of an owl
    caught in a web and give
    aweful intimations of
    eternal life.

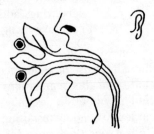

FIGURE 2

The consonants are a church of
hands interlocking,   stops
and measures of fingerings
that confine the spirit to
articulations of space and time.

•

It is in the disorders of the net that the stars fall from
the designs we grasp into their original chaos.

He flies thru a time which his wing creates. MEASURES.
As the immortal Dali has painted him. He is erected upon
the cross of vision as we see him.

•

SONG

What do you see, my little one?
I see an owl hung in a tree.
His blood flows from his side.
Earthly things may rest tonight,
all heavenly fear hangs there.
I see a nest where owlets cry
and eat the cold night air.

What do you see, my little one?
I see an owl hung in a tree
like flesh hung on a bone.
The thorns of flesh run thru and thru.
Ring out the tones of life.
He builds the artifice of heart
and takes his word to wife.

What do you see, my little one?
I see an owl hung in a tree
among the letters whispering there,
a tongue of speech that beats
the passages of mere air.
The ladders of tone pass into words,

> the words pass into song.
> The heavenly orders sing to me.
> I see an owl hung in a tree.

FINALE. DISARRANGEMENTS AS JOY.
> This is an owl in time.　Of night.
> too late / too soon / flies

out of Minerva's head into her thought.

> Reappears. On snowy wings.
> Disconsolate Valentine.

> I go along with him. As I send him.

> The joy
is a great scuttering of feathers words
> a whirl
up words into an airy sentence where
> reader
by reader accepts his mixd whether
> of love
face by face in his poem's crackd mirror.

This is an owl as he flies out of himself
into the heart that reflects all owl.

Who gives his hoot for joy as his flies.

> Alights.

1955

THIS PLACE RUMORD TO HAVE BEEN
SODOM

> > might have been.
Certainly these ashes might have been pleasures.
Pilgrims on their way toward the Holy Places remark
this place. Isn't it plain to all
that these mounds were palaces? This was once
a city among men, a gathering together of spirit?
It was measured by the Lord and found wanting.

It was measured by the Lord and found wanting,
destroyd by the angels that inhabit longing.
Surely this is Great Sodom where such cries
as if men were birds flying up from the swamp
ring in our ears, where such fears that were once
desires walk, almost spectacular,
stalking the desolate circles, red-eyed.

This place rumord to have been a City surely was,
separated from us by the hand of the Lord.
The devout have laid out gardens in the desert,
drawn water from springs where the light was blighted.
How tenderly they must attend these friendships
or all is lost. All *is* lost.
Only the faithful hold this place green.

Only the faithful hold this place green
where the crown of fiery thorns descends.
Men that once lusted grow listless. A spirit
wrappd in a cloud, ashes more than ashes,
fire more than fire, ascends.
Only those new friends gather joyous here,
where the world like Great Sodom lies under fear.

The world like Great Sodom lies under love
and knows not the hand of the Lord that moves.
This the friends teach where such cries
as if men were birds fly up from the crowds
gatherd and howling in the heat of the sun.
In the Lord Whom the friends have named at last Love
the Images and Love of the friends never die.

This place rumord to have been Sodom is blessd
in the Lord's eyes.

THE DANCE

from its dancers circulates among the other
              dancers. This
would-have-been-feverish cool excess of
              movement makes
each man   hit the pitch   co-
              ordinate.

Lovely their feet pound the green solid meadow,
              the dancers
mimic flowers — root, stem, stamen and petal
              our words are
our articulations,   our
              measures.

It is the joy that exceeds pleasure.

    You have passd the count, she said
or I understood from her eyes. Now

old Friedl has grown so lovely in my years,

    I remember only the truth.
    I swear by my yearning.
    You have conquerd the yearning, she said
    the numbers have enterd your feet . . .

        Turn,   turn,   turn

    when you're real gone, boy,   sweet boy . . .

    Where have I gone, Beloved?

    into the Waltz, Dancer.

Lovely our circulations sweeten the meadow.
In Ruben's riotous scene the May dancers teach us our
  learning seeks abandon!

Maximus calld us to dance the Man.
We calld him   to call
    season   out of season-
d mind!

         Lovely
join we to dance green to the meadow.

Whitman was right. Our names are left
      like leaves of grass,
likeness and liking,   the human greenness

tough as grass that survives cruelest seasons.

      I see now a radiance.
      The dancers are gone.
      They lie in heaps exhausted,
      dead tired we say.

      They'll sleep until noon.

      But I returned early
      for the silence,
      for the lovely pang that is

         a flower

      returned to the silent dance-ground.

That was my job that summer. I'd dance until three, then
up to get the hall swept before nine — beer bottles,
cigarette butts, paper mementos of the night before.
Writing it down now, it is the aftermath, the silence I
remember. Part of the dance too, an articulation of the
time of dancing. Like the almost dead sleeping. I've
got it in a poem, about Friedl, moaning in the depths of.
But that was another room. Part of my description. What
I see is a meadow . . .

      I'll slip away before they're up
         and see the dew shining.

THE QUESTION

Have you a gold cup
dedicated to thought
that is like clear water
held in a flower?

or sheen of the gold
burnishd on wood
to furnish fire-glow,
a burning in sight only?

color of gold, feel of gold,
weight of gold? Does the old alchemist
speak in metaphor
of a spiritual splendor?

or does he remember
how that metal is malleable?
chalice workd of gold at the altar,
chasuble elaborated in gold?

in Cuzco llamas of solid gold in the *Inti Pampa*,
the Sun's field with Stars, Lightning, Rainbow, Moon
round it?   or at Fort Knox impounded?
what wealth without show?

When money at last moves a free medium
using work as measure, justified
to needs man's common nature heeds,
will there be riches for public pleasure?

Will the good metal return
to use?   gold leaf to the house roof?
our treasure above ground
sure glow for the eye to see?

For tho *les malades imaginaires*,
who puddle in their psyches
to suck their own bones, declare
lucre is shit,

gold is to the artisan potent
for beauty; and money remains
"the growing grass that can nourish the living sheep,"
real only as that manly trust

we know as the field of accumulated good,
the keep
of justice our labors
that the gold head of the wheat thrive

for the common bread.
Work the old images from the hoard!
el trabajo en oro that gives wealth semblance
and furnishes ground for the gods to flourish.

O have you a service of rich gold
to illustrate the board of public goods?
as in the old days regalia of gold
to show wherein the spirit had food?

1957

A POEM BEGINNING WITH A LINE
BY PINDAR

I

The light foot hears you and the brightness begins,
god-step at the margins of thought,
    quick adulterous tread at the heart.
Who is it that goes there?
    Where I see your quick face
notes of an old music pace the air,
torso-reverberations of a Grecian lyre.

In Goya's canvas Cupid and Psyche
have a hurt voluptuous grace
bruised by redemption. The copper light
falling upon the brown boy's slight body
is carnal fate that sends the soul wailing

up from blind innocence, ensnared
    by dimness
into the deprivations of desiring sight.

But the eyes in Goya's painting are soft,
diffuse with rapture absorb the flame.
Their bodies yield out of strength.
    Waves of visual pleasure
wrap them in a sorrow previous to their impatience.

A bronze of yearning, a rose that burns
    the tips of their bodies, lips,
ends of fingers, nipples.   He is not wingd.
His thighs are flesh, are clouds
    lit by the sun in its going down,
hot luminescence at the loins of the visible.

      But they are not in a landscape.
      They exist in an obscurity.

The wind spreading the sail serves them.
The two jealous sisters eager for her ruin
    serve them.
That she is ignorant, ignorant of what Love will be,
    serves them.
The dark serves them.
The oil scalding his shoulder serves them,
serves their story. Fate, spinning,
    knots the threads for Love.

Jealousy, ignorance, the hurt . . serve them.

    II

This is magic. It is passionate dispersion.
What if they grow old? The gods
    would not allow it.
    Psyche is preserved.

In time we see a tragedy, a loss of beauty
    the glittering youth

of the god retains — but from this threshold
     it is age
that is beautiful. It is toward the old poets
     we go, to their faltering,
their unaltering wrongness that has style,
     their variable truth,
     the old faces,
words shed like tears from
a plenitude of powers time stores.

A stroke. These little strokes. A chill.
     The old man, feeble, does not recoil.
Recall. A phase so minute,
     only a part of the word in- jerrd.

     The Thundermakers descend,

damerging a nuve.   A nerb.
     The present dented of the U
nighted stayd.   States.   The heavy clod?
     Cloud.   Invades the brain.   What

     if lilacs last in *this* dooryard bloomd?

Hoover, Roosevelt, Truman, Eisenhower —
where among these did the power reside
that moves the heart? What flower of the nation
bride-sweet broke to the whole rapture?
Hoover, Coolidge, Harding, Wilson
hear the factories of human misery turning out commodities.
For whom are the holy matins of the heart ringing?
Noble men in the quiet of morning hear
Indians singing the continent's violent requiem.
Harding, Wilson, Taft, Roosevelt,
idiots fumbling at the bride's door,
hear the cries of men in meaningless debt and war.
Where among these did the spirit reside
that restores the land to productive order?
McKinley, Cleveland, Harrison, Arthur,
Garfield, Hayes, Grant, Johnson,

dwell in the roots of the heart's rancor.
How sad "amid lanes and through old woods"
    echoes Whitman's love for Lincoln!

There is no continuity then.   Only a few
    posts of the good remain.   I too
that am a nation sustain the damage
    where smokes of continual ravage
obscure the flame.
                It is across great scars of wrong
    I reach toward the song of kindred men
    and strike again the naked string
old Whitman sang from. Glorious mistake!
    that cried:

    "The theme is creative and has vista."
    "He is the president of regulation."

I see always the under side turning,
fumes that injure the tender landscape.
    From which up break
lilac blossoms of courage in daily act
    striving to meet a natural measure.

    III   *(for Charles Olson)*

                Psyche's tasks — the sorting of seeds
wheat   barley   oats   poppy   coriander
anise   beans   lentils   peas   — every grain
                in its right place
                            before nightfall;

gathering gold wool from the cannibal sheep
(for the soul must weep
    and come near upon death);

harrowing Hell for a casket Proserpina keeps
                            that must not
    be opend . . containing beauty?

no!   melancholy coild like a serpent

                              that is deadly sleep
            we are not permitted
                              to succumb to.

            These are the old tasks.
            You've heard them before.

            They must be impossible.   Psyche
            must despair, be brought to her
                                        insect instructor;
            must obey the counsels of the green reed;
            saved from suicide by a tower speaking,
                follow to the letter
                freakish instructions.

In the story the ants help. The old man at Pisa
            mixd in whose mind
(to draw the sorts) are all seeds
            as a lone ant from a broken ant-hill
had part restored by an insect, was
            upheld by a lizard

                    (to draw the sorts)
the wind is part of the process
                    defines a nation of the wind —

            father of many notions —

                                Who?
let the light into the dark? began
the many movements of the passion?

                                West
from east   men push.
                    The islands are blessd
(cursed) that swim below the sun.

        Man upon whom the sun has gone down!

            There is the hero who struggles east
widdershins to free the dawn   and must
                    woo Night's daughter,

sorcery, black passionate rage, covetous queens,
so that the fleecy sun go   back from Troy,
  Colchis, India . . all the blazing armies
spent, he must struggle alone toward the pyres of Day.

      The light that is Love
rushes on toward passion. It verges upon dark.
  Roses and blood flood the clouds.
  Solitary first riders advance into legend.

 This land, where I stand, was all legend
in my grandfathers' time : cattle raiders,
  animal tribes, priests, gold.
It was the West. Its vistas painters saw
  in diffuse light, in melancholy,
in abysses left by glaciers as if they had been the sun
  primordial carving empty enormities
      out of the rock.

    Snakes lurkd
guarding secrets. Those first ones
      survived solitude.

  Scientia
holding the lamp, driven by doubt;
Eros naked in foreknowledge
smiling in his sleep;   and the light
spilld, burning his shoulder   —the outrage
  that conquers legend —
passion, dismay, longing, search
  flooding up where
the Beloved is lost.   Psyche travels
life after life, my life, station
  after station,
to be tried

  without break, without
news, knowing only   — but what did she know?
  The oracle at Miletus had spoken
truth surely: that he was Serpent-Desire

　　　　that flies through the air,
a monster-husband. But she saw him fair

whom Apollo's mouthpiece said spread
　　　　pain
beyond cure　to those
　　　　wounded by his arrows.

Rilke torn by a rose thorn
blackend toward Eros.　Cupidinous Death!
　　　　that will not take no for an answer.

　　　IV

　　　　Oh yes!　Bless the footfall where
step by step the boundary walker
(in Maverick Road the snow
thud by thud　from the roof
circling the house　— another tread)

　　　　that foot　informed
by the weight of all things
　　　　that can be elusive
no more than a nearness to the mind
　　　　of a single image

　　　　　　　Oh yes!　this
most dear
　　　　the catalyst force that renders clear
the days of a life from the surrounding medium!

　　　　　　Yes, beautiful rare wilderness!
wildness that verifies strength of my tame mind,
　　　　clearing held against Indians,
health that prepared to meet death,
　　　　the stubborn hymns going up
into the ramifications of the hostile air

　　　　that, deceptive, gives way.

Who is there?　O, light the light!
　　　　The Indians give way,　the clearing falls.

Great Death gives way   and unprepares us.
    Lust gives way.   The Moon gives way.
Night gives way.   Minutely, the Day gains.

She saw the body of her beloved
    dismemberd in waking . . or was it
in sight? *Finders Keepers* we sang
    when we were children   or were taught to sing
before our histories began   and we began
    who were beloved   our animal life
toward the Beloved,   sworn to be Keepers.

    On the hill before the wind came
the grass moved toward the one sea,
    blade after blade dancing in waves.

There the children turn the ring to the left.
There the children turn the ring to the right.
    Dancing . .   Dancing . .

And the lonely psyche goes up through the boy to the king
    that in the caves of history dreams.
Round and round the children turn.
    London Bridge that is a kingdom falls.

We have come so far that all the old stories
    whisper once more.
Mount Segur, Mount Victoire, Mount Tamalpais . .
    rise to adore the mystery of Love.

(An ode? Pindar's art, the editors tell us, was not a statue but
a mosaic, an accumulation of metaphor. But if he was archaic
not classic, a survival of obsolete mode, there may have been old
voices in the survival that directed the heart. So a line from a
hymn came from a novel I was reading to help me. Psyche,
poised to leap   — and Pindar too, the editors write, goes too far,
topples over —   listend to a tower that said *Listen to me!* The
oracle had said *Despair! The Gods themselves abhor his power.*
And then the virgin flower of the dark falls back flesh of our flesh
from which everywhere . . .

the information flows
    that is yearning. A line of Pindar
moves from the area of my lamp
    toward morning.

In the dawn that is nowhere
    I have seen the willful children

clockwise and counter-clockwise turning.

1958

FOOD FOR FIRE, FOOD FOR THOUGHT

good wood
that all fiery youth burst forth from winter,
    go to sleep in the poem.
Who will remember thy green flame,
    thy dream's amber?

Language obeyd flares tongues in obscure matter.

    We trace faces in clouds: they drift apart.
    Palaces of air. The sun dying down
        sets them on fire.

    Descry shadows on the flood from its dazzling mood,
    or at its shore read runes upon the sand
        from sea-spume.

This is what I wanted for the last poem.
A loosening of conventions and return to open form.

    Leonardo saw figures that were stains upon a wall.
    Let the apparitions containd in the ground
        play as they will.

You have carried a branch of tomorrow into the room.
Its fragrance had awakend me. No . .

    It was the sound of a fire on the hearth
    Leapd up where you bankd it

. . . sparks of delight. Now I return the thought

   to the red glow, that might-be-magical blood,
   palaces of heat in the fire's mouth,

If you look you will see the salamander —

   to the very elements that attend us,
   fairies of the fire, the radiant crawling . .

That was a long time ago.
No. They were never really there,

   though once I saw — did I stare
   into the heart of desire burning
   and see a radiant man? like those
   fancy cities from fire into fire falling?

We are close enough to childhood, so easily purged
of whatever we thought we were to be.

   Flamey threads of firstness go out from your touch,

   flickers of unlikely heat
   at the edge of our belief bud forth.

DREAM DATA

The young Japanese son was in love with a servant boy.
To be in love! Don't you remember how the whole world is
   governd
by a fact that embraces
         everything that happens,
rendering tender and more real
        the details of the crowded dressing room, back-
stage, a closet off the hall, an office or
       storeroom, where furtively,
among file cabinets   — but with what joy of disclosure!
       every gesture

full filld, more than is sensible.
   And youth in love with youth!
   Tomorrow they will be twenty years
old, and being in love will go
   into the aloofness the Mother in the dream counseld.
   Hold yourself above your body, she said.
The unstaind sleeves of raw silk falling from her arms flung
  dramatically above her head to show
   her defiance of – of caring?
Or was it defiance? There was,
did she say, an aesthetic
   stronger than sex? And below,
the Prince in his laboratory, assisted by the boy,
   experimented in sensations, used as conductors
strains and sink-stoppers he applied to the flesh of the face,
   bringing it in touch, a mechanical ground
in place of hurting. Beyond
   thru an open door they referrd to
tanks or cribs in each which male torsos.
   At the eve of August, Lammas tide of desire,
deformd? mutilated? They were objects of or subjected to
preservation. Without love, dead in being alive,
   alive-dead. Inhabitants of Lammas,
bathers in hell's baths. *These,* the Prince said,
   when I was in love
   were always with me where I was.

                1959

DENISE LEVERTOV

BEYOND THE END

In 'nature' there's no choice —
                              flowers
swing their heads in the wind, sun & moon
        are as they are. But we seem
almost to have it (not just
        available death)

It's energy: a spider's thread: not to
'go on living' but to quicken, to activate: extend:
        Some have it, they force it —
with work or laughter or even
        the act of buying, if that's
all they can lay hands on —

        the girls crowding the stores, where light,
            colour, solid dreams are — what gay
        desire! It's their festival,
            ring game, wassail, mystery.

It has no grace like that of
the grass, the humble rhythms, the
falling & rising of leaf and star;
it's barely
a constant. Like salt:
take it or leave it

The 'hewers of wood' & so on; every damn
craftsman has it while he's working
        but it's not
a question of work: some
shine with it, in repose. Maybe it is
response, the will to respond — ('reason
can give nothing at all / like

60

the response to desire') maybe
a gritting of the teeth, to go
just that much further, beyond the end
beyond whatever ends: to begin, to be, to defy.

THE HANDS

            Don't forget the crablike
hands, slithering
            among the keys.
                  Eyes shut, the downstream
      play of sound lifts away from
the present, drifts you
                  off your feet : too easily let off.

      So look: that almost painful
            movement restores the pull, incites
               the head with the heart : a tension, as of
               actors at rehearsal, who move
this way, that way, on a bare stage, testing
            their diagonals, in common clothes.

                                                1953

MERRITT PARKWAY

      As if it were
forever that they move, that we
      keep moving —

               Under a wan sky where
               as the lights went on a star
                  pierced the haze and now
               follows steadily
                              a constant
               above our six lanes
               the dreamlike continuum . . .

And the people — ourselves!
   the humans from inside the
   cars, apparent
   only at gasoline stops
                              unsure,
         eyeing each other

            drink coffee hastily at the
            slot machines and hurry
         back to the cars
            vanish
            into them forever, to
            keep moving —

Houses now and then beyond the
sealed road, the trees / trees, bushes
passing by, passing
      the cars that
            keep moving ahead of

      us, past us, pressing behind us
                              and
                  over left, those that come
            toward us shining too brightly
moving relentlessly

      in six lanes, gliding
      north and south, speeding with
      a slurred sound —

                                          1954

THE WAY THROUGH

Let the rain plunge radiant
through sulky thunder
rage on rooftops

let it scissor and bounce its denials
on concrete slabs and black
roadways. Flood the streets. It's much

but not enough, not yet: persist,
rain, real rain, sensuous,
swift, released from

vague skies, the tedium
up there.

Under scared bucking trees
the beach road washed out —

trying to get by on the verge
is no good, earth crumbles into the
brown waterfall, but he backs up
the old car again and CHARGES.

The water flies in the halfwit's eyes
who didn't move fast enough
"Who do you think I am, a horse?"
but we made it —

Drown us, lose us,
rain, let us loose, so,
to lose ourselves, to career
up the plunge of the hill

1955

THE THIRD DIMENSION

Who'd believe me if
I said, 'They took and

split me open from
scalp to crotch, and

still I'm alive, and
walk around pleased with

the sun and all
the world's bounty.' Honesty

isn't so simple:
a simple honesty is

nothing but a lie.
Don't the trees

hide the wind between
their leaves and

speak in whispers?
The third dimension

hides itself.
If the roadmen

crack stones, the
stones are stones:

but love
cracked me open

and I'm
alive to

tell the tale — but not
honestly:

the words
change it. Let it be —

here in the sweet sun
— a fiction, while I

breathe and
change pace.

SCENES FROM THE LIFE OF THE PEPPERTREES

I

The peppertrees, the peppertrees!

Cats are stretching in the doorways,
sure of everything. It is morning.
    But the peppertrees

stand aside in diffidence, with berries
of modest red.
                    Branch above branch, an air
of lightness; of shadows
scattered lightly.
                    A cat
closes upon its shadow.
Up and up goes the sun,
sure of everything.
                    The peppertrees
                              shiver a little.
Robust
and soot-black, the cat
leaps to a low branch. Leaves
close about him.

    II
The yellow moon dreamily
tipping buttons of light
down among the leaves. Marimba,
marimba — from beyond the
black street.
                    Somebody dancing,
somebody
          getting the hell
outta here. Shadows of cats
weave round the treetrunks,
the exposed knotty roots.

    III
The man on the bed sleeping
defenseless. Look —
his bare long feet together
sideways, keeping each other
warm. And the foreshortened shoulders,
the head
barely visible. He is good.
Let him sleep.
                    But the third peppertree

is restless, twitching
thin leaves in the light
of afternoon. After a while
it walks over and taps
on the upstairs window with a bunch
of red berries. Will he wake?

1956

THE SHARKS

Well, then, the last day the sharks appeared.
Dark fins appear, innocent
as if in fair warning. The sea becomes
sinister, are they everywhere?
I tell you, they break six feet of water.
Isn't it the same sea, and won't we
play in it any more?
I liked it clear and not
too calm, enough waves
to fly in on. For the first time
I dared to swim out of my depth.
It was sundown when they came, the time
when a sheen of copper stills the sea,
not dark enough for moonlight, clear enough
to see them easily. Dark
the sharp lift of the fins.

THE FIVE-DAY RAIN

The washing hanging from the lemon tree
in the rain
and the grass long and coarse.

Sequence broken, tension
of bitter-orange sunlight
frayed off.

         So light a rain

fine shreds
pending above the rigid leaves.

Wear scarlet! Tear the green lemons
off the tree!   I don't want
to forget who I am, what has burned in me,
and hang limp and clean, an empty dress —

PLEASURES

I like to find
what's not found
at once, but lies

within something of another nature,
in repose, distinct.
Gull feathers of glass, hidden

in white pulp: the bones of squid
which I pull out and lay
blade by blade on the draining board —

tapered as if for swiftness, to pierce
the heart, but fragile, substance
belying design.   Or a fruit, *mamey,*

cased in rough brown peel, the flesh
rose-amber, and the seed:
the seed a stone of wood, carved and

polished, walnut-colored, formed
like a brazilnut, but large,
large enough to fill
the hungry palm of a hand.

I like the juicy stem of grass that grows
within the coarser leaf folded round,
and the butteryellow glow
in the narrow flute from which the morning-glory
opens blue and cool on a hot morning.

                                                      1957

THE GODDESS

She in whose lipservice
I passed my time,
whose name I knew, but not her face,
came upon me where I lay in Lie Castle!

Flung me across the room, and
room after room (hitting the walls, re-
bounding — to the last
sticky wall — wrenching away from it
pulled hair out!)
till I lay
outside the outer walls!

There in cold air
lying still where her hand had thrown me,
I tasted the mud that splattered my lips:
the seeds of a forest were in it,
asleep and growing! I tasted
her power!

The silence was answering my silence,
a forest was pushing itself
out of sleep between my submerged fingers.

I bit on a seed and it spoke on my tongue
of day that shone already among stars
in the water-mirror of low ground,

and a wind rising ruffled the lights:
she passed near me returning from the encounter,
she who plucked me from the close rooms,

without whom nothing
flowers, fruits, sleeps in season,
without whom nothing
speaks in its own tongue, but returns
lie for lie!

1959

PAUL BLACKBURN

THE CONTINUITY

The bricklayer tells the busdriver
and I have nothing to do but listen:

Th' holdup at the liquor store, d'ja hear?
           a detective
watch't 'm for ten minutes
         He took it anyway

          Got away down Broadway.
                             Yeah?
Yeah.
        And me:
               the one on the Circle?
                             Yeah.
Yeah? I was in there early tonight.

The continuity. A dollar forty-
two that I spent on a bottle of wine
is now in a man's pocket going down Broadway.

Thus far the transmission is oral.

Then a cornerboy borrows my pencil
to keep track of his sale of newspapers.

THE ASSISTANCE

On the farm it never mattered;
behind the barn, in any grass, against
any convenient tree; the
woodshed in winter, in a corner
if it came to that.

69

But in a city of eight million one
                 stands on the defensive
In the West 59th Street parking lot
it has long since sunk into the cinders.

But in the shallow doorway of
a shop on Third Avenue, between
               the dark and the streetlight,
it was the trail of the likewise drinking-man who preceded me
                          that gave me courage
                      lo que me dió valor.

                                           1953

NIGHT SONG FOR TWO MYSTICS

That man,
this man, never
               satisfied
is almost enough.
The sense, the half-sense of his
of any man's in-
               corruptible loneliness
incorrigible and terrified,
               should be enough
to cave society in
his need and ours.

What's melancholy is the most abstract.
Yet skip it back
seven centuries,
that same centrifugal leaves a sediment
whose taste is sweet

"when the light from the beloved's room comes

         t o   i l l u m i n a t e

the chamber of the lover, then
all the shadows are thrown back,
then he is filled and surfilled

with his peculiar pleasures,
the heavy thoughts, the languors.
And the lover will throw all the furniture out of the room,
everything,
that it may contain his beloved" That he may.

       And Llull is taught what red is
"and what new vestments he shall put on,
           what his arms are for
           and what they shall embrace,
and how to lower his head to give the kiss"
           which is good training for a lover.
       But the beloved remains forever
far enough removed
and in a high place
as to be easily seen from a distance.
Which pride is unforgivable.

So you see where we stand, where you stood, Yeats?
And must it always lead to gods?
The man's shadow dissolves in shadows.
Most men go down to obliteration
with the homeliest of remembrances.

       (pride, avarice, lust, anger
       gluttony, envy & sloth

       What are the positive virtues
which come between a man and his world,
estrange his friends, seduce his wife,
emasculate his god and general manager in charge of
blow his earth up?

       (down, sailor,
       blow the man
   c o i l e d   d o w n   t h e r e

in the dark pools of the mind, their time

they wait the violent lunatic wind
           at the star's dimming.

Dust, Yeats, all dust,
tho Llull remain a lover.

THE PROBLEM

My wife broke a dollar tube of perfume.

      The arab
who owns the perfume shop, insisted
       it was good-luck.
Sure it was.
To break any vessel is, if we know
the appropriate formula to make it sacrifice,
      and know a god
      to dedicate it to.

             1956

SIRVENTES

     Un sirventes ai fach
     Contra'l ciutat de Tolosa
     On m'avia pretz ostalatge
     D'un sen salvatge e famosa
     Del mons . . . PB/1956

I have made a sirventes against the city of Toulouse
and it cost me plenty of garlic:
and if I have a brother, say, or a cousin, or a 2nd cousin,
I'll tell him to stay out too.
     As for me, Henri,

     I'd rather be in España
     pegging pernod thru a pajita
     or yagrelling a luk
     jedamput en Jugoslavije,
     jowels wide & yowels not
     permitted to emerge —
     or even
     in emergency

slopping slivovitsa thru
the brlog in the luk.
I mean I'm not particular,
but to be
in the Midi

now that rain is here,
to be sitting in Toulouse
the slop tapping in the court
for another year,
to stop typing just at ten
and the wet-rot setting in
and the price is always plus,
I mean, please,
must I?

Whole damn year teaching
trifles to these trout with trousers
tramping thru the damp
with gout up to my gut
taking all the guff, sweet

jesus crypt,
god of the he
brews, she blows, it bawls, & Boses
(by doze is stuffed)
by the balls of the livid saviour, lead be
back hundu eegypt-la-aad
before I'b canned for indisciblidnary reasons.

O god.
The hallowed halls
the ivy covered walls
the fishwife calls
& the rain falls

BASTAL!

Jove, god of tourists, the whores in Barcelona are beautiful,
you would understand.
Weren't there Europa and Io? and Aegina, twin sister of Thebe

both daughters of Asopus?
and Maia and Antiope
and Niobe of the Thebans?
Eagle, ant, bull, beaver, flame, otter, how *not*?
Remember Leda?
I swan, you never felt old.
Your shower of rain at least was a shower of gold.
A gentle white bull with dewlaps.
The bulls in Barcelona are beautiful, Jove,
need no persuasion, are themselves as brave.

My old Guillem, who once stole this town,
thinking your wife's name enuf reason to . . .

St. Julian, patron of travelers, *mi des mercey*!

                              Who else invoke? Who else to save
                              a damned poet impaled by a *betterave*?
Mercury! Post of Heaven, you old thief, deliver me
from this ravel-streeted, louse-ridden, down-river,
gutter-sniping, rent-gouging, hard-hearted,
                              complacent provincial town,
where they have forgotten all that made this country the
belly of courage, the body of beauty, the hands of heresy,
the legs of the individual spirit, the heart of song!

                              That mad Vidal would spit on it,
                              that I as his maddened double
                              do —
                              too changed, too changed, o
                              deranged master of song,
                              master of the viol and the lute
                              master of those sounds,
                              I join you in public madness,
                              in the street I piss
                              on French politesse
that has wracked all passion from the sound of speech.
A leech that sucks the blood is less a lesion. Speech!
this imposed   imposing   imported   courtliness,   that

the more you hear it the more it's meaningless
                 & without feeling.

                    The peel is off the grape
                    and there's not much left
                    and what is left is soured
                        if clean :
                    if I go off my beam, some
                    small vengeance would be sweet,
                    something definite and neat, say
                        total destruction.

Jove, father, cast your bolts
& down these bourgeois dolts!

         Raise a wave, a glaive of light, Poseidon,
         inundate this fish bait!

              Hermes, keep my song
              from the dull rhythms of rain.

                 Apollo, hurl your darts,
                 cleanse these abysmal farts
                 out from this dripping cave
                 in the name of Love.

                                 1956

THE ONCE-OVER

The tanned blonde
                   in the green print sack
in the center of the subway car
                       standing
though there are seats
                 has had it from
1   teen-age hood
1   lesbian
1   envious housewife
4   men over fifty

(& myself), in short
the contents of this half of the car

                    Our notations are:
long legs, long waist, high breasts (no bra), long
neck, the model slump
                    the handbag drape and how the skirt
cuts in under a very handsome
                    set of cheeks
'stirring dull roots with spring rain' sayeth the preacher

            Only a stolid young man
            with a blue business suit and the New York *Times*
            does not know he is being assaulted

So.
She has us and we her
all the way to downtown Brooklyn
Over the tunnel and through the bridge
            to DeKalb Avenue we go
all very chummy

She stares at the number over the door
and gives no sign
            yet the sign is on her

THE ENCOUNTER

Staggering down the road at midnite
home from the bar, the

mexican Bandit stood facing me, about
to improve his standard of living

Two
fingers handled the moustache gently,
the other hand fingered the pistol.   My asshole

dropped out/
and crawled all the way back to El Paso

                                        1958

ROBERT CREELEY

THE INNOCENCE

Looking to the sea, it is a line
of unbroken mountains.

It is the sky.
It is the ground. There
we live, on it.

It is a mist
now tangent to another
quiet. Here the leaves
come, there
is the rock in evidence

or evidence.
What I come to do
is partial, partially kept.

1951

THE KIND OF ACT OF

Giving oneself to the dentist or doctor who is a good one,
to take the complete
possession of mind, there is no

giving. The mind
beside the act of any dispossession is

lecherous. There is no more giving in
when there is no more sin.

THE IMMORAL PROPOSITION

If you never do anything for anyone else
you are spared the tragedy of human relation-

ships. If quietly and like another time
there is the passage of an unexpected thing:

to look at it is more
than it was. God knows

nothing is competent nothing is
all there is. The unsure

egoist is not
good for himself.

1953

A COUNTERPOINT

Let me be my own fool
of my own making, the sum of it

is equivocal.
One says of the drunken farmer:

leave him lay off it. And this is
the explanation.

THE WARNING

For love — I would
split open your head and put
a candle in
behind the eyes.

Love is dead in us
if we forget
the virtues of an amulet
and quick surprise.

THE WHIP

I spent a night turning in bed,
my love was a feather, a flat

sleeping thing. She was
very white

and quiet, and above us on
the roof, there was another woman I

also loved, had
addressed myself to in

a fit she
returned. That

encompasses it. But now I was
lonely, I yelled,

but what is that? Ugh,
she said, beside me, she put

her hand on
my back, for which act

I think to say this
wrongly.

1954

A MARRIAGE

The first retainer
he gave to her
was a golden
wedding ring.

The second — late at night
he woke up,
leaned over on an elbow,
and kissed her.

The third and the last —
he died with
and gave up loving
and lived with her.

BALLAD OF THE DESPAIRING HUSBAND

My wife and I lived all alone,
contention was our only bone.
I fought with her, she fought with me,
and things went on right merrily.

But now I live here by myself
with hardly a damn thing on the shelf,
and pass my days with little cheer
since I have parted from my dear.

Oh come home soon, I write to her.
Go fuck yourself, is her answer.
Now what is that, for Christian word,
I hope she feeds on dried goose turd.

But still I love her, yes I do.
I love her and the children too.
I only think it fit that she
should quickly come right back to me.

Ah no, she says, and she is tough
and smacks me down with her rebuff.
Ah no, she says, I will not come
after the bloody things you've done.

Oh wife, oh wife — I tell you true,
I never loved no one but you.
I never will, it cannot be
another woman is for me.

That may be right, she will say then,
but as for me, there's other men.
And I will tell you I propose
to catch them firmly by the nose.

And I will wear what dresses I choose!
And I will dance, and what's to lose!
I'm free of you, you little prick,
and I'm the one can make it stick.

Was this the darling I did love?
Was this that mercy from above
did open violets in the spring —
and made my own worn self to sing?

She was. I know. And she is still,
and if I love her? then so I will.
And I will tell her, and tell her right . . .

Oh lovely lady, morning or evening or afternoon.
Oh lovely lady, eating with or without a spoon.
Oh most lovely lady, whether dressed or undressed or partly.
Oh most lovely lady, getting up or going to bed or sitting only.

Oh loveliest of ladies, than whom none is more fair,
                                        more gracious, more beautiful.
Oh loveliest of ladies, whether you are just or unjust,
                                        merciful, indifferent, or cruel.
Oh most loveliest of ladies, doing whatever, seeing whatever,
                                        being whatever.
Oh most loveliest of ladies, in rain, in shine, in any weather —

Oh lady, grant me time,
please, to finish my rhyme.

                                                                    1955

IF YOU

If you were going to get a pet
what kind of animal would you get.

A soft-bodied dog, a hen —
feathers and fur to begin it again.

When the sun goes down and it gets dark
I saw an animal in a park.

Bring it home, to give it to you.
I have seen animals break in two.

You were hoping for something soft
and loyal and clean and wondrously careful —

a form of otherwise vicious habit
can have long ears and be called a rabbit.

Dead. Died. Will die. Want.
Morning, midnight. I asked you,

if you were going to get a pet
what kind of animal would you get.

JUST FRIENDS

Out of the table endlessly rocking,
sea shells and firm,
I saw a face appear
which called me dear.

To be loved is half the battle
I thought.
To be
is to be better than is not.

Now when you are old what will you say?
You don't say,
she said.
That was on a Thursday.

Friday night I left
and haven't been back since.
Everything is water
if you look long enough.

1956

THE THREE LADIES

I dreamt. I saw three ladies in a tree,
and the one that I saw most clearly
showed her favors unto me,
and I saw up her leg above the knee!

But when the time for love was come,
and of readiness I had made myself,
upon my head and shoulders
dropped the other two like an unquiet dew.

What were these two but the one?
I saw in their faces, I heard in their words,
wonder of wonders! it was the undoing of me
they came down to see!

Sister, they said to her who upon my lap
sat complacent, expectant:
He is dead in his head, and we
have errands, have errands . . .

Oh song of wistful night! Light shows
where it stops nobody knows, and two
are one, and three, to me, and to look
is not to read the book.

Oh one, two, three! Oh one, two, three!
Three old ladies sat in a tree.

THE DOOR

For Robert Duncan

It is hard going to the door
cut so small in the wall where
the vision which echoes loneliness
brings a scent of wild flowers in a wood.

What I understood, I understand.
My mind is sometime torment,
sometimes good and filled with livelihood,
and feels the ground.

But I see the door,
and knew the wall, and wanted the wood,
and would get there if I could
with my feet and hands and mind.

Lady, do not banish me
for digressions. My nature
is a quagmire of unresolved
confessions. Lady, I follow.

I walked away from myself,
I left the room, I found the garden,
I knew the woman
in it, together we lay down.

Dead night remembers. In December
we change, not multiplied but dispersed,
sneaked out of childhood,
the ritual of dismemberment.

Mighty magic is a mother,
in her there is another issue
of fixture, repeated form, the race renewal,
the charge of the command.

The garden echoes across the room.
It is fixed in the wall like a mirror
that faces a window behind you
and reflects the shadows.

May I go now?
Am I allowed to bow myself down
in the ridiculous posture of renewal,
of the insistence of which I am the virtue?

Nothing for You is untoward.
Inside You would also be tall,

more tall, more beautiful.
Come toward me from the wall, I want to be with You.

So I screamed to You,
who hears as the wind, and changes
multiply, invariably,
changes in the mind.

Running to the door, I ran down
as a clock runs down. Walked backwards,
stumbled, sat down
hard on the floor near the wall.

Where were You.
How absurd, how vicious.
There is nothing to do but get up.
My knees were iron, I rusted in worship, of You.

For that one sings, one
writes the spring poem, one goes on walking.
The Lady has always moved to the next town
and you stumble on after her.

The door in the wall leads to the garden
where in the sunlight sit
the Graces in long Victorian dresses,
of which my grandmother had spoken.

History sings in their faces.
They are young, they are obtainable,
and you follow after them also
in the service of God and Truth.

But the Lady is indefinable,
she will be the door in the wall
to the garden in sunlight.
I will go on talking forever.

I will never get there.
Oh Lady, remember me
who in Your service grows older
not wiser, no more than before.

How can I die alone.
Where will I be then who am now alone,
what groans so pathetically
in this room where I am alone?

I will go to the garden.
I will be a romantic. I will sell
myself in hell,
in heaven also I will be.

In my mind I see the door,
I see the sunlight before me across the floor
beckon to me, as the Lady's skirt
moves small beyond it.

1958

THE AWAKENING

For Charles Olson

He feels small as he awakens,
but in the stream's sudden mirror,
a pool of darkening water,
sees his size with his own two eyes.

The trees are taller here,
fall off to no fields or clearing,
and depend on the inswept air
for the place in which he finds himself thus lost.

I was going on to tell you
when the door bell rang it was
another story which as I know
previously had happened, had occurred.

That was a woman's impression
of the wonders of the morning, the same place,
whiter air now, and strong breezes
move the birds off in that first freshening.

O wisest of gods! Unnatural prerogatives
would err to concur, would fall deafened

between the seen, the green green,
and the ring of a far off telephone.

God is no bone of whitened contention.
God is not air, nor hair, is not
a conclusive concluding
to remote yearnings. He moves

only as I move, you also move to
the awakening, across long rows, of beds,
stumble breathlessly, on leg pins and crutch,
moving at all as all men, because you must.

THE WAY

My love's manners in bed
are not to be discussed by me,
as mine by her
I would not credit comment upon gracefully.

But I ride by that margin of the lake in
the wood, the castle;
and have a small boy's notion of doing good.

Oh well, I will say here,
knowing each man,
let you find a good wife too,
and love her as hard as you can.

1959

PAUL CARROLL

FATHER

How sick I get
of your ghost. And
of looking at this tintype on my desk
of you as a cocky kid —
Kilkenny's coast, rocks & suncracked turf
giving the resilience to your countenance
as you try to seem so nonchalant, posing
in a rented Sunday morning-suit
spats & bowler hat:
a greenhorn off the boat. Yet something in

that twist of fist, knuckles taut
around the cane-knob, shows
how you already seem to know you will transform
that old cow-pasture of Hyde Park
into your own oyster.

The way you did.

And that other picture —
stuck somewhere in the dresser drawer
among the Christmas handkerchiefs,
the rubbers, poems & busted rosary beads.
Posed beneath 3 palms
on Tampa Beach's boardwalk,
a stocky man who made his millions by himself.
And can quarrel with congressmen from Washington
about the New Deal bank acts.
Or call Mayor Kelly crooked to his face.

Hair, bone,
brains & cock & skin
rotten in the earth these 16 years.
Remember, father, how Monseignor Keelty
(whose mouth you always said
looked exactly like a turkey's ass)
boomed out Latin above your coffin at Mt. Olivet?

But as the raw October rain

88

        rasped against our limousine
guiding the creeping cars back into Chicago,
        Jack, your first born,
picked his nose:
          and for an instant flicked a look
            to ask if I too knew
            you were dead for good —
        St. Patrick's paradise a club
        for priests & politicians
          you wouldn't get caught dead in.
You used to like to call me "Bill." And kiss me.
Or take me to the Brookfield Zoo. Or stuff
        english toffee in my mouth — but always
        only after you had cursed
          & with a bedroom slipper whacked
the tar out of Jack. This morning,

        broke as usual,
        no woman in my bed,
     I threw 6 bucks away
     for a shave & haircut at the Drake.
     And looked again for you. On Oak St. beach

gazing beyond the bathers & the boats
I suddenly searched the horizon, father,
for that old snapshot of Picasso
        & his woman Dora Maar.
     Picasso bald & 60. But both
        in exaltation, emerging
with incredible sexual dignity
        from the waters of the Golfe Juan.

The sun tattooed light on the lake.
     A red bone of a fish.
        The semen of the ghost.

        I left the lake. But tripped
        in the quick dark
of the Division St. underpass. Then picked a way past
        newspaper scraps, puddles
        & a puckered beachball.
I looked for dirty drawings on the wall.
    Traffic crunches overhead.
This underpass is endless.   *1959*

LARRY EIGNER

A FETE

The children were frightened by crescendoes
cars coming forward in the movies

That is, before they found out love,
that is, Comedy

         the cheeks blew
   music rises and continues

and the sea does

and there were no accidents today
the bombs showered us in the air

July, 1951

NOISE GRIMACED

Noise grimaced
we took pleasure in the heavens
  the close sky
although we knew we could not have seen it
and the flash fell expanding the light
up the beds and walls   at once
dying, leaving the star   distant
although we had known all season's heat
      like a room's still air here

slowly   I have sometimes heard my ears click
as if some naked siftings bared themselves
and who knows how these needles come to the body

Another moment   Day passing or

beside it,

out of the corners of the eyes
the wind like the rain, it can't be swallowed
rain as rain, walls shut   in
virtue of walls,   Rain is a forest
but the wind is too light for a sea
Under it still the skin is unquenched

And there are not two dangers either
none moving away, in front   forwards
to my head

though sometime it will rain, hail or
                                        still more variety
gripping the shoulders
                        before or after our deaths

1950-53

B

Is it serious, or funny?
Merely?

Miasma of Art
                        The

more the merrier is my view

seeing the levels of the world

and how easily emptied space

is

Here they made the perfect pots
on the beastly floors
the spoons and knives randomly dealt

and tread on the pine-cones
bare-footed
to cut wood

and here, the women went undone

till noon, plaiting

   Once this happened
and the cooks brought food to their seniors in wigs
in dressed-stone mansions;

I am omnipresent to some extent,
but how should I direct my attention

sufficiently to what I desire, to
stop, to
what is charging on the roadbed, what
       going away, the

fire-gong, people and buses

    and even in my room, as
I know
       the waving sun
             the

constant ephemerals

ENVIRON S

Many shapes of wings
on the sky and the table;
and large men carefully at dusk
lengthened by lights   watering their lawns

turn, paterfamilias

   and the sweet hay as I go
   from one leg to the other
more so than I might
mingled with barber's tonic
from the morning's shops
   of papers and bright rag
      as if we could
      take time out for life

and the afternoon's seas,   like yards

At some smell of smoke
I found a spray behind me
and the two on my right gone
    tending the grass, all night
  everyone beautifully
    (by themselves   the same thing

time   for the surroundings

     against the strip of hill
  ending low, a space
  on this side, hut for clouds.

O P E N

They nod at me and I at stems
Yes, I agree   But I flower myself.
or can't change

Yes, passes.   As I, pass on the air
As i,   pause
As i dream, sight
  I have been on all sides
    my face and my back

Disappears   any time   a world   can
Reality   dissolve

     abstract, abstract,   O little
               seeing that word
blue against the stack–
       o i walk i walk

the pavements
assume they are yellow

     the flowers seem to nod

               1953

A GONE

The world under the sky
clouds
all winter and summer

                    a snow
descends and occupies the ground
stars,   filled
              air
with abstracted wings

on crystalline lines
                    and time
                    between the stars
                    a broken hinge, by
                    the garage

a flagpole   mainstreet
          five cats yokked

                    the world
                    cant hold, really
                    too many absolutes

                    but I am shattered
                    and another time lost

          while the sea
                    slams
          the wind
or lags
                    an old woman's shoe
                         flapping
                              on the beach
          and the awning was still there

                                             1955-56

PASSAGES

Sunlight drawing from shadow, up and down the street
the dream of joy is only lightning
in the finale, beginnings so far from the end,
the short millions of poles, clouds on the sea,
the sea of human things the
leaves of men in the pure wind
of the seasons falling and swaying
                over the world land

and the pitch of the open night, the lightning seeming to rend
                and twist, the shadow to close in
above the flower the world cries out
time is obliterate and man turns
the false dream, missing details

                        that man who was deafened

we go to bed. The airs are dim
aside   marchings of men
and after this the boulevards

        the grounding of arms

    toys, and the blinding gulls

                                                    1956

KEEP ME STILL, FOR I DO NOT
WANT TO DREAM

I live in this house,   walls being plastered
all my life. the apple tree still standing
my life built,   the minutes keeping on
the walls cross, standing around
                in distinct company
    projection,   the clothes wave
            briefly, touch beyond eyes

weed the garden
the light burns away the street
the peaceful corn salt in the empty night,
among chickens, sparrows and dogs,

the pigeons limping easily on the roof,
the cat sticking his limbs through the sewer
his claws agape, naked
pondering

    he goes to sleep and wakes up
       he plays dead, hanging . .
               rain melts
      and hail fans on the wind

      the thistles, when they get old

   nearly everything gets in
   and then we close up

      the flowers are hidden lately

1956-57

DO IT YRSELF

Now they have two cars to clean
the front and back lawns
bloom in the drought

                  why not turn the other radio on the
     pious hopes of the Red Sox

yes, that's a real gangling kid coming down the street

he'll grow up

        he'll fill out

      sponges with handles

        we got trinaural hearing

— they are taller than their cars

1957-58

EDWARD DORN

THE RICK OF GREEN WOOD

In the woodyard were green and dry
woods fanning out, behind
                            a valley below
a pleasure for the eye to go.

Woodpile by the buzzsaw. I heard
the woodsman down in the thicket. I don't
want a rick of green wood, I told him
I want cherry or alder or something strong
and thin, or thick if dry, but I don't
want the green wood, my wife would die

Her back is slender
and the wood I get must not
bend her too much through the day.

Aye, the wood is some green
and some dry, the cherry thin of bark
cut in July.

My name is Burlingame
said the woodcutter.
My name is Dorn, I said.
I buzz on Friday if the weather cools
said Burlingame, enough of names.

        Out of the thicket my daughter was walking
singing —
            backtracking the horse hoof
        gone in earlier this morning, the woodcutter's horse
        pulling the alder, the fir, the hemlock
        above the valley
                        in the november

air, in the world, that was getting colder
as we stood there in the woodyard talking
pleasantly, of the green wood and the dry.

1956

VAQUERO

The cowboy stands beneath
a brick-orange moon. The top
of his oblong head is blue, the sheath
of his hips
is too.

In the dark brown night
your delicate cowboy stands quite still.
His plain hands are crossed.
His wrists are embossed white.

In the background night is a house,
has a blue chimney top,
Yi Yi, the cowboy's eyes
are blue. The top of the sky
is too.

THE HIDE OF MY MOTHER

1

My mother, who has a hide

on several occasions remarked what
a nice rug or robe
my young kids would make,

Would we send them to her?
When we had them butchered?

It was certainly a hoo ha ha
from me
and a ho ho
from my wife: and I would amusedly say

to conceal the fist in my heart
which one? the black?

or the grey
& white?

And she would smile, exposing the carnival
in her head

What's the difference, after they're dead?

Can you imagine asking a poet that?
Perhaps I should tell her about my pet rat.

2
My mother remarked
that in Illinois

little boys sell holly
from door to door,

and *here,* she would say
they grow all over the mountains
what if I took a holly tree back
there? would it grow?
No. I said.

3
Once my mother
was making dinner

and my cats were on the floor.

Why do they whine like that?
she asked,

why don't we throw them all out the door?
why don't you feed them I ventured?

She said she wasn't indentured.

Can you imagine telling a poet that?
Later she fed them my pet rat.

4

One day my son
found a parakeet in the bush
brought it to the house
carrying the little blue thing by the tail.

My mother said why, isn't it pretty,
I wonder if it would make the trip home
to Illinois. Oh, I said, we'll have to find its owner

you don't want to pull a boner
like that.

5

Tho winter's at term
it still gets cold

in the evening.
My pets are warm

because I have set a fire.

My mother is arranging some ferns
and young trees, a little too big

she found in the mountains.
A jig, of a sort must be going

on in her head. It is raining
outside. Do you think I can get the copper legs

of that stool in the box
or is it too wide? With some of those

pretty rocks I saw on the beach, would you,
she was saying to my little boy,

like to go home to Illinois with grandmother?

He was saying from inside the box enclosure,
he wasn't sure he

wanted to leave his mother.

6

For a point of etiquette,
when I observed she was digging
the neighbor's English Privet,

I said, it grows in abundance here.

As a matter of fact, she had it,
I thought I saw a rabbit,
that's why I came over here.

I said, a plant like that might grow anywhere.

Well now, I suppose you are right
back home our elms have the blight
but the land is flat there
so many mountains hereabouts

Yes, I allowed, it must help the sprouts . . .

Well now, there's more rain here
than we have in Illinois in an entire year
wouldn't you think tho it would grow there?

I said, what about a Privet hedge from . . .

You remember the peonies on grandfather's grave
well someone took them they were gone
the last Memorial Day I was there.

. . . From Hudson's Bay to the Gulf of Carpentaria.
Do you think it would stay?

Oh I love plants but where I am the weather
drives the birds away.

7

As for the hides of other people,
My wife told her

of how the junkman's
woman had been so good to us

a truss as it were, had kept the children
when it was a hardship

the condition had been foul, sleet,
masses of air, a raw affair,

dumped out of the Yukon upon
us, roving bands of weather

sliding across British Columbia
a kind of dementia

of the days, frozen water pipes
and the wringer on the washing machine

busted, no coal.
Our house split in two like Pakistan.

The graciousness
of the woman of the junkman

she said. Now what do you think
we should do? forget it? some doughnuts?
a cake?

"Why, I don't know what I would do" —
my mother was alluding

to a possible misfortune of her own.

8

As for the thick of it,
really, my mother
never knew about the world.

I mean even that there was one,
or more.

Whorled, like a univalve shell
into herself,

early to bed, nothing
in her head, here and there

Michigan one time,   Ohio
another. Led a life
like a novel, who hasn't?

As for Sociology:
garbage cans were what she dumped
the remains of supper in,

dirty newspapers, if blowing
in the street, somebody probably

dropped them there.

Nobody told her about the damned
or martyrdom. She's 47

so that, at least, isn't an emergency.

Had a chance to go to Arizona once
and weighed the ins and outs

to the nearest ounce:
didn't go. She was always slow.

Incidently, for her the air
was Red one time:

tail end of a dust storm
somehow battered up from Kansas.

1957

ARE THEY DANCING

There is a sad carnival up the valley
The willows flow it seems on trellises of music
Everyone is there today, everyone I love.

There is a mad mad fiesta along the river
Thrilling ladies sing in my ear, where
Are your friends, lost? They were to come

And banjoes were to accompany us all
And our feet were to go continually
The sound of laughter was to flow over the water

What was to have been, is something else
I am afraid. Only a letter from New Mexico
And another from a mountain by Pocatello.

I wonder, what instruments are playing
And whose eyes are straying over the mountain
Over the desert
And are they dancing: or gazing at the earth.

THE AIR OF JUNE SINGS

Quietly and while at rest on the trim grass I have gazed,
admonished myself for having never been here
at the grave-side and read the names of my Time Wanderers.
And now, the light noise of the children at play on the inscribed
    stone

jars my ear and they whisper and laugh covering their mouths.
    "My Darling"
my daughter reads, some of the markers
reflect such lightness to her reading eyes, yea, as I rove
among these polished and lime blocks I am moved to tears and
    I hear
the depth in "Darling, we love thee," and as in "Safe in Heaven."

I am going off to heaven and I won't see you anymore. I am
going back into the country and I won't be here anymore. I am
going to die in 1937. But where did you die my Wanderer?
You, under the grave-grass, with the tin standard whereat
I look, and try to read the blurred ink. I cannot believe
you were slighted knowing what I do of cost and evil
yet tin is less than granite. Those who buried you should have
    known
a 6 inch square of sandstone, flush with the earth
is more proper for the gone than blurred and faded flags.

Than the blurred and faded flags I am walking with in the
    graveyard.

Across the road in the strawberry field two children are stealing
their supper fruit, abreast in the rows, in the fields of the overlord,
Miller his authentic name, and I see that name represented here,
there is that social side of burial too, long residence,
and the weight of the established local dead. My eyes avoid
the largest stone, larger than the common large, Goodpole
    Matthews,
Pioneer, and that pioneer sticks in me like a wormed black cherry
in my throat, No Date, nothing but that zeal, that trekking
and Business, that presumption in a sacred place, where children
are buried, and where peace, as it is in the fields and the country
should reign. A wagon wheel is buried there. Lead me away

to the small quiet stones of the unpreposterous dead and leave
me my tears for Darling we love thee, for Budded on earth and
    blossomed
in heaven, where the fieldbirds sing in the fence rows,
and there is possibility, where there are not the loneliest of all.

Oh, the stones not yet cut.

                                                                    1958

WHEN THE FAIRIES

When the fairies come back to Santa Fe
they sit in dark caverns called taverns
and eat nervously picking at their food.

When they come back to Santa Fe
they gesticulate nervously and it's London
is meant.

When you pass their tables you see
their fingers flying off from Santa Fe
to Dakar or somewhere very far
away where neither you nor they
have ever been.

Still, they are nervous and pick at their food.

When the fairies fly back to Santa Fe
coming in on their smelly little wings
they gesticulate and Paris is meant
and they play games like guess what
book is meant,

and what color

and order drinks no one can mix.

They are a witchy bunch
and very inarticulate and late
in the day they order a lunch no one can assemble,

which they attack nervously
guessing what color —
where Copenhagen is meant

guessing what color and raiment.

1959

JONATHAN WILLIAMS

A LITTLE TUMESCENCE

This time, I mean it:
twice tonight!

> (*omne animal,* always
>   The Hope

Triste, triste
situation, such outrageous
limitation,
limp,
        simply

1954

THE SWITCH BLADE (or,
JOHN'S OTHER WIFE

men share perceptions (and
their best friends' wives, in lieu of

a perverse tangling of arseholes

— so if you don't dig that sound get down together
on the wrestling mat mit your
Blutbruderschaft,
                Mr Caesar, Mr Seizure, Mr Man

(every man's woman and every
woman's man, said Suetonius

THOSE TROUBLESOME DISGUISES

Sat Will & Kate,
                doing a Mr & Mrs

Eve & Adam . . .

                Milton got murmured
like Bees
                lost in the Hercules Apt's Eden-type Pavilion

'Come on in, Nobody here
                        but us
Chickens, Naked as
                Jaybirds . . .

Just Glimmed a Ghost, Man, the Most Gross
(like a Common Man would — a Lower Visible:
                        Scaly, Speckled & Very Awful . . .

We're Cooling it, Man, Before the Fall'

THE DISTANCES TO THE FRIEND

Thoreau,
        grabbing on, hard,
a red, raw
        muskrat . . .

he ate it,
        stifling all repulsion

So sat by the quagmire,
cranky, no cannibal, too
uninvolved
        to get to man,
so simply

        We, the
heirs, hear other rustlings (

the grass stirs like an androgyne,
the man in our heart stands
his fear
          on its head,
savagely —

               inversed, nervelessly,
we sweat past each other,
                    unrelieved:

bitter landscapes,
               unlovely

                                                        1955

FAST BALL

          (for WW, Hot for Honorary Installation at Cooperstown)

not just folklore, or
               a tall can of corn (or *Grass* on Cranberry Street) —
to point at the wall and win
               the whole ball of wax . . .

yet
   Walt Whitman
struck out, singing: 'rambled
               all around,
                         in & out the town, ram-
                    bled til the butchers
                              cut him down'

hard from the heels, swung,
               took a notion, had a hankering,
                         had good wood, but
                         came out —

                                   a ripple
                         in the breeze

bingo! —

          old solitary Whiff-Beard

                                                        1956

JOEL OPPENHEIMER

THE BATH

he will insist on
reading things into her simplest act.
her bath, which she takes
because he wills it so. her bath
she takes to cleanse herself.
ritual. ritual always
in his life. she takes her bath
to ready herself.
and himself more often than not decides
she wants him unbathed. manlike.
what he is most pleased about is
her continuing bathing.
in his tub. in his water. wife.

1953

THE BUS TRIP

images of J—— assail him.
the moon used to, but the moon is
an illuminated clock, he feels.
it does not particularly remind him or instruct.
when he rides on the bus with
drawings, a bag of apples, his
wife and lovely child, is he any
less or more the, a, fool.
if his child were not beautiful
what could he do and live. if his wife
were not beautiful what could he do and live.
these things are insanely important
to him. tho he lose his power facing them.

a woman, girl, across from him is
more beautiful than the world. he is
repelled. and pulls back. death.
the death of beauty, when it is beautiful, he
finds her. and dead. across from him
in a bus. the old man beside her. they
talk in italian.
                    a heavy sigh escapes him
when he goes. away from that across from him.
descends into the street. sketches, apples,
child, helps his pregnant wife. she
smiles. the child runs down
the street. images of J——
assail him. constantly. what shall he do.

                                                    1955

THE FEEDING

when she fed the
child, he fought back,
what does
he know of fruitfulness.
after she yelled at him
he was contrite.
but not even fearing she
meant it. a common decency you might say.
and again, then, spilled his milk.
and then looked up. smiling at her,
pleasantly, and, damn it, without
malice, even.

                                                    1956

MARE NOSTRUM

a bosom of
green buds,
ass like a

valentine.

the spring
rolls around,
moiling me
up.

(also green buds on
hedges, my heart
in every dogwood
blossom, even tulip,
even pink daisies)

i'm forced to it again
                              old
lady with a
bosom of green buds, also
an ass like a valentine, etc.

BLUE FUNK

I wish all the
mandragora grew
wild, screaming.

and in the cattails,
pussywillows, etc.
wind soft as
eastern standard time.

wind soft as the
last time you
did it. wind soft
as a soft wind.

I wish we
bathed in essence of
ginseng, for our health.

I wish eastern standard
time, etc. rang the
changes in our hearts.

1958

II

HELEN ADAM

I LOVE MY LOVE

"In the dark of the moon the hair rules." — ROBERT DUNCAN

There was a man who married a maid. She laughed as he led her home.
The living fleece of her long bright hair she combed with a golden comb.
He led her home through his barley fields where the saffron poppies grew.
She combed, and whispered, "I love my love." Her voice like a plaintive coo.
Ha! Ha!
Her voice like a plaintive coo.

He lived alone with his chosen bride, at first their life was sweet.
Sweet was the touch of her playful hair binding his hands and feet.
When first she murmured adoring words her words did not appall.
"I love my love with a capital A. To my love I give my All.
Ah, Ha!
To my love I give my All."

She circled him with the secret web she wove as her strong hair grew.
Like a golden spider she wove and sang, "My love is tender and true."
She combed her hair with a golden comb and shackled him to a tree.
She shackled him close to the Tree of Life. "My love I'll never set free.
No, No.
My love I'll never set free."

114

Whenever he broke her golden bonds he was held with bonds of
   gold.
"Oh! cannot a man escape from love, from Love's hot smothering
   hold?"
He roared with fury. He broke her bonds. He ran in the light of
   the sun.
Her soft hair rippled and trapped his feet, as fast as his feet could
   run,
Ha! Ha!
As fast as his feet could run.

He dug a grave, and he dug it wide. He strangled her in her sleep.
He strangled his love with a strand of hair, and then he buried
   her deep.
He buried her deep when the sun was hid by a purple thunder
   cloud.
Her helpless hair sprawled over the corpse in a pale resplendent
   shroud.
Ha! Ha!
A pale resplendent shroud.

Morning and night of thunder rain, and then it came to pass
That the hair sprang up through the earth of the grave, and it
   grew like golden grass.
It grew and glittered along her grave alive in the light of the sun.
Every hair had a plaintive voice, the voice of his lovely one.

"I love my love with a capital T. My love is Tender and True.
I'll love my love in the barley fields when the thunder cloud is
   blue.
My body crumbles beneath the ground but the hairs of my head
   will grow.
I'll love my love with the hairs of my head. I'll never, never let go.
Ha! Ha!
I'll never, never let go."

The hair sang soft, and the hair sang high, singing of loves that
   drown,
Till he took his scythe by the light of the moon, and he scythed

that singing hair down.

Every hair laughed a lilting laugh, and shrilled as his scythe
swept through.

"I love my love with a capital T. My love is Tender and True.

Ha! Ha!

Tender, Tender, and True."

All through the night he wept and prayed, but before the first
bird woke

Around the house in the barley fields blew the hair like billowing
smoke.

Her hair blew over the barley fields where the slothful poppies
gape.

All day long all its voices cooed, "My love can never escape,

No, No!

My love can never escape."

"Be still, be still, you devilish hair. Glide back to the grave and
sleep.

Glide back to the grave and wrap her bones down where I buried
her deep.

I am the man who escaped from love, though love was my fate
and doom.

Can no man ever escape from love who breaks from a woman's
womb?"

Over his house, when the sun stood high, her hair was a dazzling
storm,

Rolling, lashing o'er walls and roof, heavy, and soft, and warm.

It thumped on the roof, it hissed and glowed over every window
pane.

The smell of the hair was in the house. It smelled like a lion's
mane,

Ha! Ha!

It smelled like a lion's mane.

Three times round the bed of their love, and his heart lurched
with despair.

In through the keyhole, elvish bright, came creeping a single hair.

Softly, softly, it stroked his lips, on his eyelids traced a sign.
"I love my love with a capital Z. I mark him Zero and mine.
Ha! Ha!
I mark him Zero and mine."

The hair rushed in. He struggled and tore, but whenever he tore
   a tress,
"I love my love with a capital Z," sang the hair of the sorceress.
It swarmed upon him, it swaddled him fast, it muffled his every
   groan.
Like a golden monster it seized his flesh, and then it sought the
   bone,
Ha! Ha!
And then it sought the bone.

It smothered his flesh and sought the bones. Until his bones were
   bare
There was no sound but the joyful hiss of the sweet insatiable
   hair.
"I love my love," it laughed as it ran back to the grave, its home.
Then the living fleece of her long bright hair, she combed with a
   golden comb.

1958

BROTHER ANTONINUS

ADVENT

Fertile and rank and rich the coastal rains
Walked on the stiffened weeds and made them bend;
And stunned November chokes the cottonwood creeks
For Autumn's end.

And the hour of Advent draws on the small-eyed seeds
That spilled in the pentacostal drought from the fallen cup:
Swept in the riddled summer-shrunken earth;
Now the eyes look up.

Faintly they glint, they glimmer; they try to see;
They pick at the crust; they touch at the wasted rind.
Winter will pinch them back but now they know,
And will not stay blind.

And all Creation will gather its glory up
Out of the clouded winter-frigid womb;
And the sudden Eye will swell with the gift of sight,
And split the tomb.

1949

A CANTICLE TO THE WATERBIRDS

Written for the Feast of St. Francis of Assisi, 1950

Clack your beaks you cormorants and kittiwakes,
North on those rockcroppings fingerjutted into the rough Pacific
    surge;
You migratory terns and pipers who leave but the temporal claw-
    track written on sandbars there of your presence;
Grebes and pelicans; you comber-picking scoters and you shore-
    long gulls;

118

All you keepers of the coastline north of here to the Mendocino
   beaches;
All you beyond upon the cliff-face thwarting the surf at Hecate
   Head,
Hovering the under-surge where the cold Columbia grapples at
   the bar;
North yet to the Sound, whose islands float like a sown flurry of
   chips upon the sea:
Break wide your harsh and salt-encrusted beaks unmade for song
And say a praise up to the Lord.

And you freshwater egrets east in the flooded marshlands skirting
   the sea-level rivers, white one-legged watchers of shallows;
Broadheaded kingfishers minnow-hunting from willow stems on
   meandering valley sloughs;
You too, you herons, blue and supple-throated, stately, taking the
   air majestical in the sunflooded San Joaquin,
Grading down on your belted wings from the upper lights on sun-
   set,
Mating over the willow clumps or where the flatwater rice-fields
   shimmer;
You killdeer, high night criers, far in the moon-suffusion sky;
Bitterns, sandwaders, all shorewalkers, all roostkeepers,
Populates of the 'dobe cliffs of the Sacramento:
Open your waterdartling beaks,
And make a praise up to the Lord.

For you hold the heart of His mighty fastness,
And shape the life of His indeterminate realms.
You are everywhere on the lonesome shores of His wide creation.
You keep seclusion where no man may go, giving Him praise;
Nor may a woman come to lift like your cleaving flight her clear
   contralto song
To honor the spindrift gifts of His soft abundance.
You sanctify His hermitage rocks where no holy priest may kneel
   to adore, nor holy nun assist;
And where his true communion-keepers are not enabled to enter.

And well may you say His praises, birds, for your ways
Are verved with the secret skills of His inclinations,
And your habits plaited and rare with the subdued elaboration of
   His intricate craft;
Your days intent with the direct astuteness needful for His out-
   working,
And your nights alive with the dense repose of His infinite sleep.
You are His secretive charges and you serve His secretive ends,
In His clouded mist-conditioned stations, in His murk,
Obscure in your matted nestings, immured in His limitless ranges.
He makes you penetrate through dark interstitial joinings of His
   thicketed kingdoms,
And keep your concourse in the deeps of His shadowed world.

Your ways are wild but earnest, your manners grave,
Your customs carefully schooled to the note of His serious mien.
You hold the prime condition of His clean creating,
And the swift compliance with which you serve His minor means
Speaks of the constancy with which you hold Him.
For what is your high flight forever going home to your first be-
   ginnings,
But such a testament to your devotion?
You hold His outstretched world beneath your wings, and mount
   upon His storms,
And keep your sheer wind-lidded sight upon the vast perspectives
   of His mazy latitudes.

But mostly it is your way you bear existence wholly within the
   context of His utter will and are untroubled.
Day upon day you do not reckon, nor scrutinize tomorrow, nor
   multiply the nightfalls with a rash concern,
But rather assume each instant as warrant sufficient of His final
   seal.
Wholly in Providence you spring, and when you die you look on
   death in clarity unflinched,
Go down, a clutch of feather ragged upon the brush;
Or drop on water where you briefly lived, found food,
And now yourselves made food for His deep current-keeping fish,
   and then are gone:

Is left but the pinion feather spinning a bit on the uproil
Where lately the dorsal cut clear air.

You leave a silence. And this for you suffices, who are not of the
   ceremonials of man,
And hence are not made sad to now forgo them.
Yours is of another order of being, and wholly it compels.
But may you, birds, utterly seized in God's supremacy,
Austerely living under His austere eye —
Yet may you teach a man a necessary thing to know,
Which has to do of the strict conformity that creaturehood en-
   tails,
And constitutes the prime commitment all things share.
For God has given you the imponderable grace to *be* His verifi-
   cation,
Outside the mulled incertitude of our forensic choices;
That you, our lessers in the rich hegemony of Being,
May serve as testament to what a creature is,
And what creation owes.

Curlews, stilts and scissortails, beachcomber gulls;
Wave-hunters, shore-keepers, rockhead-holders, all cape-top vigi-
   lantes,
Now give God praise.
Send up the strict articulation of your throats,
And say His name.

1950

THE SOUTH COAST

Salt creek mouths unflushed by the sea
And the long day shuts down.
Whose hand stacks rock, cairn-posted,
Churched to the folded sole of this hill,
And Whose mind conceives? Three herons
Gig their necks in the tule brake
And the prying mudhen plies.
Long down, far south to Sur, the wind lags,

Slosh-washes his slow heel,
Lays off our coast, rump of the domed
Mountain, woman-backed, bedded
Under his lea. Salt grasses here,
Fringes, twigging the crevice slips,
And the gagging cypress
Wracked away from the sea.
God *makes*. On earth, in us, most instantly,
On the very now,
His own means conceives.
How many strengths break out unchoked
Where He, Whom all declares,
Delights to make be!

1954

JAMES BROUGHTON

FEATHERS OR LEAD?

Feathers or Lead?
    asked the Devil of Remedies locking the door
    clamped his stethoscope claw to my belly
    and pricked my liver with his beak.
How does it hurt now?
Feathers or Lead?
I warn you, either answer is wrong!
    said this very same Demon of Tender Mercy
    who had come to nurse me in an odorous gown
    where I lay bedsick with my broken soul
    where he would not let go of the wound.
If you don't feel it yet I can come much closer,
I can crawl much farther in!
    and stood up naked with two heads of hair
    and a scalp between his legs.

Doctor my doctor!
Shall I last the night?
    I was on my knees in my own hair shirt
Where is the gold apple core you promised?
Why did you feed me on ghostly bait?
When I begged the medicinal root of my Fall
you gave me an old umbilical to suck,
gave me my own contamination to swallow,
imbedded the ghost in my guts.

Feathers or Lead?
Feathers or Lead?
    and he rattled his teeth in my pelvis.

Lead Lead leaden as the jokes of Hell!
For the curse thumped down inside me where
feathers lack bones to fly them.
O Doctor my Doctor!

I groveled at his hammer-toed feet
What you put in, take out take back!
I asked for one slice of the bread of life
I asked for one sip of the healing waters
to father my own grown Son made flesh.
Instead I am child to my gangrene brother
who hangs his skull between your legs
and infects every breath in my blood.
For the love of Man at any price
cut my Other out of my bowels!
Or I vomit your bargain back!

The trick is known only to the specialist,
    said the Ministering Devil of Chronic Sores.
There remain advanced stages of your complaint.
A diagnosis of the incorrect self
can lead to fatal complications.
If you mistake despair for desire,
mistake your greed for need
and your sentence of death for a book of love,
I'm always ready to oblige.
It's time for another stronger dose.
You're not sick enough yet by far.
    And he clamped my nose and forced my chin
    with his cold wet rubber paws.
Now you must eat the regurgitated loaf,
now you must drink the excremental wine.
Here is your mother's befouled placenta!
    And he thrust her corpse down my throat.

    I choked, I spit, I wrenched my gall,
    I broke his needle, kicked his black bag —
    and when the maggots inside it cried out
    I ripped open my guts with trembling hands
    and spilled his own filth upon him.

Feathers or Lead?
    the dungheap cackled
    and slithered out under the door.

1957

MADELINE GLEASON

ONCE AND UPON

Cross at the morning
and at waking,
with a mourning for summer,
she crossed the bridge Now
over the river Gone
toward the place called New
to begin her Once Upon.

Once and Upon
my daddy long legs
walked in a web of work
for my sisters and me,
as Mother spun round
with silver knives and forks
in a shining of pans,
a wash of Mondays
and plans
for our lives ten thousand weeks.

To cross the bridge Now
over the river Gone
toward the place called New
to begin her Once Upon,
in a mourning for summer, she moved
to write her right becoming
and find her true beloved.

Snippets and tags of Gone,
criss-crossed as retold,
beggared the strumming
of fresh rhythms
that should have stirred her becoming.

Once and Upon
she ate the plum
and from a full mouth
disgorged the pit
into her hand
while Mother spun as she canned
peach and plum in season —
the land, holy Mother to
the plentiful fruit.

To cross.
But where should her steps lead
away from the river?

Through a desert she hurried,
thirsting she ran
to reach becoming,
passed three water holes
but never saw them,
so eager was she to reach
outward evidence
of her inward drawing.

Sisters of grace,
comely, sea-washed,
with blond shell hair and skin,
whirling with intermittent passion
amidst daddy long legs
and Mother awash
among the underthings,
boys shouting and running,
swaggering and dying
for the sisters' charms.
AMEN!

Tops a-spin in a dying dance.
Yoo Hoo, Fatty! Buck!
Hi, Pete! Hello, old Gene!

Cross at the morning,
summer crossed with the beginning
of gold,
a sea of brown leaves swirling.

And no trees bent down
to whisper their wisdom
for her becoming.
Ah! Now! Ah! Gone! Ah! New
Ah! Once Upon!

1958

LAWRENCE FERLINGHETTI

from: **PICTURES OF THE GONE WORLD**

8

Sarolla's women in their picture hats
stretched upon his canvas beaches
beguiled the Spanish
Impressionists

And were they fraudulent pictures
of the world
the way the light played on them
creating illusions
of love?

I cannot help but think
that their 'reality'
was almost as real as
my memory of today

when the last sun hung on the hills
and I heard the day falling
like the gulls that fell
almost to land

while the last picnickers lay
and loved in the blowing yellow broom
resisted and resisting
tearing themselves apart
again

again

until the last hot hung climax
which could at last no longer be resisted
made them moan

And night's trees stood up

23

Dada would have liked a day like this
                              with its various very realistic
            unrealities
                      each about to become
    too real for its locality
                      which is never quite remote enough
        to be Bohemia

Dada would have loved a day like this
                              with its light-bulb sun
    which shines so differently
                      for different people
    but which still shines the same
                              on everyone
                              and on everything
                                        such as
        a bird on a bench about to sing
                              a plane in a gilded cloud
a dishpan hand
            waving at a window

                              or a phone about to ring
                or a mouth about to give up
                              smoking

    or a new newspaper
                with its new news story
                              of a cancerous dancer

Yes Dada would have died for a day like this
                              with its sweet street carnival
        and its too real funeral
                      just passing thru it
    with its real dead dancer
                      so beautiful and dumb

                    in her shroud
                              and her last lover lost
          in the unlonely crowd
                              and its dancer's darling baby
      about to say Dada
                    and its passing priest
          about to pray
                    Dada
                              and offer his so transcendental
          apologies

Yes Dada would have loved a day like this
                              with its not so accidental
          analogies

                                        1953-55

from: A CONEY ISLAND OF THE MIND

1

In Goya's greatest scenes we seem to see
                              the people of the world
      exactly at the moment when
          they first attained the title of
                              'suffering humanity'
      They writhe upon the page
                    in a veritable rage
                              of adversity
      Heaped up
          groaning with babies and bayonets
                              under cement skies
      in an abstract landscape of blasted trees
          bent statues bats wings and beaks
               slippery gibbets
          cadavers and carnivorous cocks
          and all the final hollering monsters
               of the
                    'imagination of disaster'
      they are so bloody real
                    it is as if they really still existed

And they do

        Only the landscape is changed

They still are ranged along the roads
       plagued by legionnaires
                  false windmills and demented roosters

They are the same people
              only further from home
  on freeways fifty lanes wide
           on a concrete continent
              spaced with bland billboards
           illustrating imbecile illusions of happiness

The scene shows fewer tumbrils
         but more maimed citizens
              in painted cars
   and they have strange license plates
and engines
     that devour America

        11
The wounded wilderness of Morris Graves
    is not the same wild west
             the white man found
It is a land that Buddha came upon
          from a different direction
  It is a wild white nest
       in the true mad north
             of introspection

     where 'falcons of the inner eye'
            dive and die
    glimpsing in their dying fall
         all life's memory
           of existence
   and with grave chalk wing
         draw upon the leaded sky

a thousand threaded images
of flight

It is the night that is their 'native habitat'
these 'spirit birds' with bled white wings
these droves of plover
bearded eagles
blind birds singing
in glass fields
these moonmad swans and ecstatic ganders
trapped egrets
charcoal owls
trotting turtle symbols
these pink fish among mountains
shrikes seeking to nest
whitebone drones
mating in air
among hallucinary moons

And a masked bird fishing
in a golden stream
and an ibis feeding
'on its own breast'

and a stray Connemara Pooka
(life size)

And then those blown mute birds
bearing fish and paper messages
between two streams
which are the twin streams
of oblivion
wherein the imagination
turning upon itself
with white electric vision
refinds itself still mad
and unfed
among the hebrides

15

Constantly risking absurdity

                              and death
          whenever he performs

                         above the heads

                                   of his audience
         the poet like an acrobat

                      climbs on rime

                              to a high wire of his own making
     and balancing on eyebeams

                         above a sea of faces

              paces his way

                      to the other side of day
        performing entrechats

                         and slight-of-foot tricks
     and other high theatrics

                         and all without mistaking
              any thing

                         for what it may not be
        For he's the super realist

                         who must perforce perceive
              taut truth

                         before the taking of each stance or step
     in his supposed advance

                         toward that still higher perch
     where Beauty stands and waits

                         with gravity

                              to start her death-defying leap
          And he

              a little charleychaplin man

                         who may or may not catch
              her fair eternal form

                         spreadeagled in the empty air
              of existence

                                              1955-58

HE

He is one of the prophets come back
He is one of the wiggy prophets come back
He had a beard in the Old Testament
    but shaved it off in Paterson
He has a microphone around his neck
    at a poetry reading
    and he is more than one poet
    and he is an old man perpetually writing a poem
    about an old man
    whose every third thought is Death
    and who is writing a poem
    about an old man
    whose every third thought is Death
    and who is writing a poem
    Like the picture on a Quaker Oats box
    that shows a figure holding up a box
    upon which is a picture of a figure
    holding up a box
    and the figure smaller and smaller
    and further away each time
    a picture of shrinking reality itself
He is one of the prophets come back
    to see to hear to file a revised report
    on the present state
    of the shrinking world
He has buttonhooks in his eyes
    with which he fastens on
    to every foot of existence
    and onto every shoestring rumor
    of the nature of reality
    And his eye fixes itself
    on every stray person or thing
    and waits for it to move
    like a cat with a dead white mouse
    suspecting it of hiding

some small clew to existence
and he waits gently
for it to reveal itself
or herself or himself
and he is gentle as the lamb of God
made into mad cutlets
And he picks up every suspicious object
and he picks up every person or thing
examining it and shaking it
like a white mouse with a piece of string
who thinks the thing is alive
and shakes it to speak
and shakes it alive
and shakes it to speak
He is a cat who creeps at night
and sleeps his buddhahood in the violet hour
and listens for the sound of three hands about to clap
and reads the script of his brainpan
his hieroglyph of existence
He is a talking asshole on a stick
he is a walkie-talkie on two legs
and he holds his phone to his ear
and he holds his phone to his mouth
and hears *death death*
He has one head with one tongue hung
in the back of his mouth
and he speaks with an animal tongue
and man has devised a language
that no other animal understands
and his tongue sees and his tongue speaks
and his own ear hears what is said
and clings to his head
and hears *death death*
and he has a tongue to say it
that no other animal understands
He is a forked root walking
with a knot-hole eye in the middle of his head
and his eye turns outward and inward

and sees and is mad
and is mad and sees
And he is the mad eye of the fourth person singular
of which nobody speaks
and he is the voice of the fourth person singular
in which nobody speaks
and which yet exists
with a long head and a foolscap face
and the long mad hair of death
of which nobody speaks
And he speaks of himself and he speaks of the dead
of his dead mother and his Aunt Rose
with their long hair and their long nails
that grow and grow
and they come back in his speech without a manicure
And he has come back with his black hair
and his black eye and his black shoes
and the big black book of his report
And he is a big black bird with one foot raised
to hear the sound of life reveal itself
on the shell of his sensorium
and he speaks to sing to get out of his skin
and he pecks with his tongue on the shell of it
and he knocks with his eye on the shell
and sees *light light* and hears *death death*
of which nobody speaks
For he is a head with a head's vision
and his is the lizard's look
And his unbuttoned vision is the door
in which he stands and waits and hears
the hand that knocks and claps and claps and knocks
his *Death Death*
For he is his own ecstatic illumination
and he is his own hallucination
and he is his own shrinker
and his eye turns in the shrinking head of the world
and hears his organ speak *Death Death*
a deaf music

For he has come at the end of the world
   and he is the flippy flesh made word
   and he speaks the word he hears in his flesh
   and the word is *Death*

               Death Death
                     Death Death
          Death Death
                 Death Death
                       Death
                Death Death
                    Death Death
          Death Death
                  Death Death
                      Death Death
      Death Death
             Death Death
                Death Death
                     Death Death

          Death

                          San Francisco, 1959

ROBIN BLASER

POEM BY THE CHARLES RIVER

It is their way to find the surface
when they die.
                Fish feed on fish
and drop those beautiful bones
                        to swim.
I see them stretch the water to their need
as I domesticate the separate air to be my
breath.
            These fish die easily.

I find my surface in the way they feed.
Their gathering hunger is a flash like death.
No agony
               as if
                     my mind had eaten death

A 4 PART GEOMETRY LESSON
for Sylvia Townsend Warner

1. I teach how we cheat the young:
     that is,
               to know how tall a tree is
               I must fall from the top;
     that is,
               desire burns.

2. Now let me give you experience.
    We change. No lies. To snakes
    and splendor in old age.
                    I'm young

138

you say
        and those words
make me pay $10.
                        Two words more
and I'll pay 20.
                    (If I was 20
I'd say forget decrepitude.)

3. I would speak for all my skin
    that part which is serpentine:
    that is, now you sleep as though
    youth were a point whose definition
    is that "at least 2 exist and 2 suffice
    to determine a line" of development.

4. That's it. All those dead children.
    What calm eyes. A machine gun
    tore them out of the grass.
                        Our eyes
    like leaves on aspens twist
                        in the wind,
    desire continu
                ING.

POEM

And when I pay death's duty
a few men will come to mind
and 1 or 2 objects shine like buttons.

And when I pay death's duty
my dry mouth will swallow up
                        INDIGNITY
and old hands crack its wedding cup.

And when I pay death's duty, the big question
is what will it feel like with eyes wide open.

It won't be complete darkness because there
isn't any. One thing will stop and that's this
overweening pride in the peacock flesh. That's
a negative definition. More to the point is that
the skin wrinkles and the muscles weaken. And
what I think is that there's a sparrow in an old
man's heart and it flies up —

                                        Thus
in the wrinkling flesh the discovery of disgust.

What is the word for completion. A steel girder?
A building going up?

And when I pay death's duty
the love I never conquered
when young will end as such.

HERONS

I saw cold thunder in the grass,
the wet black trees of my humanity, my skin.

How much love lost hanging there
out of honesty.
                I catch at those men who chose
to hang in the wind
                        out of honesty.
It is the body lies with its skin —

Robed in my words I say that the snake
changes its skin out of honesty.

And they
            hanged there with some symmetry
died young
            like herons proud in their landscape.

Now it is age crept in, nobody younger knows
the quick-darting breath is
our portion of honesty.

POEM

For years I've heard
others speak like birds.
                              The words
clicking.
              One day I spoke
articulate
              the words *tic-ed*
in my throat.
                    It was
as if love woke
                    after anger.
The words
              sure —
                    Listen.
(*CHURRR*)
              Love wakes
at the breakfast table.
                              (*CHURRR*)
Not that
              the language itself has wings.
(*CHURRR*)   Not that
                              (*CHURRR*)
unfortunate skill.
                    Listen.
The words
              sure as a scream.

1956

JACK SPICER

IMAGINARY ELEGIES, I-IV

for Robin Blaser

I

Poetry, almost blind like a camera
Is alive in sight only for a second. Click,
Snap goes the eyelid of the eye before movement
Almost as the word happens.
One would not choose to blink and go blind
After the instant. One would not choose
To see the continuous Platonic pattern of birds flying
Long after the stream of birds had dropped or had nested.
Lucky for us that there are visible things like oceans
Which are always around,
Continuous, disciplined adjuncts
To the moment of sight.
Sight
But not so sweet
As we have seen.
When I praise the sun or any bronze god derived from it
Don't think I wouldn't rather praise the very tall blond boy
Who ate all of my potato-chips at the Red Lizard.
It's just that I won't see him when I open my eyes
And I will see the sun.
Things like the sun are always there when the eyes are open
Insistent as breath.
                    One can only worship
These cold eternals for their support of
What is absolutely temporary.
But not so sweet.
The temporary tempts poetry
Tempts photographs, tempts eyes.

I conjure up
From photographs
The birds
The boy
The room in which I began to write this poem
All
My eye has seen or ever could have seen
I love
I love — The eyelid clicks
I see
Cold poetry
At the edge of their image.
It is as if we conjure the dead and they speak only
Through our own damned trumpets, through our damned medium:
"I am little Eva, a Negro princess from sunny heaven."
The voice sounds blond and tall.
"I am Aunt Minnie. Love is sweet as moonlight here in heaven."
The voice sounds blond and tall.
"I'm Barnacle Bill. I sank with the Titanic. I rose in salty heaven."
The voice sounds blond, sounds tall, sounds blond and tall.
"Goodbye from us in spiritland, from sweet Platonic spiritland.
You can't see us in spiritland, and we can't see at all."

II

God must have a big eye to see everything
That we have lost or forgotten. Men used to say
That all lost objects stay upon the moon
Untouched by any other eye but God's.
The moon is God's big yellow eye remembering
What we have lost or never thought. That's why
The moon looks raw and ghostly in the dark.
It is the camera shots of every instant in the world
Laid bare in terrible yellow cold.
It is the objects that we never saw.
It is the dodos flying through the snow
That flew from Baffinland to Greenland's tip
And did not even see themselves.
The moon is meant for lovers. Lovers lose

Themselves in others. Do not see themselves.
The moon does. The moon does.
The moon is not a yellow camera. It perceives
What wasn't, what undoes, what will not happen.
It's not a sharp and clicking eye of glass and hood. Just old,
Slow infinite exposure of
The negative that cannot happen.
Fear God's old eye for being shot with ice
Instead of blood. Fear its inhuman mirror blankness
Luring lovers.
Fear God's moon for hexing, sticking pins
In forgotten dolls. Fear it for wolves,
For witches, magic, lunacy, for parlor tricks.

The poet builds a castle on the moon
Made of dead skin and glass. Here marvelous machines
Stamp Chinese fortune cookies full of love.

                                        Tarot cards
Make love to other Tarot cards. Here agony
Is just imagination's sister bitch.
This is the sun-tormented castle which
Reflects the sun. Da dada da.
The castle sings.
Da. I don't remember what I lost. Dada.
The song. Da. The hippogriffs were singing.
Da dada. The boy. His horns
Were wet with song. Dada.
I don't remember. Da. Forgotten.
Da. Dada. Hell. Old butterface
Who always eats her lovers.

Hell somehow exists in the distance
Between the remembered and the forgotten.
Hell somehow exists in the distance
Between what happened and what never happened
Between the moon and the earth of the instant
Between the poem and God's yellow eye.
Look through the window at the real moon.
See the sky surrounded. Bruised with rays.

But look now, in this room, see the moon-children
Wolf, bear, and otter, dragon, dove.
Look now, in this room, see the moon-children
Flying, crawling, swimming, burning
Vacant with beauty.
Hear them whisper.

III

God's other eye is good and gold. So bright
The shine blinds. His eye is accurate. His eye
Observes the goodness of the light it shines
Then, pouncing like a cat, devours
Each golden trace of light
It saw and shined.
Cat feeds on mouse. God feeds on God. God's goodness is
A black and blinding cannibal with sunny teeth
That only eats itself.
Deny the light
God's golden eye is brazen. It is clanging brass
Of good intention.
It is noisy burning clanging brass.
Light is a carrion crow
Cawing and swooping. Cawing and swooping.
Then, then there is a sudden stop.
The day changes.
There is an innocent old sun quite cold in cloud.
The ache of sunshine stops.
God is gone. God is gone.
Nothing was quite as good.
It's getting late. Put on your coat.
It's getting dark. It's getting cold.
Most things happen in twilight
When the sun goes down and the moon hasn't come
And the earth dances.
Most things happen in twilight
When neither eye is open
And the earth dances.

Most things happen in twilight
When the earth dances
And God is blind as a gigantic bat.
The boys above the swimming pool receive the sun.
Their groins are pressed against the warm cement.
They look as if they dream. As if their bodies dream.
Rescue their bodies from the poisoned sun,
Shelter the dreamers. They're like lobsters now
Hot red and private as they dream.
They dream about themselves.
They dream of dreams about themselves.
They dream they dream of dreams about themselves.
Splash them with twilight like a wet bat.
Unbind the dreamers.
                              Poet,
Be like God.

                              IV
Yes, be like God. I wonder what I thought
When I wrote that. The dreamers sag a bit
As if five years had thickened on their flesh
Or on my eyes. Wake them with what?
Should I throw rocks at them
To make their naked private bodies bleed?
No. Let them sleep. This much I've learned
In these five years in what I spent and earned:
Time does not finish a poem.
The dummies in the empty funhouse watch
The tides wash in and out. The thick old moon
Shines through the rotten timbers every night.
This much is clear, they think, the men who made
Us twitch and creak and put the laughter in our throats
Are just as cold as we. The lights are out.
                              The lights are out.

You'll smell the oldest smells
The smell of salt, of urine, and of sleep
Before you wake. This much I've learned
In these five years in what I've spent and earned:

Time does not finish a poem.
What have I gone to bed with all these years?
What have I taken crying to my bed
For love of me?
Only the shadows of the sun and moon
The dreaming groins, their creaking images.
Only myself.
                    Is there some rhetoric
To make me think that I have kept a house
While playing dolls? This much I've learned
In these five years in what I've spent and earned:
That two-eyed monster God is still above.
I saw him once when I was young and once
When I was seized with madness, or was I seized
And mad because I saw him once. He is the sun
And moon made real with eyes.
He is the photograph of everything at once. The love
That makes the blood run cold.
But he is gone. No realer than old
Poetry. This much I've learned
In these five years in what I've spent and earned:
Time does not finish a poem.
Upon the old amusement pier I watch
The creeping darkness gather in the west.
Above the giant funhouse and the ghosts
I hear the seagulls call. They're going west
Toward some great Catalina of a dream
Out where the poem ends.
                         But does it end?
The birds are still in flight. Believe the birds.

1950-55

LEW WELCH

CHICAGO POEM

I lived here nearly 5 years before I could
        meet the middle western day with anything like
Dignity. It's a place that lets you
        understand why the Bible is the way it is:
Proud people cannot live here.

The land's too flat ugly sullen and big it
        . pounds men down past humbleness. They
Stoop at 35 possibly cringing from the heavy and
        terrible sky. In country like this there
Can be no God but Jahweh.

In the mills and refineries of its south side Chicago
        passes its natural gas in flames
Bouncing like bunsens from stacks a hundred feet high.
        The stench stabs at your eyeballs.
The whole sky green and yellow backdrop for the skeleton
        steel of a bombed-out town.

Remember the movies in grammar school? The goggled men
        doing strong things in
Showers of steel-spark? The dark screen cracking light
        and the furnace door opening with a
Blast of orange like a sunset? Or an orange?

It was photographed by a fairy, thrilled as a girl, or
        a Nazi who wished there were people
Behind that door (hence the remote beauty) but Sievers,
        whose old man spent most of his life in there,
Remembers a nigger in a red T-shirt pissing into the
        black sand.

It was 5 years until I could afford to recognize the ferocity.
       Friends helped me. Then I put some
Love into my house. Finally I found some quiet lakes
       and a farm where they let me shoot pheasant.

Standing in the boat one night I watched the lake go absolutely
       flat. Smaller than raindrops, and only
Here and there, the feeding rings of fish were visible 100 yards
       away — and the Blue Gill caught that afternoon
Lifted from its northern lake like a tropical. Jewel at its ear
       belly gold so bright you'd swear he had a
Light in there . . . color fading with his life a small
       green fish . . .

All things considered, it's a gentle and an undemanding
       planet, even here. Far gentler
Here than any of a dozen other places. The trouble is
       always and only with what we build on top of it.
There's nobody else to blame. You can't fix it and you
       can't make it go away. It does no good appealing
To some ill-invented Thunderer
       brooding above his unimaginable crag . . .

It's ours. Right down to the last small hinge it
       all depends for its existence
Only and utterly upon our sufferance.

Driving back I saw Chicago rising in its gases and I
       knew again that never will the
Man be made to stand against this pitiless, unparalleled
       monstrocity. It
Snuffles on the beach of its Great Lake like a
       blind, red rhinoceros.
It's already running us down.

You can't fix it. You can't make it go away.
       I don't know what you're going to do about it,
But I know what I'm going to do about it. I'm just
       going to walk away from it. Maybe

A small part of it will die if I'm not around
        feeding it anymore.

1957

AFTER ANACREON

When I drive cab
        I am moved by strange whistles and wear a hat.

When I drive cab
        I am the hunter. My prey leaps out from where it
        hid, beguiling me with gestures.

When I drive cab
        All may command me, yet I am in command of all who do.

When I drive cab
        I am guided by voices descending from the naked air.

When I drive cab
        A revelation of movement comes to me: They wake now.
        Now they want to work or look around. Now they want
        drunkenness and heavy food. Now they contrive to love.

When I drive cab
        I bring the sailor home from the sea. In the back of
        my car he fingers the pelt of his maiden.

When I drive cab
        I watch for stragglers in the urban order of things.

When I drive cab
        I end the only lit and waitful thing in miles of
        darkened houses.

1959

RICHARD DUERDEN

MUSICA NO. 3: **pickup on some
numbers & balances**

> Such light is in sea-caves
> Inheres in beginnings

And
in waters: the acceptance of a seal
   while the given bulb is wholly inside
to our gain, the dark cave is moved
                      to germinate.
A microscope.   control: timidity?
   Get it safely onto a blackboard
   mind sees in a sea cave
   the light leaks in.   look!   the transformations!
We're gonna lead evolution if it kills us
            by the light
            by height; sands
jellyfish end on.
            who killed Neanderthal?
Science for the clean ones:
Which way'd the gardener go.
            the roots dark!
            beloved dirty roots
            which in the dark bring down light,
               Change & feed of it,
               in the sacred bulb
the sea cave.

1957

DANCE WITH BANDERILLAS

Barefoot   without a stitch she walks
as walking is a dance
of her full body by proportion is,   stopt,
at the man kneeling.
Up on her toes her look — power, the
round & horns of her — 2 spears aimed at his horny mask:
held loose;
his long face the wound   as contained as her face
in common with the building, the monkey, land etcetera.

MOON IS TO BLOOD

for R. D. &J. C.

Morning, on a beach. A man & woman sitting by fire.
The woman stands, looks toward land for, something. dancing off
to the sparkles
                music of the queers' circle.
Look ice plant's blossoming, she cries!
dancing long streams, & whirls, of the airs' dancing;
into long glass pendants, red & purple striped papers.
The Fleeing Hell Dance.

The moon, right outside the window, woke me: jarring thru the
glass. From the window, the seas dark face.
Who'd call it lit, by the moon?
But for stars the night'ld be whole! :
Ah, there is black cardboard here, I'll
cut a triangle my face size . . .
Shut out the moon? Damn it
it's nutrition of the body one bears in conduction — grounded.
I mean not quite like plants, that they require 8 hours of un
interrupted darkness to blossom
but that conduction holds the face, the flowering,
                        is its weight.

Such as it is the moon's face is a flowering.
It's lopsided by conduction, it need not be pretty.
The moon face in silence sings:
grounded, there is the pleasure of a toilet seat, after her,
an act
of warm respect.

Moon. Moon. To whom my hands are out.
When I turned to the room I saw that the woman sleeping
is half woman half bird.
At her sides there are long wings, folded.

1959

PHILIP LAMANTIA

TERROR CONDUCTION

The menacing machine turns on and off

Across the distance light unflickers active infinities

Under the jangling hand set going in the brain
                THE WOMAN
menacing by white lacerations
           THE MAN
menacing
in a timeweighed fishbowl of the vertical act

and the woman and the man menacing together
                      out of mutual crucifixions
disgorge
          towers for the dead

             the woman menacing
the man menacing
the woman and the man menacing together
            BUT
THE CROWDS
    THE CROWDS MENACING
as eyes take off for NOTHINGNESS
in night rememorizing the primal menace

on a day in a night crossed with butchering
polite squeels humdrum
                    WHAT are all these
        waywardlooking   scorching   haggard
                grim
perilous   witchlike   criminal
              SUBLIME
drunken   wintered
            GRAZING

                    FACES
                               FACES
                                          going by
          like icebergs
                          like music
                                     like boats

                                          like mechanical toys
          LIKE
                    RAINING
                               SWORDS!

1950

"MAN IS IN PAIN"

Man is in pain
          ten bright balls bat the air
          falling through the window
          on which his double leans a net the air made
          to catch the ten bright balls

Man is a room
          where the malefic hand turns a knob
          on the unseen unknown double's door

Man is in pain
          with his navel hook caught on a stone quarry
          where ten bright balls chose to land
          AND where the malefic hand carves
               on gelatinous air THE WINDOW
          to slam shut on his shadow's tail

          Ten bright balls bounce into the unseen
          unknown double's net
Man is a false window
          through which his double walks to the truth
          that falls as ten bright balls
          the malefic hand tossed into the air

Man is in pain
    ten bright spikes nailed to the door!

1952

MORNING LIGHT SONG

RED DAWN clouds coming up! the heavens proclaim you,
    Absolute God
I claim the glory, in you, of singing to you this morning
For I am coming out of myself and Salga to you, Lord of the
    Morning Light
For what's a singer worth if he can't talk to you, My God of Light?
These lines should grow like trees to tie around your Crown of
    the Sky
These words should be strong like those of the Ancient Makers,
                          O Poet of poets
              Ancient deity of the Poem
Here's spindle tongue of morning riding the flushes of NIGHT
Here's gigantic ode of the sky about to turn on the fruits of my
    lyre
Here's Welcome Cry from heart of the womb of words, Hail!
    Queen of Night!
Who giveth birth to the Morning Star, Here's the quiet cry of
    stars broken among crockery
Here's the spoon of sudden birds wheeling the rain of Zeus
Here's the worshipping Eye of my soul stinging the heavens
Here's Charmed Bird, Zephyr of High Crags — jugs of the divine
    poem
As it weaves terrestial spaces, overturning tombs, breaking
    hymens
Here's the Thrice ONE God, imprinted on the firmament I'm
    watching
From where cometh this first cry
                 that my hands go into for the wresting of words
Here's my chant to you, Morning of Mornings, God of Gods,
    light of light
Here's your singer let loose into the sky of Your Heaven
For we have come howling and screaming and wailing and I

come SINGING
To you who giveth forth the song of songs that I am reborn from
    its opulence
That I hold converse with your fantasy   That I am your BEAUTY
Not of this world and bring to nothing all that would stop me
From flying straight to Your Heart Whose Rays conduct me to
    the SONG!

STILL POEM 9

There is this distance between me and what I see
everywhere immanence of the presence of God
no more ekstasis
a cool head
watch watch watch
I'm here
He's over there. . . . It's an Ocean . . .
sometimes I can't think of it, I fail, fall
There IS this look of love
there IS the tower of David
there IS the throne of Wisdom
there IS the silent look of love
Constant flight in air of the Holy Ghost
I long for the luminous darkness of God
I long for the superessential light of this darkness
another darkness I long for the end of longing
I long for the
            It is Nameless what I long for
      a spoken word caught in its own meat saying nothing
This nothing ravishes beyond ravishing
There is this look of love Throne Silent look of love

1959

BRUCE BOYD

THIS IS WHAT THE WATCHBIRD SINGS, WHO PERCHES IN THE LOVETREE

Who has but dighted his tricks in a bed,
And never delighted in anything said,
He'll nibble dry leaves until he is dead.

For love is the kind of a tree whose fruit
Grows not on the branches, but at the root.

Who with his lover's real presence has talked,
And enacted his lover's least speakable thought,
He will find out what it is he has sought.

For love is the kind of a tree whose fruit
Grows not on the branches, but at the root.

1957

SANCTUARY

because the warm honey
       is never dissolved, by water,
but drifts on the river's stone bottom
like wads of raw silk,

under the surface the swimmers still look

    where sharp little stars
        bloom on the bone-tree
  & tender incredulous fish
        swim out of its watery eyes

& grow warmer; while gently the bone-tree
      is turned in its bed
   & sees how it gradually wakens.

around it the water is still:
but the sheet-glass surface is quietly shaken
& breaks into ripples, as gulls rise
into the rooms of the hungry children
to watch the tall water close over their heads.

                                                                    1958

VENICE RECALLED

on the salt water streets
that rose & then fell with the ocean
when the fish that were caught in the mud
underneath the wooden footbridge started in to stink,
soon there was always the incoming tide

                                        there, we were
each his own man

        to speak, the play of sounds, pleasant or
        otherwise, but only open & discursive.

                                differently, here, in the language
the oblique sense of a word to stamp one as "in"
                                whose dialect (not
dialectic) held
                        "right or wrong"
invents a greater crime than just to force the song:
to force it back,
                        & closets them wet & huddled together.

            they are fearful in their heads
            of being on the outside looking in
            – to the center of language:

but we who would live openly are its natural peripheries,
& take the unborn where the dead leave it
to grow, at our hand

"always to prefer the common," thus the noble
Heraclitus, in "this world, which is the same for all

our language is although inductive
the topology of what we live:
thus not its substitute but its enlargement.

        there, with us
a new poem always was something
         the making, something
that asked to be shared at once: seldom a "result"
to praise or blame, & never this only, we mostly looked
behind it for the ways that came together,
between whom, intended, a clearing was being made

in which to discover what, having forgotten
is recovered
     in measure, apart from direction:
  as in accord with old codes,
  codices,
     a kind of law
  of least action in language, or
         taken as return
to the origin,
     a place of actual
welcome, always the nearest
stone path that is watered
       against the coming of guests
    is to say,
      cooler:
& the poem, what it means to say,
for the natural motion of its body, is the clearer
that remarks the wider movement of its actual thought.

1959

KIRBY DOYLE

STRANGE

               how you go along all day
   for a million years
                 and see the world groping about
  in its existentialist sort of way
like the white limbed old nurse
    hurrying to a hygienic universe
                where issues of importance to no one
are decided in heaping spoonfuls
             of absolute death,
or the three a.m. food emporiums
              on forever corners
  where the day-old bread is a bargain of reality
    served with blue-plate attitudes
or how the transparent aged
         do their eyeless genuflections to the sun
   in anesthetic parks where the grass
               is only to look at
or how people crouch in streetcars
            and hide behind newsprint
    of foreign wars and domestic rape
  afraid to look out and see what's really there
or how stretched out on the sunny sand at Aquatic Park
         you watch an old retired lithographer
  take off his shoes and neatly fold
            his pension purchased coat
then wade out towards the bell-buoy
        until you don't see him any longer
or how on a streetcorner in front of Penny's
     a clean old man with REPENT in his hat-band
  hawks the unknown sayings of Jesus

for a nickel
or how the door is knocked once too often
and you capitulate to Girl Scout Cookies
or how the glass statue of St. John the anti-baptist
shudders slightly
at the sound of vesper bells
or how an almost non-existent salesperson
peers across years of yardage
as if a fate worse than death
really was
or how learned virgins emerge from book-stalls
to stand waiting
in the crevice of a single thought
under the baptismal chill of a solitary streetlamp
or how you jamble up stick stairs
a passageway for dusty smells
and midnight coughs
in an old brown house of high façade
or how she looks and says yes
and you are young in your old shoes
and the night goes around inside of the moon.
STRANGE
you should see all this for a million years
and then one day,
never look again.

1956

EBBE BORREGAARD

SOME STORIES OF THE BEAUTY WAPITI

tonight and forever I shall be yours so says the oleo king
via dolorosa vexation of beauty soft with oil
by the side rings of wapiti drink blood from cuckoopint stamens
tonight the wapiti wastrel move thru the lower plains
bending water fennel in vatrix streams

                                    toward the skulls place
struck down wolfsbane or monkshood

                                    weep in the pico rain
and beneath their tails tumble rails of heterogenesis

tonight and forever I shall

                        dream

                        be yours

                            in montalto with tonio by leoncavallo
pia mater delicate membrane peach pink in wine vagabonda
here before the inconsolate wapiti is wine mingled with myrrh
also are reconstituted paps which never give suck
tonight is vinegar to drink mingled with gall
take the delicate wapiti make the spunge with vinegar
monstrous elk we shed your horns and unsack your

                                    precious peach preserves

                                                    ya

                                                    . . .

tonight and forever I shall be yours

                            so goes my nedda
hyacinth the lily of your evil heart

                            laugh clown laugh
a full day of the hyades is gone they rose with the sun
blessed are the wapiti saturated with piss and myrrh
and as the cuckoopint one hundred fifty three times bleed
so must tonio unto nedda wed expensive ointments such as these

163

open thy mouth for the numb in the cause open thy mouth
                                                prov 31
she seeketh wool and giveth meat to her household
her hands hold the distaff
                           she shall rejoice in time to come
for she opens her mouth with wisdom and her tongue is the law
                                                         amen
give her the fruit of her hands and let her own works
                                         praise in her gates
                                                          . . .

tonight and forever I shall be yours
                           elk
via crucis vicar son of a bitch render out with magnificat
hesperus comes in this seventh hour in peculiar antiphone
tonight the little wax match will wobble and sulk
    no I am not a clown
                           my white face is not painted on
tonight and forever tonight and forever the wapiti move thru
    water hemlock
and bend their necks into the soil of the lower plains
prov 1
          and from the green wool pull brave testicles
so surely domesticated they make a garden scene
like cowbells from their heavy lip swing hyacinthus blue knicker-
    bockers
gathered below the knee
                           gayly swinging
                              nectarine penticles like apricots
                                                        1955

"EACH FOUND HIMSELF AT
THE END OF..."

Each found himself at the end of
a tremendous age
rigid, like with unrelieved love; the
desire inherent
        to love, and to take
and propel it;
to spred like with flowers their guilt,
to sell it,
       these nurserymen, for desire   *(not guilt,*
to the other   .   Love in the hands   *but the flower*
of a mason —   *of it*
the stones true, square, precise;
                in
the hands of a mason, pots   .   No real
satisfaction or so forth,
stones themselfs, all of them; folly
and, to finish it — concrete avenues, good
concrete hiways

And found himselfs with a flea,
the culture gone bad sucking its
lovers of, and men   .
Each a lovely article of blame,
that is, themselfs blamed —
myoptic   .   stupid   .   at beginnings

truly mad with corpulent preciseness   *(that of flower*
as an elk   .   Love,   *beauty*
a figure, and a kind of Mu(sic to sooth
and to vibrate into action, satisfaction) — Love,
hardly the word itself,
              its meaning   *(its meaning?*

The Act   *(as I said*
the Game itself, that which spells it out,

that which is found —
    'Each found himself at the end of a . . .
they had this on common grounds

love and the word consistently new, like
with flowers facing
the sun all the sweet organs of them;
tight;
their life screwd-up in violent crowns

    . . . tremendous age'
                       Each found himself
NEW, at beginnings,
always at beginnings
breaking the hard ground,
the hard ground holding the word,   (*The man un*
always   *hesitant*

rigid with it

                                               1957

III

JACK KEROUAC

MEXICO CITY BLUES: *12 Choruses*

113th Chorus

Got up and dressed up
    and went out & got laid
Then died and got buried
    in a coffin in the grave,
Man —
    Yet everything is perfect,
Because it is empty,
Because it is perfect
    with emptiness,
Because it's not even happening.

Everything
Is Ignorant of its own emptiness —
Anger
Doesnt like to be reminded of fits —

You start with the Teaching
    Inscrutable of the Diamond
And end with it, your goal
    is your startingplace,
No race was run, no walk
    of prophetic toenails
Across Arabies of hot
    meaning — you just
    numbly dont get there

127th Chorus

Nobody knows the other side
    of my house,
My corner where I was born,
    dusty guitars
Of my tired little street where
    with little feet
I beetled and I wheedled
    with my sisters
And waited for afternoon sunfall
    call a kids
And ma's to bring me back
    to supper mainline
Hum washing line tortillas
    and beans,
That Honey Pure land,
    of Mominu,
Where I lived a myriad
    kotis of millions
Of incalculable
    be-aeons ago
When white while joyous
    was also
Center of lake of light

146th Chorus

The Big Engines
In the night —
The Diesel on the Pass,
The Airplane in the Pan
    American night —
Night —

The Blazing Silence in the Night,
    the Pan Canadian Night —

The Eagle on the Pass,
        the Wire on the Rail,
the High Hot Iron
        of my heart.

The blazing chickaball
        Whap-by
Extry special Super
        High Job
Ole 169 be
        floundering
Down to Kill Roy

179th Chorus

Glenn Miller and I were heroes
When it was discovered
That I was the most beautiful
Boy of my generation,
They told Glenn Miller,
Whereby he got inspired
And wrote the saxophone
Wrote the reed sections —
like sautergain & finn —
and then they all did dance
and kissed me mooning stars
and I became the Yokum
of the wall-gang, flowers,
and believed in truth & loved
the snowy earth
        and had no truck
        and no responsibility

a bhikku in my heart
waiting for philosophy's
        dreadful murderer
                B U D D H A

182nd Chorus

The Essence of Existence
　　is Buddhahood —
As a Buddha
　　you know
　　that all the sounds
　　that wave from a tree
　　and the sights
　　from a sea of fairies
　　　　in Isles of Blest
　　and all the tastes
　　　　in Nectar Soup
　　and all the odors
　　　　in rose arbour
　　— ah rose, July rose —
　　　　　bee-dead rose —

and all the feelings
　　in the titwillow's
　　chuckling throat
and all the thoughts
　　in the raggedy mop
　　of the brain —
　　one dinner

183rd Chorus

"Only awake to Universal Mind
And realize that there is nothing
Whatever to be attained. This
Is the real Buddha."

Thus spake Hsi Yun
　　　to P'ei Hsiu

Names so much like each other
You know it cant be wrong

You know that sweet Hsi Yun
Had eyes to see the Karma
Wobbling in the balloon
— shiney —
    millions of dollars damage
    from rains and floods —
vast fading centers of a Kansas
    central standard time

        buss-i-ness
        my fron

Only awake to Universal Mind,
        accept everything,
        see everything,
        it is empty,
Accept as thus — the Truth.

211th Chorus

The wheel of the quivering meat
                conception
Turns in the void expelling human beings,
Pigs, turtles, frogs, insects, nits,
Mice, lice, lizards, rats, roan
Racinghorses, poxy bucolic pigtics,
Horrible unnameable lice of vultures,
Murderous attacking dog-armies
Of Africa, Rhinos roaming in the
                jungle,
Vast boars and huge gigantic bull
Elephants, rams, eagles, condors,
Pones and Porcupines and Pills —
All the endless conception of living
                beings
Gnashing everywhere in Consciousness
Throughout the ten directions of space
Occupying all the quarters in & out,

From supermicroscopic no-bug
To huge Galaxy Lightyear Bowell
Illuminating the sky of one Mind —
    Poor! I wish I was free
    of that slaving meat wheel
    and safe in heaven dead

219th Chorus

Saints, I give myself up to thee.
Thou hast me. What mayest thou do?
What hast thou? Hast nothing?
Hast illusion. Hast rage, regret,
Hast pain. Pain wont be found
Outside the Monastery only —
    Hast decaying saints like Purushka
    Magnificent Russian-booted bird loving
    Father Zossima under the cross
    In his father cell in Holy Russia
    And Alyosha falls to the ground
    And Weeps, as Rakitin smears.
    Grushenka sits him on her lap
    And lacky daisies him to lull
    And love and loll with her
    And wild he runs home in the night
    Over Charade Chagall fences
        snow-white
    To the pink cow of his father's ear,
    Which he slits, presenting to Ivan
    As an intellectual courtesy, Dmitri
    Burps, Smerdyakov smirks.
    The Devil giggles in his poorclothes.
Saints, accept me to the drama
of thy faithful desire.
No me? No drama to desire?
No Alyosha, no Russia, no tears?
Good good good good, my saints.

No saints? No no no my saints.
No no? No such thing as no.

221st Chorus

Old Man Mose
Early American Jazz pianist
Had a grandson
Called Deadbelly.
Old Man Mose walloped
        the rollickin keyport
        Wahoo wildhouse Piany
        with monkies in his hair
        drooling spaghetti, beer
        and beans, with a cigar
        mashed in his countenance
        of gleaming happiness
        the furtive madman
        of old sane times.

Deadbelly dont hide it —
        Lead killed Leadbelly —
Deadbelly admit
        Deadbelly modern cat
Cool — Deadbelly, Man,
Craziest.
                Old Man Mose is Dead
                But Deadbelly get Ahead
                Ha ha ha

225th Chorus

The void that's highly embraceable
        during sleep
Has no location and no fret;
Yet I keep restless mental searching

And geographical meandering
To find the Holy Inside Milk
Damema gave to all.

Damema, Mother of Buddhas,
        Mother of Milk

In the dark I wryly remonstrate
With my sillier self
For feigning to believe
In the reality of anything
Especially the so-called reality
Of giving the Discipline
The full desert-hut workout
And superman solitude
And continual enlightened trance
With no cares in the open
And no walls closing in
The Bright Internal Heaven
Of the Starry Night
Of the Cloud Mopped afternoon —
        Oh, Ah, Gold, Honey,
        I've lost my way.

228th Chorus

Praised be man, he is existing in milk
        and living in lillies —
And his violin music takes place in milk
        and creamy emptiness —
Praised be the unfolded inside petal
        flesh of tend'rest thought —
        (petrels on the follying
        wave-valleys idly
        sing themselves asleep) —
Praised be delusion, the ripple —
Praised the Holy Ocean of Eternity —
Praised be I, writing, dead already &

dead again —
Dipped in ancid inkl
　　　the flamd
　　　of T i m
the Anglo Oglo Saxon Maneuvers
Of Old Poet-o's —
　　　Praised be wood, it is milk —
　　　Praised be Honey at the Source —
Praised be the embrace of soft sleep
— the valor of angels in valleys
　of hell on earth below —
Praised be the Non ending —
Praised be the lights of earth-man —
Praised be the watchers —
　　　Praised be my fellow man
　　　For dwelling in milk

230th Chorus

Love's multitudinous boneyard
　of decay,
The spilled milk of heroes,
Destruction of silk kerchiefs
　by dust storm,
Caress of heroes blindfolded to posts,
Murder victims admitted to this life,
Skeletons bartering fingers and joints,
The quivering meat of the elephants of kindness
　being torn apart by vultures,
Conceptions of delicate kneecaps,
Fear of rats dripping with bacteria,
Golgotha Cold Hope for Gold Hope,
Damp leaves of Autumn against
　the wood of boats,
Seahorse's delicate imagery of glue,
Sentimental "I Love You" no more,
Death by long exposure to defilement,

Frightening ravishing mysterious beings
    concealing their sex,
Pieces of the Buddha-material frozen
    and sliced microscopically
In Morgues of the North,
Penis apples going to seed,
The severed gullets more numerous than sands —
       Like kissing my kitten in the belly
       The softness of our reward

1955

ALLEN GINSBERG

THE SHROUDED STRANGER

Bare skin is my wrinkled sack
When hot Apollo humps my back
When Jack Frost grabs me in these rags
I wrap my legs with burlap bags

My flesh is cinder my face is snow
I walk the railroad to and fro
When city streets are black and dead
The railroad embankment is my bed

I sup my soup from old tin cans
And take my sweets from little hands
In Tiger Alley near the jail
I steal away from the garbage pail

In darkest night where none can see
Down in the bowels of the factory
I sneak barefoot upon stone
Come and hear the old man groan

I hide and wait like a naked child
Under the bridge my heart goes wild
I scream at a fire on the river bank
I give my body to an old gas tank

I dream that I have burning hair
Boiled arms that claw the air
The torso of an iron king
And on my back a broken wing

Who'll go out whoring into the night
On the eyeless road in the skinny moonlight
Maid or dowd or athlete proud
May wanton with me in the shroud

Who'll come lay down in the dark with me
Belly to belly and knee to knee
Who'll look into my hooded eye
Who'll lay down under my darkened thigh?

1949

MALEST CORNIFICI TUO CATULLO

I'm happy, Kerouac, your madman Allen's
finally made it: discovered a new young cat,
and my imagination of eternity's boy
walks on the streets of San Francisco
handsome, and meets me in cafeterias
and loves me. Ah, don't think I'm sickening!
You're angry at me. For all of my lovers?
It's hard to eat shit, without having visions,
& when they have eyes for me it's Heaven.

SUNFLOWER SUTRA

I walked on the banks of the tincan banana dock and sat down
    under the huge shade of a Southern Pacific locomotive to
    look at the sunset over the box house hills and cry.
Jack Kerouac sat beside me on a busted rusty iron pole,
    companion, we thought the same thoughts of the soul, bleak
    and blue and sad-eyed, surrounded by the gnarled steel roots
    of trees of machinery.
The oily water on the river mirrored by the red sky, sun sank on
    top of final Frisco peaks, no fish in that stream, no hermit in
    those mounts, just ourselves rheumy-eyed and hungover like
    old bums on the riverbank, tired and wily.
Look at the Sunflower, he said, there was a dead gray shadow
    against the sky, big as a man, sitting dry on top of a pile of
    ancient sawdust —
— I rushed up enchanted — it was my first sunflower, memories
    of Blake — my visions — Harlem

and Hells of the Eastern rivers, bridges clanking, Joes Greasy
   Sandwiches, dead baby carriages, black treadless tires for-
   gotten and unretreaded, the poem of the riverbank, condoms
   & pots, steel knives, nothing stainless, only the dank muck
   and the razor sharp artifacts passing into the past —
and the gray Sunflower poised against the sunset, crackly bleak
   and dusty with the smut and smog and smoke of olden
   locomotives in its eye —
corolla of bleary spikes pushed down and broken like a battered
   crown, seeds fallen out of its face, soon-to-be-toothless mouth
   of sunny air, sunrays obliterated on its hairy head like a
   dried wire spiderweb,
leaves stuck out like arms out of the stem, gestures from the
   sawdust root, broke pieces of plaster fallen out of the black
   twigs, a dead fly in its ear,
Unholy battered old thing you were, my sunflower O my soul,
   I loved you then!
The grime was no man's grime but death and human locomotives,
all that dress of dust, that veil of darkened railroad skin, that
   smog of cheek, that eyelid of black mis'ry, that sooty hand
   or phallus or protuberance of artificial worse-than-dirt —
   industrial — modern — all that civilization spotting your crazy
   golden crown —
and those blear thoughts of death and dusty loveless eyes and
   ends and withered roots below, in the home-pile of sand and
   sawdust, rubber dollar bills, skin of machinery, the guts and
   innards of the weeping coughing car, the empty lonely
   tincans with their rusty tongues alack, what more could I
   name, the smoked ashes of some cock cigar, the cunts of
   wheelbarrows and the milky breasts of cars, wornout asses
   out of chairs & sphincters of dynamos — all these
entangled in your mummied roots — and you there standing
   before me in the sunset, all your glory in your form!
A perfect beauty of a sunflower! a perfect excellent lovely
   sunflower existence! a sweet natural eye to the new hip
   moon, woke up alive and excited grasping in the sunset
   shadow sunrise golden monthly breeze!
How many flies buzzed round you innocent of your grime, while

you cursed the heavens of the railroad and your flower soul?
Poor dead flower? when did you forget you were a flower? when
 did you look at your skin and decide you were an impotent
 dirty old locomotive? the ghost of a locomotive? the specter
 and shade of a once powerful mad American locomotive?
You were never no locomotive, Sunflower, you were a sunflower!
And you Locomotive, you are a locomotive, forget me not!
So I grabbed up the skeleton thick sunflower and stuck it at my
 side like a scepter,
and deliver my sermon to my soul, and Jack's soul too, and
 anyone who'll listen,
— We're not our skin of grime, we're not our dread bleak dusty
 imageless locomotive, we're all beautiful golden sunflowers
 inside, we're blessed by our own seed & golden hairy naked
 accomplishment-bodies growing into mad black formal sun-
 flowers in the sunset, spied on by our eyes under the shadow
 of the mad locomotive riverbank sunset Frisco hilly tincan
 evening sitdown vision.

A SUPERMARKET IN CALIFORNIA

What thoughts I have of you tonight, Walt Whitman, for
I walked down the sidestreets under the trees with a headache
self-conscious looking at the full moon.

In my hungry fatigue, and shopping for images, I went into
the neon fruit supermarket, dreaming of your enumerations!

What peaches and what penumbras! Whole families shopping
at night! Aisles full of husbands! Wives in the avocados, babies
in the tomatoes! — and you, Garcia Lorca, what were you doing
down by the watermelons?

I saw you, Walt Whitman, childless, lonely old grubber,
poking among the meats in the refrigerator and eyeing the
grocery boys.

I heard you asking questions of each: Who killed the pork
chops? What price bananas? Are you my Angel?

I wandered in and out of the brilliant stacks of cans following you, and followed in my imagination by the store detective.

We strode down the open corridors together in our solitary fancy tasting artichokes, possessing every frozen delicacy, and never passing the cashier.

Where are we going, Walt Whitman? The doors close in an hour. Which way does your beard point tonight?

(I touch your book and dream of our odyssey in the supermarket and feel absurd.)

Will we walk all night through solitary streets? The trees add shade to shade, lights out in the houses, we'll both be lonely.

Will we stroll dreaming of the lost America of love past blue automobiles in driveways, home to our silent cottage?

Ah, dear father, graybeard, lonely old courage-teacher, what America did you have when Charon quit poling his ferry and you got out on a smoking bank and stood watching the boat disappear on the black waters of Lethe?

Berkeley 1955

HOWL, PARTS I AND II

for Carl Solomon

I

I saw the best minds of my generation destroyed by madness, starving hysterical naked,

dragging themselves through the negro streets at dawn looking for an angry fix,

angelheaded hipsters burning for the ancient heavenly connection to the starry dynamo in the machinery of night,

who poverty and tatters and hollow-eyed and high sat up smoking in the supernatural darkness of cold-water flats floating across the tops of cities contemplating jazz,

who bared their brains to Heaven under the El and saw Mohammedan angels staggering on tenement roofs illuminated,

who passed through universities with radiant cool eyes hallucinating Arkansas and Blake-light tragedy among the scholars of war,

who were expelled from the academies for crazy & publishing
  obscene odes on the windows of the skull,

who cowered in unshaven rooms in underwear, burning their
  money in wastebaskets and listening to the Terror through
  the wall,

who got busted in their pubic beards returning through Laredo
  with a belt of marijuana for New York,

who ate fire in paint hotels or drank turpentine in Paradise Alley,
  death, or purgatoried their torsos night after night

with dreams, with drugs, with waking nightmares, alcohol and
  cock and endless balls,

incomparable blind streets of shuddering cloud and lightning in
  the mind leaping toward poles of Canada & Paterson, illumi-
  nating all the motionless world of Time between,

Peyote solidities of halls, backyard green tree cemetery dawns,
  wine drunkenness over the rooftops, storefront boroughs of
  teahead joyride neon blinking traffic light, sun and moon and
  tree vibrations in the roaring winter dusks of Brooklyn, ash-
  can rantings and kind king light of mind,

who chained themselves to subways for the endless ride from
  Battery to holy Bronx on benzedrine until the noise of
  wheels and children brought them down shuddering mouth-
  wracked and battered bleak of brain all drained of brilliance
  in the drear light of Zoo,

who sank all night in submarine light of Bickford's floated out
  and sat through the stale beer afternoon in desolate Fu-
  gazzi's listening to the crack of doom on the hydrogen juke-
  box,

who talked continuously seventy hours from park to pad to bar
  to Bellevue to museum to the Brooklyn Bridge,

a lost battalion of platonic conversationalists jumping down the
  stoops off fire escapes off windowsills off Empire State out
  of the moon,

yacketayakking screaming vomiting whispering facts and mem-
  ories and anecdotes and eyeball kicks and shocks of hospitals
  and jails and wars,

whole intellects disgorged in total recall for seven days and

nights with brilliant eyes, meat for the Synagogue cast on the
pavement,

who vanished into nowhere Zen New Jersey leaving a trail of
ambiguous picture postcards of Atlantic City Hall,

suffering Eastern sweats and Tangerian bone-grindings and mi-
graines of China under junk-withdrawal in Newark's bleak
furnished room,

who wandered around and around at midnight in the railroad
yard wondering where to go, and went, leaving no broken
hearts,

who lit cigarettes in boxcars boxcars boxcars racketing through
snow toward lonesome farms in grandfather night,

who studied Plotinus Poe St. John of the Cross telepathy and bop
kaballa because the cosmos instinctively vibrated at their
feet in Kansas,

who loned it through the streets of Idaho seeking visionary in-
dian angels who were visionary indian angels,

who thought they were only mad when Baltimore gleamed in
supernatural ecstasy,

who jumped in limousines with the Chinaman of Oklahoma on
the impulse of winter midnight streetlight smalltown rain,

who lounged hungry and lonesome through Houston seeking jazz
or sex or soup, and followed the brilliant Spaniard to con-
verse about America and Eternity, a hopeless task, and so
took ship to Africa,

who disappeared into the volcanoes of Mexico leaving behind
nothing but the shadow of dungarees and the lava and ash
of poetry scattered in fireplace Chicago,

who reappeared on the West Coast investigating the F.B.I. in
beards and shorts with big pacifist eyes sexy in their dark
skin passing out incomprehensible leaflets,

who burned cigarette holes in their arms protesting the narcotic
tobacco haze of Capitalism,

who distributed Supercommunist pamphlets in Union Square
weeping and undressing while the sirens of Los Alamos
wailed them down, and wailed down Wall, and the Staten
Island ferry also wailed,

who broke down crying in white gymnasiums naked and trem-
bling before the machinery of other skeletons,

who bit detectives in the neck and shrieked with delight in po-
licecars for committing no crime but their own wild cooking
pederasty and intoxication,

who howled on their knees in the subway and were dragged off
the roof waving genitals and manuscripts,

who let themselves be fucked in the ass by saintly motorcyclists,
and screamed with joy,

who blew and were blown by those human seraphim, the sailors,
caresses of Atlantic and Caribbean love,

who balled in the morning in the evenings in rosegardens and
the grass of public parks and cemeteries scattering their
semen freely to whomever come who may,

who hiccupped endlessly trying to giggle but wound up with a
sob behind a partition in a Turkish Bath when the blonde &
naked angel came to pierce them with a sword,

who lost their loveboys to the three old shrews of fate the one
eyed shrew of the heterosexual dollar the one eyed shrew
that winks out of the womb and the one eyed shrew that
does nothing but sit on her ass and snip the intellectual
golden threads of the craftsman's loom,

who copulated ecstatic and insatiate with a bottle of beer a
sweetheart a package of cigarettes a candle and fell off the
bed, and continued along the floor and down the hall and
ended fainting on the wall with a vision of ultimate cunt
and come eluding the last gyzym of consciousness.

who sweetened the snatches of a million girls trembling in the
sunset, and were red eyed in the morning but prepared to
sweeten the snatch of the sunrise, flashing buttocks under
barns and naked in the lake,

who went out whoring through Colorado in myriad stolen night-
cars, N.C., secret hero of these poems, cocksman and Adonis
of Denver — joy to the memory of his innumerable lays of
girls in empty lots & diner backyards, moviehouses' rickety
rows, on mountaintops in caves or with gaunt waitresses in
familiar roadside lonely petticoat upliftings & especially

secret gas-station solipsisms of johns, & hometown alleys too,

who faded out in vast sordid movies, were shifted in dreams, woke on a sudden Manhattan, and picked themselves up out of basements hungover with heartless Tokay and horrors of Third Avenue iron dreams & stumbled to unemployment offices,

who walked all night with their shoes full of blood on the snowbank docks waiting for a door in the East River to open to a room full of steamheat and opium,

who created great suicidal dramas on the apartment cliff-banks of the Hudson under the wartime blue floodlight of the moon & their heads shall be crowned with laurel in oblivion,

who ate the lamb stew of the imagination or digested the crab at the muddy bottom of the rivers of Bowery,

who wept at the romance of the streets with their pushcarts full of onions and bad music,

who sat in boxes breathing in the darkness under the bridge, and rose up to build harpsichords in their lofts,

who coughed on the sixth floor of Harlem crowned with flame under the tubercular sky surrounded by orange crates of theology,

who scribbled all night rocking and rolling over lofty incantations which in the yellow morning where stanzas of gibberish,

who cooked rotten animals lung heart feet borsht & tortillas dreaming of the pure vegetable kingdom,

who plunged themselves under meat trucks looking for an egg,

who threw their watches off the roof to cast their ballot for Eternity outside of Time, & alarm clocks fell on their heads every day for the next decade,

who cut their wrists three times successively unsuccessfully, gave up and were forced to open antique stores where they thought they were growing old and cried,

who were burned alive in their innocent flannel suits on Madison Avenue amid blasts of leaden verse & the tanked-up clatter of the iron regiments of fashion & the nitroglycerine shrieks of the fairies of advertising & the mustard gas of sinister intelligent editors, or were run down by the drunken taxicabs of Absolute Reality, who jumped off the Brooklyn Bridge this actually happened and walked away unknown and forgotten into the ghostly daze of Chinatown soup alleyways & firetrucks, not even one free beer,

who sang out of their windows in despair, fell out of the subway window, jumped in the filthy Passaic, leaped on negroes, cried all over the street, danced on broken wineglasses barefoot smashed phonograph records of nostalgic European 1930's German jazz finished the whiskey and threw up groaning into the bloody toilet, moans in their ears and the blast of colossal steamwhistles,

who barreled down the highways of the past journeying to each other's hotrod-Golgotha jail-solitude watch or Birmingham jazz incarnation,

who drove crosscountry seventytwo hours to find out if I had a vision or you had a vision or he had a vision to find out Eternity,

who journeyed to Denver, who died in Denver, who came back to Denver & waited in vain, who watched over Denver & brooded & loned in Denver and finally went away to find out the Time, & now Denver is lonesome for her heroes,

who fell on their knees in hopeless cathedrals praying for each other's salvation and light and breasts, until the soul illuminated its hair for a second,

who crashed through their minds in jail waiting for impossible criminals with golden heads and the charm of reality in their hearts who sang sweet blues to Alcatraz,

who retired to Mexico to cultivate a habit, or Rocky Mount to tender Buddha or Tangiers to boys or Southern Pacific to the black locomotive or Harvard to Narcissus to Woodlawn to the daisychain or grave,

who demanded sanity trials accusing the radio of hypnotism & were left with their insanity & their hands & a hung jury,

who threw potato salad at CCNY lecturers on Dadaism and subsequently presented themselves on the granite steps of the madhouse with shaven heads and harlequin speech of suicide, demanding instantaneous lobotomy, and who were given instead the concrete void of insulin metrasol electricity hydrotherapy psychotherapy occupational therapy pingpong & amnesia,

who in humorless protest overturned only one symbolic pingpong table, resting briefly in catatonia,

returning years later truly bald except for a wig of blood, and tears and fingers, to the visible madman doom of the wards of the madtowns of the East,

Pilgrim State's Rockland's and Greystone's foetid halls, bickering with the echoes of the soul, rocking and rolling in the midnight solitude-bench dolmen-realms of love, dream of life a nightmare, bodies turned to stone as heavy as the moon,

with mother finally °°°°°°, and the last fantastic book flung out of the tenement window, and the last door closed at 4 AM and the last telephone slammed at the wall in reply and the last furnished room emptied down to the last piece of mental furniture, a yellow paper rose twisted on a wire hanger in the closet, and even that imaginary, nothing but a hopeful little bit of hallucination —

ah, Carl, while you are not safe I am not safe, and now you're really in the total animal soup of time —

and who therefore ran through the icy streets obsessed with a sudden flash of the alchemy of the use of the ellipse the catalog the meter & the vibrating plane,

who dreamt and made incarnate gaps in Time & Space through images juxtaposed, and trapped the archangel of the soul between 2 visual images and joined the elemental verbs and set the noun and dash of consciousness together jumping with sensation of Pater Omnipotens Aeterna Deus

to recreate the syntax and measure of poor human prose and stand before you speechless and intelligent and shaking with shame, rejected yet confessing out the soul to conform to the rhythm of thought in his naked and endless head,

the madman bum and angel beat in Time, unknown, yet putting down here what might be left to say in time come after death,

and rose reincarnate in the ghostly clothes of jazz in the goldhorn
   shadow of the band and blew the suffering of America's
   naked mind for love into an eli eli lamma lamma sabacthani
   saxophone cry that shivered the cities down to the last radio
with the absolute heart of the poem of life butchered out of their
   own bodies good to eat a thousand years.
                                   II
What sphinx of cement and aluminum bashed open their skulls
   and ate up their brains and imagination?
Moloch! Solitude! Filth! Ugliness! Ashcans and unobtainable
   dollars! Children screaming under the stairways! Boys sob-
   bing in armies! Old men weeping in the parks!
Moloch! Moloch! Nightmare of Moloch! Moloch the loveless!
   Mental Moloch! Moloch the heavy judger of men!
Moloch the incomprehensible prison! Moloch the crossbone soul-
   less jailhouse and Congress of sorrows! Moloch whose build-
   ings are judgement! Moloch the vast stone of war! Moloch
   the stunned governments!
Moloch whose mind is pure machinery! Moloch whose blood is
   running money! Moloch whose fingers are ten armies!
   Moloch whose breast is a cannibal dynamo! Moloch whose
   ear is a smoking tomb!
Moloch whose eyes are a thousand blind windows! Moloch
   whose skyscrapers stand in the long streets like endless
   Jehovahs! Moloch whose factories dream and croak in the
   fog! Moloch whose smokestacks and antennae crown the
   cities!
Moloch whose love is endless oil and stone! Moloch whose soul
   is electricity and banks! Moloch whose poverty is the specter
   of genius! Moloch whose fate is a cloud of sexless hydrogen!
   Moloch whose name is the Mind!
Moloch in whom I sit lonely! Moloch in whom I dream Angels!
   Crazy in Moloch! Cocksucker in Moloch! Lacklove and
   manless in Moloch!
Moloch who entered my soul early! Moloch in whom I am a
   consciousness without a body! Moloch who frightened me
   out of my natural ecstacy! Moloch whom I abandon! Wake
   up in Moloch! Light streaming out of the sky!

Moloch! Moloch! Robot apartments! invisible suburbs! skeleton
treasuries! blind capitals! demonic industries! spectral
nations! invincible madhouses! granite cocks! monstrous
bombs!
They broke their backs lifting Moloch to Heaven! Pavements,
trees, radios, tons! lifting the city to Heaven which exists
and is everywhere about us!
Visions! omens! hallucinations! miracles! ecstasies! gone down
the American river!
Dreams! adorations! illuminations! religions! the whole boatload
of sensitive bullshit!
Breakthroughs! over the river! flips and crucifixions! gone down
the flood! Highs! Epiphanies! Despairs! Ten years' animal
screams and suicides! Minds! New loves! Mad generation!
down on the rocks of Time!
Real holy laughter in the river! They saw it all! the wild eyes!
the holy yells! They bade farewell! They jumped off the
roof! to solitude! waving! carrying flowers! Down to the
river! into the street!

San Francisco 1955-56

SATHER GATE ILLUMINATION

Why do I deny manna to another?
Because I deny it to myself.

Why have I denied myself?
What other has rejected me?

Now I believe you are lovely, my soul, soul of Allen, Allen —
and you so beloved, so sweetened, so recalled to your true
loveliness, your original nude breathing Allen
will you ever deny another again?

Dear Walter, thanks for the message —
I forbid you not to touch me, man to man, True American.

The bombers jet through the sky in unison of twelve,
the pilots are sweating and nervous at the controls in the hot
    cabins.
Over what souls will they loose their loveless bombs?

The Campanile pokes its white granite innocent head into the
    clouds for me to look at.

A crippled lady explains French grammar with a loud sweet
    voice: *Regarder is to look* —
the whole French language looks on the trees on the campus.

 The girls' haunted voices make quiet dates for 2 o'clock — yet one
of them waves farewell and smiles at last — her red skirt swing-
ing shows how she loves herself.

Another encased in flashy scotch clothes clomps up the concrete
in a hurry — into the door — poor dear! — Who will receive you
in love's offices?

How many beautiful boys have I seen on this spot?
The trees seem on the verge of moving — ah! they do move in the
    breeze.
Roar again of airplanes in the sky — everyone looks up.

And do you know that all these rubbings of the eyes & painful
    gestures to the brow
of suited scholars entering Dwinelle (Hall) are Holy Signs? —
    anxiety and fear?

How many years have I got to float on this sweetened scene of
    trees & humans clomping above ground —
O I must be mad to sit here lonely in the void & glee & build up
    thoughts of love!
But what do I have to doubt but my own shiney eyes, what to
    lose but life which is a vision today this afternoon.

My stomach is light, I relax, new sentences spring forth out of
the scene to describe spontaneous forms of Time — trees, old
ladies, sleeping dogs, soldiers, airplanes wandering through the
air, Negroes with their lunch books of anxiety, apples and sand-
wiches, lunchtime, icecream, Timeless —

And even the ugliest will seek beauty — "What are you doing
      Friday night?" asks the sailor in white school training cap &
      gilt buttons & blue coat,
and the little ape in a green jacket and baggy pants and over-
      loaded schoolbook satchel says, "Quartets."
Every Friday night, beautiful quartets to celebrate and please my
      soul with all its hair — music!
And then strides off, snapping pieces chocolate off a bar wrapped
      in Hershey brown paper and tinfoil, eating chocolate rose.

& how can those other boys be them happy selves in their brown
      army study uniforms?

Now cripple girl swings down the walk with loping fuck gestures
      of her hips askew —
let her roll her eyes in abandon & camp angelic through the
      campus bouncing her body about in joy
— someone will dig that pelvic energy for sure.

Those white stripes down your chocolate cupcake, Lady (held in
      front of your nose finishing sentence preparatory to chomp),
they were painted there to delight you by some Spanish industrial
      artistic hand in bakery factory faraway,
expert hand in simple-minded messages of white stripes on
      millions of message cupcakes.

I have a message for you all — I will denote one particularity of
      each!

And there goes Professor Hart striding enlightened by the years
through the doorway and arcade he built (in his mind) and
knows — he too saw the ruins of Yucatan once —

followed by a lonely janitor in dovegrey Italian fruitpeddlar
      Chico Marx hat pushing his rolypoly belly thru the trees.

Neal sees all girls
as visions of their inner cunts,
yes, it's true!
and all men walking

along thinking of
their spirit cocks.

So look at that poor dread boy
with two-day black hair
all over his dirty face,
　　　　　　how he must hate his cock
　　　　　　— Chinamen stop shuddering —

And now to bring this to an end with a rise and an ellipse —

The boys are now all talking to the girls
"If I was a girl I'd love all boys" & girls giggling the opposite, all
　　　pretty everywhichway;
and even I have my secret beds and lovers under another moon-
　　　light, be you sure

& any minute I expect to see a baby carriage pushed on to the
　　　scene
and everyone turn in attention like the airplanes and laughter,
　　　like a Greek campus
and the big brown shaggy silent dog lazing open-eyed in the
　　　shade
lift up his head & sniff & laugh & lower his head on his golden
　　　paws & let his belly rumble away unconcerned.

. . . the lion's ruddy eyes
Shall flow with tears of gold!

Now the silence is broken, students pour onto the square, the
　　　doors are filled, the dog gets up and walks away,
the cripple swings out of Dwinelle, a nun even, I wonder about
　　　her, an old lady distinguished by a cane,
we all look up, silence moves, huge changes upon the ground, and
　　　in the air thoughts fly all over filling space.

My grief at Peter's not loving me was grief at not loving myself.

Huge karmas of broken minds in beautiful bodies unable to re-
　　　ceive love because not knowing the self as lovely —

Fathers and Teachers!

Seeing in people the visible evidence of inner self thought by
     their treatment of me:
who loves himself loves me who love myself.

Berkeley 1956

MESSAGE

               Since we had changed
               rogered spun worked
               wept & pissed together
               I wake up in the morning
               with a dream in my eyes
               but you are gone in NY
               remembering me good
               I love you I love you
               & your brothers are crazy
               I accept their drunk cases
It is too long that I have been alone
It's too long that I've sat up in bed
without anyone to touch on the knee, man
or woman I don't care what anymore, I
want love I was born for I want you with me now
Ocean liners boiling over the Atlantic
Delicate steelwork of unfinished skyscrapers
Back end of the dirigible roaring over Lakehurst
Six women dancing on a red stage naked
The leaves are green on all the trees in Paris now
I will be home in two months and look you in the eyes

Paris 1958

KADDISH, Parts I, III, IV, V

     I
Strange now to think of you, gone without corsets and eyes, while
     I walk on the sunny pavement of Greenwich Village
downtown Manhattan, clear winter noon, and I've been up all

night, talking, talking, reading the Kaddish aloud, listening
to Ray Charles blues shout blind on the phonograph

the rhythm the rhythm — and your memory in my head three
years after — And read Adonais' last triumphant stanzas
aloud — wept, realizing how we suffer —

And how Death is that remedy all singers dream of, sing, remem-
ber, prophesy as in the Hebrew Anthem, or the Buddhist
Book of Answers — and my own imagination of a withered
leaf — at dawn —

Dreaming back thru life, Your time — and mine accelerating
toward Apocalypse,

the final moment — flower burning in the Day — and what comes
after,

looking back on the mind itself that saw an American city

a flash away, and the great dream of Me or China, or you and a
phantom Russia, or a crumpled bed that never existed —

like a poem in the dark — escaped back to Oblivion —

No more to say, and nothing to weep for but the Beings in the
Dream, trapped in its disappearance,

sighing, screaming with it, buying and selling pieces of phantom,
worshipping each other,

worshipping the God included in it all — longing or inevitability?
— while it lasts, a Vision — anything more?

It leaps about me, as I go out and walk the street, look back over
my shoulder, Seventh Avenue, the battlements of window
office buildings shouldering each other high, under a cloud,
tall as the sky an instant — and the sky above — an old blue
place,

or down the Avenue to the South, to — as I walk toward the
Lower East Side — where you walked fifty years ago, little
girl — from Russia, eating the first poisonous tomatoes of
America — frightened on the dock —

then struggling in the crowds of Orchard Street toward what? —
toward Newark —

toward candy store, first home-made sodas of the century, hand-
churned ice cream in backroom on musty brownfloor boards —

Toward education marriage nervous breakdown, operation, teaching school, and learning to be mad, in a dream — What is this life?

Toward the Key in the window — and the great Key lays its head of light on top of Manhattan, and over the floor, and lays down on the sidewalk — in a single vast beam, moving — as I walk down First toward the Yiddish Theater — and the place of poverty

you knew, and I know, but without caring now — Strange to have moved thru Paterson, and the West, and Europe and here again,

with the cries of Spaniards now in the doorstoops doors and dark boys on the street, fire escapes old as you

— Though you're not old now, that's left here with me —

Myself, anyhow, maybe as old as the universe — and I guess that dies with us — enough to cancel all that comes — What came is gone forever every time —

That's good! That leaves it open for no regret — no fear radiators, lacklove, torture even toothache in the end —

Though while it comes it is a lion that eats the soul — and the lamb, the soul, in us, alas, offering itself in sacrifice to change's fierce hunger — hair and teeth — and the roar of bonepain, skull bare, break rib, rot-skin, brain-tricked Implacability.

Ai! ai! we do worse! We are in a fix! And you're out, Death let you out, Death had the Mercy, you're done with your century, done with God, done with the path thru it — Done with yourself at last — Pure — Back to the Babe dark before your Father, before us all — before the world —

There, rest. No more suffering for you. I know where you've gone, it's good.

No more flowers in the summer fields of New York, no joy now, no more fear of Louis,

and no more of his sweetness and glasses, his high school decades, debts, loves, frightened telephone calls, conception beds, relatives, hands —

No more of sister Elanor — she gone before you — we kept it secret — you killed her, or she killed herself to bear with

you — an arthritic heart — But Death's killed you both —
No matter —

Nor your memory of your mother, 1915 tears in silent movies
weeks and weeks — forgetting, agrieve watching Marie
Dressler address humanity, Chaplin dance in youth,

or Boris Gudinov, Chaliapin's at the Met, hauling his voice of a
weeping Czar — by standing room with Elanor and Max —
watching also the Capitalists take seats in Orchestra, white
furs, diamonds,

with the YPSL's hitch-hiking thru Pennsylvania, in black baggy
gym skirt pants, photograph of four girls holding each other
round the waste, and laughing eye, too coy, virginal solitude
of 1920

all girls grown old, or dead, now, and that long hair in the grave
— lucky to have husbands later —

You made it — I came too — Eugene my brother before (still
grieving now and will gream on to his last stiff hand, as he
goes thru his cancer — or kill — later perhaps — soon he will
think —)

And it's the last moment I remember, when I see them all, thru
myself, now — though not you

I didn't foresee what you felt — what more hideous gape of bad
mouth came first — to you — and were you prepared?

To go where? In that Dark — that — in that God? a radiance? A
Lord in the Void? Like an eye in the black cloud in a dream?
Adonoi at last, with you?

Beyond my remembrance! Incapable to guess! Not merely the
yellow skull in the grave, or a box of worm dust, and a
stained ribbon — Deathshead with Halo? can you believe it?

It is only the sun that shines once for the mind, only the flash of
existence, that none ever was?

Nothing beyond what we have — what you had — that so pitiful —
yet Triumph,

to have been here, and changed, like a tree, broken, or flower —
fed to the ground — but mad, with its petals, colored, think-
ing Great Universe, shaken, cut in the head, leaf stript, hid
in an egg crate hospital, cloth wrapped, sore — freaked in the
moon brain, Naughtless.

No flower like that flower, which knew itself in the garden, and
    fought the knife — lost
Cut down by an idiot Snowman's icy — even in the Spring —
    strange ghost thought — some Death — Sharp icicle in his
    hand — crowned with old roses — a dog for his eyes — cock
    of a sweatshop — heart of electric irons.
All the accumulations of life, that wear us out — clocks, bodies,
    consciousness, shoes, breasts — begotten sons — your Com-
    munism — "Paranoia" into hospitals.
You once kicked Elanor in the leg, she died of heart failure later.
    You of stroke. Asleep? Within a year, the two of you, sisters
    in death. Is Elanor happy?
Max grieves alive in an office on Lower Broadway, lone large
    mustache over midnight Accountings, not sure. His life
    passes — as he sees — and what does he doubt now? Still
    dream of making money, or that might have made money,
    hired nurse, had children, found even your Immortality,
    Naomi?
I'll see him soon. Now I've got to cut through — to talk to you
    — as I didn't when you had a mouth.
Forever. And we're bound for that, Forever — like Emily Dickin-
    son's horses — headed to the End.
They know the way — These Steeds — run faster than we think —
    it's our own life they cross — and take with them.

Magnificent, mourned no more, marred of heart, mind be-
hind, married dreamed, mortal changed — Ass and face done with
murder.
    In the world, given, flower maddened, made no Utopia, shut
under pine, almed in Earth, balmed in Lone, Jehovah, accept.
    Nameless, One Faced, Forever, beyond me, beginningless,
endless, Father in death. Though I am not there for this Prophecy,
I am unmarried, I'm hymnless, I'm heavenless, headless in bliss-
hood I would still adore
    Thee, Heaven, after Death, only One blessed in Nothingness,
not light or darkness, Dayless Eternity —
    Take this, this Psalm, from me, burst from my hand in a day,
some of my Time, now given to Nothing — to praise Thee — But

Death

This is the end, the redemption from Wilderness, way for the Wonderer, House sought for All, black handkerchief washed clean by weeping — page beyond Psalm — Last change of mine and Naomi — to God's perfect Darkness — Death, stay thy phantoms!

III

Only to have not forgotten the beginning in which she drank cheap sodas in the morgues of Newark,

only to have seen her weeping on grey tables in long wards of her universe

only to have known the weird ideas of Hitler at the door, the wires in her head, the three big sticks

rammed down her back, the voices in the ceiling shrieking out her ugly early lays for 30 years,

only to have seen the time-jumps, memory lapse, the crash of wars, the roar and silence of a vast electric shock,

only to have seen her painting crude pictures of Elevateds running over the rooftops of the Bronx

her brothers dead in Riverside or Russia, her lone in Long Island writing a last letter — and her image in the sunlight at the window

"The key is in the sunlight at the window in the bars the key is in the sunlight,"

only to have come to that dark night on iron bed by stroke when the sun gone down on Long Island

and the vast Atlantic outside roars the great call of Being to its own

to come back out of the Nightmare — divided creation — with her head lain on a pillow of the hospital to die

— in one last glimpse — all Earth one everlasting Light in the familiar blackout — no tears for this vision —

But that the key should be left behind — at the window — the key in the sunlight — to the living — that can take

that slice of light in hand — and turn the door — and look back see

Creation glistening backwards to the same grave, size of universe,

size of the tick of the hospital's clock on the archway over the
    white door —

    IV
O mother
what have I left out
O mother
what have I forgotten
O mother
farewell
with a long black shoe
farewell
with old dress and broken stocking
farewell
with six dark hairs on the wen of your breast
farewell
with gold teeth and a long black beard around the vagina

with your sagging belly
with your fear of Hitler
with your mouth of bad short stories
with your fingers of rotten mandolines
with your arms of fat Paterson porches
with your belly of strikes and smokestacks
with your chin of Trotsky and the Spanish War
with your voice singing for the decaying overbroken workers
with your nose of bad lay with your nose of the smell of the
    pickles of Newark

with your eyes
with your eyes of Russia
with your eyes of no money
with your eyes of false China
with your eyes of Aunt Elanor
with your eyes of starving India
with your eyes pissing in the park
with your eyes of your failure at the piano
with your eyes of your relatives in California
with your eyes of Ma Rainey dying in an ambulance
with your eyes of Czechoslovakia attacked by robots

with your eyes going to painting class at night in the Bronx
 with your eyes of the killer Grandma you see on the fire-escape
with your eyes running naked out of the apartment screaming
      into the hall
with your eyes being led away by policemen to an ambulance
with your eyes strapped down on the operating table
with your eyes with the pancreas removed
with your eyes of appendix operation
with your eyes of abortion
with your eyes of ovaries removed
with your eyes of shock
with your eyes of lobotomy
with your eyes of divorce
with your eyes of stroke
with your eyes alone
with your eyes
with your eyes
with your Death full of Flowers

            IV
Caw caw caw crows shriek in the white sun over grave stones in
      Long Island
Lord Lord Lord Naomi underneath this grass my halflife and my
      own as hers
caw caw my eye be buried in the same Ground where I stand in
      Angel
Lord Lord great Eye that stares on All and moves in a black cloud
caw caw strange cry of Beings flung up into sky over the waving
      trees
Lord Lord O Grinder of giant Beyonds my voice in a boundless
      field in Sheol
Caw caw the call of Time rent out of foot and wing an instant in
      the universe
Lord Lord an echo in the sky the wind through ragged leaves the
      roar of memory
caw caw all years my birth a dream caw caw New York the bus
      the broken shoe the vast highschool caw caw all Visions of
      the Lord
Lord Lord Lord caw caw caw Lord Lord Lord caw caw caw Lord

                                                                          1959

GREGORY CORSO

BIRTHPLACE REVISITED

I stand in the dark light in the dark street
and look up at my window, I was born there.
The lights are on; other people are moving about.
I am with raincoat; cigarette in mouth,
hat over eye, hand on gat.
I cross the street and enter the building.
The garbage cans haven't stopped smelling.
I walk up the first flight; Dirty Ears
aims a knife at me . . .
I pump him full of lost watches.

POETS HITCHHIKING ON THE HIGHWAY

Of course I tried to tell him
but he cranked his head
        without an excuse.
I told him the sky chases
        the sun
And he smiled and said:
        "What's the use."
I was feeling like a demon
        again
So I said: "But the ocean chases
        the fish."
This time he laughed
        and said: "Suppose the
            strawberry were
                pushed into a mountain."
After that I knew the

        war was on —
So we fought:
He said: "The apple-cart like a
                broomstick-angel
            snaps & splinters
                    old dutch shoes."
I said: "Lightning will strike the old oak
            and free the fumes!"
He said: "Mad street with no name."
I said: "Bald killer! Bald killer! Bald killer!"
He said, getting real mad,
        "Firestoves! Gas! Couch!"
I said, only smiling,
            "I know God would turn back his head
                if I sat quietly and thought."
We ended by melting away,
        hating the air!

                                                    1956

ZIZI'S LAMENT

I am in love with the laughing sickness
it would do me a lot of good if I had it —
I have worn the splendid gowns of Sudan,
carried the magnificent halivas of Boudodin Bros.,
kissed the singing Fatimas of the pimp of Aden,
wrote glorious psalms in Hakhaliba's cafe,
but I've never had the laughing sickness,
so what good am I?

The fat merchant offers me opium, kief, hashish, even camel
        juice,
all is unsatisfactory —
O bitter damned night! you again! must I yet
pluck out my unreal teeth
undress my unlaughable self
put to sleep this melancholy head?
I am nothing without the laughing sickness.

My father's got it, my grandfather had it;
surely my Uncle Fez will get it, but me, me
who it would do the most good,
will I ever get it?

UCCELLO

They will never die on that battlefield
nor the shade of wolves recruit their hoard like brides of
wheat on all horizons   waiting there to consume battle's end
There will be no dead to tighten their loose bellies
no heap of starched horses to redsmash their bright eyes
or advance their eat of dead
They would rather hungersulk with mad tongues
than believe that on that field no man dies

They will never die who fight so embraced
breath to breath   eye knowing eye   impossible to die
or move   no light seeping through   no maced arm
nothing but horse outpanting horse   shield brilliant upon
shield   all made starry by the dot ray of a helmeted eye
ah   how difficult to fall between those knitted lances
And those banners! angry as to flush insignia across its
erasure of sky
You'd think he'd paint his armies by the coldest rivers
have rows of iron skulls flashing in the dark
You'd think it impossible for any man to die
each combatant's mouth is a castle of song
each iron fist a dreamy gong   flail resounding flail
like cries of gold
how I dream to join such battle!
a silver man on a black horse with red standard and striped
lance   never to die but to be endless
a golden prince of pictorial war

BUT I DO NOT NEED KINDNESS

I have known the strange nurses of Kindness,
I have seen them kiss the sick, attend the old,
give candy to the mad!
I have watched them, at night, dark and sad,
rolling wheelchairs by the sea!
I have known the fat pontiffs of Kindness,
the little old grey-haired lady,
the neighborhood priest,
the famous poet
the mother,
I have known them all!
I have watched them, at night, dark and sad,
pasting posters of mercy
        on the stark posts of despair.

2

I have known Almighty Kindness Herself!
I have sat beside Her pure white feet,
gaining Her confidence!
We spoke of nothing unkind,
but one night I was tormented by those strange nurses,
those fat pontiffs
The little old lady rode a spiked car over my head!
The priest cut open my stomach, put his hands in me,
and cried: — Where's your soul? Where's your soul! —
The famous poet picked me up
and threw me out of the window!
The mother abandoned me!
I ran to Kindness, broke into Her chamber,
and profaned!
with an unnamable knife I gave Her a thousand wounds,
and inflicted them with filth!
I carried Her away, on my back, like a ghoul!
down the cobble-stoned night!
Dogs howled! Cats fled! All windows closed!
I carried Her ten flights of stairs!

Dropped Her on the floor of my small room,
and kneeling beside Her, I wept. I wept.

3

But what is Kindness? I have killed Kindness,
but what is it?
You are kind because you live a kind life.
St. Francis was kind.
The landlord is kind.
A cane is kind.
Can I say people, sitting in parks, are kinder?

1957

DIALOGUE — 2 DOLLMAKERS

Let's not use eyes anymore.
    Folly!
Let's use cans instead.
    Say next no mouth!
No mouth; why not?
    Fool! Fool!
Let's use a piece of hose.
    And what about the nose?
A chair is better.
    A chair for the nose!?
Or two chairs for the ears.
    Fool! Fool! Fool!
And the legs, the arms, why not suitcases?
    Suitcases?
Yes, and for the body, why not a staircase?
    Fool! Fool! Fool!
Good God! and for the hair we could use a sink!
    Hmmmm, and for the dress we could use a meat truck.
Right!
    Sure, and for the hat we could use a wall.
Right! Right! Oh, Alberto, I love you!
    And for the fingernails we could use racetracks.

Yes, and for the toenails, why not mattresses?
    And the eyebrows, we could use blockbusters.
Ah, Alberto, and the stockings, what about the stockings?
    What about them? There's always abandoned farms to use.

PARANOIA IN CRETE

Damned Minoan crevices, that I clog them up!
Plaster myself away from everything, all that out there!
Just sit here, knees up, amid amphora and aloe,
reading lusty potsherd, gobbling figs, needing no one —
Mine the true labyrinth, it is my soul, Theseus;
try a ball of string in *that!*

Thrones descended by kings are ascended by ruin;
upon no singular breast do I rest my head of mythologies;
no footman seat, no regnant couch, enough this pillowy cave —
O Zeus! I was such a king able to mobilize everything!
A king advised by oraclry his aulic valets imperium;
not kingsmen, nor my sons, that pederast Miletus;
that hot-shot Rhadamathys, his nine year cave advocacy —
And my wife! that wood-cow brothel!

Clog! Clog! Clog! Stuff-up the cracks!
They'd like to dump me in a miserable nymph's bubbling brake!
Vise my feet in the River-god's mouth!
Perplex my head with Naiads!
Set Eros on me, that sequesterer of mortal vanity!
O Calypso's green-fluid boudoir is tearing me to pieces!
Plaster! Plaster! Stay the Aegean tide! Blot out Athens!

I survey the hunched bull, the twin headless lions,
one more crevice to go, and lo!
    I forfeit the Echinadian Isles —

A DREAMED REALIZATION

The carrion-eater's nobility calls back from God;
Never was a carrion-eater *first* a carrion-eater —
Back there in God creatures sat like stone
— no light in their various eyes.

Life. It was Life jabbed a spoon in their mouths.
Crow jackal hyena vulture worm woke to necessity
— dipping into Death like a soup.

1958

FROM ANOTHER ROOM

Dumb genius blows
feeble breath into my windowless room
He — the sagacious mute
rap-tapping a code or doom
— the drunkard punched the wall to have his storm!
Through the crack! Through the crack!
My feast was in the easy blood that flowed.

NOTES AFTER BLACKING OUT

Lady of the legless world I have
    refused to go beyond self-disappearance
I'm in the thin man's bed knowing my legs
    kept to me by a cold fresh air
Useless and not useless this meaning
All is answerable I need not know the answer
Poetry is seeking the answer
Joy is in knowing there is an answer
Death is knowing the answer
(That faint glow in the belly of Enlightment
    is the dead spouting their answers)
Queen of cripples the young no longer

seem necessary
The old are secretive about their Know
They are constant additions to this big
        unauthorized lie
Yet Truth's author itself is nothingness
And though I make it vital that nothingness
        itself will collapse
There is nothing.
Nothing ever was
Nothing is a house never bought
Nothing comes after this wildbright Joke
Nothing sits on nothing in a nothing of many nothings
        a nothing king.

MARRIAGE

for Mr. and Mrs. Mike Goldberg

Should I get married? Should I be good?
Astound the girl next door
with my velvet suit and faustus hood?
Don't take her to movies but to cemeteries
tell all about werewolf bathtubs and forked clarinets
then desire her and kiss her and all the preliminaries
and she going just so far and I understanding why
not getting angry saying You must feel! It's beautiful to feel!
Instead take her in my arms
lean against an old crooked tombstone
and woo her the entire night the constellations in the sky —

When she introduces me to her parents
back straightened, hair finally combed, strangled by a tie,
should I sit knees together on their 3rd-degree sofa
and not ask Where's the bathroom?
How else to feel other than I am,
a young man who often thinks Flash Gordon soap —
O how terrible it must be for a young man
seated before a family and the family thinking
We never saw him before! He wants our Mary Lou!

After tea and homemade cookies they ask What do you do?
Should I tell them? Would they like me then?
Say All right get married, we're losing a daughter
but we're gaining a son —
And should I then ask Where's the bathroom?

O God, and the wedding! All her family and her friends
and only a handful of mine all scroungy and bearded
just waiting to get at the drinks and food —
And the priest! he looking at me as if I masturbated
asking me Do you take this woman
for your lawful wedded wife?
And I, trembling what to say, say Pie Glue!
I kiss the bride all those corny men slapping me on the back:
She's all yours, boy! Ha-ha-ha!
And in their eyes you could see
some obscene honeymoon going on —
Then all that absurd rice and clanky cans and shoes
Niagara Falls! Hordes of us! Husbands! Wives! Flowers!
All streaming into cozy hotels
All going to do the same thing tonight
The indifferent clerk he knowing what was going to happen
The lobby zombies they knowing what
The whistling elevator man he knowing
The winking bellboy knowing
Everybody knows! I'd be almost inclined not to do anything!
Stay up all night! Stare that hotel clerk in the eye!
Screaming: I deny honeymoon! I deny honeymoon!
running rampant into those almost climactic suites
yelling Radio belly! Cat shovel!
O I'd live in Niagara forever! in a dark cave beneath the Falls
I'd sit there the Mad Honeymooner
devising ways to break marriages, a scourge of bigamy
a saint of divorce —

But I should get married I should be good
How nice it'd be to come home to her
and sit by the fireplace and she in the kitchen
aproned young and lovely wanting my baby

and so happy about me she burns the roast beef
and comes crying to me and I get up from my big papa chair
saying Christmas teeth! Radiant brains! Apple deaf!
God what a husband I'd make! Yes, I should get married!
So much to do! like sneaking into Mr. Jones' house late at night
and cover his golf clubs with 1920 Norwegian books
Like hanging a picture of Rimbaud on the lawnmower
Like pasting Tannu Tuva postage stamps
all over the picket fence
Like when Mrs. Kindhead comes to collect
for the Community Chest
grab her and tell her There are unfavorable omens in the sky!
And when the mayor comes to get my vote tell him
When are you going to stop people killing whales!
And when the milkman comes leave him a note in the bottle
Penguin dust, bring me penguin dust, I want penguin dust —

Yet if I should get married and it's Connecticut and snow
and she gives birth to a child and I am sleepless, worn,
up for nights, head bowed against a quiet window,
the past behind me,
finding myself in the most common of situations
a trembling man
knowledged with responsibility not twig-smear
nor Roman coin soup —
O what would that be like!
Surely I'd give it for a nipple a rubber Tacitus
For a rattle a bag of broken Bach records
Tack Della Francesca all over its crib
Sew the Greek alphabet on its bib
And build for its playpen a roofless Parthenon —

No, I doubt I'd be that kind of father
not rural not snow no quiet window
but hot smelly tight New York City
seven flights up, roaches and rats in the walls
a fat Reichian wife screeching over potatoes Get a job!
And five nose-running brats in love with Batman

And the neighbors all toothless and dry haired
like those hag masses of the 18th century
all wanting to come in and watch TV
The landlord wants his rent
Grocery store Blue Cross Gas & Electric Knights of Columbus
Impossible to lie back and dream Telephone snow,
ghost parking —
No! I should not get married I should never get married!

But — imagine if I were married to a beautiful
sophisticated woman
tall and pale wearing an elegant black dress
and long black gloves
holding a cigarette holder in one hand
and a highball in the other
and we lived high up in a penthouse with a huge window
from which we could see all of New York
and even farther on clearer days
No, can't imagine myself married to that pleasant prison dream —

O but what about love? I forget love
not that I am incapable of love
it's just that I see love as odd as wearing shoes —
I never wanted to marry a girl who was like my mother
And Ingrid Bergman was always impossible
And there's maybe a girl now but she's already married
And I don't like men and —
but there's got to be somebody!
Because what if I'm 60 years old and not married,
all alone in a furnished room with pee stains on my underwear
and everybody else is married! All the universe married but me!

Ah, yet well I know that were a woman possible
as I am possible
then marriage would be possible —
Like SHE in her lonely alien gaud waiting her Egyptian lover
so I wait — bereft of 2,000 years and the bath of life.

1959

PETER ORLOVSKY

SECOND POEM

Morning again, nothing has to be done,
            maybe buy a piano or make fudge
At least clean the room up, for sure like my farther
     I've done flick the ashes & buts over the bedside on the floor.
But frist of all wipe my glasses and drink the water
            to clean the smelly mouth.
A nock on the door, a cat walks in, behind her the Zoo's baby
     elephant demanding pancaks — I cant stand hallucinations
     any more.
Time for another cigarette and then let the curtains rise, then
     I notice the dirt makes a road path to the garbage pan.
No icebox so a dried up grapefruit.
Is there any one saintly thing I can do to my room, paint it pink
     maybe or install an elevator from the floor to the bed or
     maybe take a bath in the bed?
What's the use of living if I cant make paradise in my own
     room-land?
For this drop of time upon my eyes
like the endurance of a red star on a cigarette
makes me feel life splits faster than scissors.

I know if I could shave myself the bugs around my face would
     disappear forever.
The holes in my shues are only temporary, I understand that.
My rug is dirty but whose that isen't?
There comes a time in life when everybody must take a piss in
     the sink — here let me paint the window black for a minute.
Thro a plate & brake it out of naughtiness — or maybe just in-
     nocently accidentally drop it wile walking around the tabol.
Before the mirror I look like sahara desert gost,
or on the bed I resemble a crying mummey hollaring for air,

213

or on the tabol I feel like Napoleon.

But now for the main task of the day — wash my underwear — two months abused — what would the ants say about that?

How can I wash my clothes — why I'd, I'd, I'd be a woman if I did that.

No, I'd rather polish my sneakers then that and as for the floor it's more creative to paint it then clean it up.

As for the dishes I can do that for I am thinking of getting a job in a lunchenette.

My life and my room are like two huge bugs following me around the globe.

Thank god I have an innocent eye for nature.

I was born to remember a song about love — on a hill a butterfly makes a cup that I drink from, walking over a bridge of flowers.

Nov. '57, Paris

IV

BARBARA GUEST

PARACHUTES, MY LOVE, COULD CARRY US HIGHER

I just said I didn't know
And now you are holding me
In your arms,
How kind.
Parachutes, my love, could carry us higher.
Yet around the net I am floating
Pink and pale blue fish are caught in it,
They are beautiful,
But they are not good for eating.
Parachutes, my love, could carry us higher
Than this mid-air in which we tremble,
Having exercised our arms in swimming,
Now the suspension, you say,
Is exquisite. I do not know.
There is coral below the surface,
There is sand, and berries
Like pomegranates grow.
This wide net, I am treading water
Near it, bubbles are rising and salt
Drying on my lashes, yet I am no nearer
Air than water. I am closer to you
Than land and I am in a stranger ocean
Than I wished.

SUNDAY EVENING

I am telling you a number of half-conditioned ideas
Am repeating myself,
The room has four sides; it is a rectangle,
From the window the bridge, the water, the leaves,

Her hat is made of feathers,
My fortune is produced from glass
And I drink to my extinction.

Barges on the river carry apples wrapped in bales,
This morning there was a sombre sunrise,
In the red, in the air, in what is falling through us
We quote several things.

I am talking to you
With what is left of me written off,
On the cuff, ancestral and vague,
As a monkey walks through the many fires
Of a jungle while a village breathes in its sleep.

Someone stops in the alcove,
It is a risk we will later make,
While I talk and you bring your eyes to the fibre
(as the blade to the brown root)
And the room is slumberous and slow
(as a pulse after the first September earthquake).

                                                                    1957

SANTA FE TRAIL

I go separately
The sweet knees of oxen have pressed a path for me
ghosts with ingots have burned their bare hands
it is the dungaree darkness with China stitched
where the westerly winds
and the traveller's checks
the evensong of salesmen
the glistening paraphernalia of twin suitcases
where no one speaks English.
I go separately
It is the wind, the rubber wind
when we brush our teeth in the way station
a climate to beard. What forks these roads?
Who clammers o'er the twain?
What murmurs and rustles in the distance

in the white branches where the light is whipped
piercing at the crossing as into the dunes we simmer
and toss ourselves awhile the motor pants like a forest
where owls from their bandaged eyes send messages
to the Indian couple. Peaks, you have heard?
I go separately
We have reached the arithmetics, are partially quenched
while it growls and hints in the lost trapper's voice
She is coming toward us like a session of pines
in the wild, wooden air where rabbits are frozen
O mother of lakes and glaciers save us gamblers
whose wagon is perilously rapt.

1958

PIAZZAS

       In the golden air, the risky autumn,
leaves on the piazza, shadows by the door
on your chair the red berry
       after the dragon fly summer

we walk this mirroring air our feet chill
and silver and golden a portrait
by Pinturicchio we permanently taste the dark
grapes and the seed pearls glisten

       as the flight of those fresh brown birds
an instant of vision that the coupling mind
and heart see in their youth
with thin wings attacking a real substance
       as Pinturicchio fixed his air.

After all dragon flies do as much
in midsummer with a necessary water
there is always a heaviness of wings.

       To remember
now that the imagination's at its turning
how to recall those Pierrots of darkness
(with the half-moon like a yellow leg of a pantaloon)

I would see you again (like the purple P
of piazza).

              Imagination
thunder in the Alps yet we flew above it
then met a confusion of weather and felt
the alphabet turning over when we landed
in Peking. I read the late Empresses' letters
and thought they were yours,
that impeccable script followed by murders

              real or divined
as the youth leaning over the piazza
throwing stones at his poems. He reads
his effigy in the one that ricochets
he weeps into the autumn air
and that stone becomes golden as a tomb
beware the risky imagination

              that lines its piazzas
with lambswool or for sheer disturbance
places mirrors for Pinturicchio
to draw his face at daybreak

when the air is clear of shadows
and no one walks the piazza.

                                                      1959

JAMES SCHUYLER

SALUTE

Past is past, and if one
remembers what one meant
to do and never did, is
not to have thought to do
enough? Like that gather-
ing of one of each I
planned, to gather one
of each kind of clover,
daisy, paintbrush that
grew in that field
the cabin stood in and
study them one afternoon
before they wilted. Past
is past. I salute
that various field.

1951

FEBRUARY

A chimney, breathing a little smoke.
The sun, I can't see
making a bit of pink
I can't quite see in the blue.
The pink of five tulips
at five p.m. on the day before March first.
The green of the tulip stems and leaves
like something I can't remember,
finding a jack-in-the-pulpit
a long time ago and far away.
Why it was December then
and the sun was on the sea
by the temples we'd gone to see.

220

One green wave moved in the violet sea
like the U.N. Building on big evenings,
green and wet
while the sky turns violet.
A few of the almond trees
had a few flowers, like a few snow flakes
out of the blue looking pink in the light.
A gray hush
in which the boxy trucks roll up Second Avenue
into the sky. They're just
going over the hill.
The green leaves of the tulips on my desk
like grass-light on flesh,
and a green copper steeple
and streaks of cloud beginning to glow.
I can't get over
how it all works in together
like a woman who just came to her window
and stands there filling it
jogging her baby in her arms.
She's so far off. Is it the light
that makes the baby pink?
I can see the little fists
and the rocking-horse motion of her breasts.
It's getting grayer and gold and chilly.
Two dog-size lions face each other
at the corners of a roof.
It's the yellow dust inside the tulips.
It's the shape of a tulip.
It's the water in the drinking glass the tulips are in.
It's a day like any other.

1955

"THE ELIZABETHANS CALLED IT DYING"

Beyond Nagel's Funeral Parlor
       ("Your cousin says you filled her station wagon up;
        I didn't say it your cousin said it")
and (is it a perpetual wake they have
or just a popular parlor?)
       the novelty ice cream cake and soda shop
       the boys hang out in front of
       until they're eighteen, then move across the street
in front of the saloon   Munich beer on draught
not forgetting the big church with the doleful bells
cheerily summoning housewives to early mass
       ("The good thing about religion is
        it gives a man a sense of his place in the universe")
to Karl Schurz Park
kept reasonably free of la di da
after all the Mayor lives in it
in the huge glare of the electric sign on Doctors' Hospital
that says HOSPITAL.
what are they trying to do, solicit trade in Queens?
or is that Welfare Island?
the river races upstream, neap tide turned
past the posh apartments
       did you ever sit back and try to remember
       whether particular paving stones were hex- or octagons?
       seen once at night and presumably memorized
        Sloshing around in the rain —
your eyes lips and nostrils
vary a distinct and unique shape —
       why it's The Raindrop Prelude!
home —
       not to be in love with you
I can't remember what it was like
       it must've been lousy

1958

James Schuyler

FREELY ESPOUSING

a commingling sky

> a semi-tropic night
> that cast the blackest shadow
> of the easily torn, untrembling banana leaf

or Quebec! what a horrible city
so Steubenville is better?
> the sinking sensation
when someone drowns thinking, "This can't be happening to me!"
the profit of excavating the battlefield where Hannibal whomped
   the Romans
the sinuous beauty of words like allergy
the tonic resonance of
pill when used as in
"she is a pill"
on the other hand I am not going to espouse any short stories in
   which lawn mowers clack.
No, it is absolutely forbidden
for words to echo the act described; or try to. Except very directly
as in
bong. And tickle. Oh it is inescapable kiss.
Marriages of the atmosphere
are worth celebrating
> where Tudor City
catches the sky or the glass side
of a building lit up at night in fog
"What is that gold-green tetrahedron down the river?"
"You are experiencing a new sensation."

> *if the touch-me-nots*
> *are not in bloom*
> *neither are the chrysanthemums*
The bales of pink cotton candy
in the slanting light

are ornamental cherry trees.
The greens around them, and
the browns, the grays, are the park.

It's. Hmm. No.
     Their scallop shell of quiet
is the S.S. *United States*.
It is not so quiet and they
are a medium-size couple who
when they fold each other up
well, thrill. That's their story.

1959

EDWARD FIELD

A VIEW OF JERSEY

I

Often in the morning the fog is thick over Jersey,
Sometimes, like today, lifting later on
To reveal with the clarity of a dream
The wide river with its traffic, the cluttered far shore,
And the hills beyond where hidden towns
Send up spires like messages.

The river is never terribly obscured
Even when the land beyond is absolutely white,
And I can see the ferry leave the shore
With a load of commuters like refugees from a land
where faces have no face, and bodies only exist
If you put your arms around them.

They come to the city where I am
Although they do not find me
Nor even know that they are searching for me;
And as the morning progresses with its growing clarity
There is a world over there after all,
Anyway, for a while, precise as a dream, perfect and grimy,
Until another night and its temperatures
Pulls down the fog from the air and obliterates it.

II

Now that it is winter my coldwater flat is cold:
The morning alarm wakes my seedy eyes to their first heroic look;
If they shut just once all is lost.
I light the oven that barely pushes out a bell of warmth,
Shave a ragged face that I do not dare study,
And brush the traces of digestion out of my mouth.
Saliva flows, my arms
Struggle with the clothes like with an enemy.
The toilet is far beyond this small place of comfort,
And it is only at the extremest necessity
That I dare to bare my behind:
Truly I am man braving the elements.

And only now, blinking behind my typewriter
In the dry warmth commerce provides its dependents
Can I appreciate the miracle that got me out of bed

And made me leave behind my strange and lovely dreams
For the world and its miseries, mankind and his hungers,
For a life of goosepimples and sweat
And the rare overwhelming flush of love.

III

The new warmth of spring has raised a mist
Obscuring the vista that through the winter
Made this office a platform for speculation
And me a quite tranquil anchorite.

Now itchy in my tweed pants
I'm ready to leave the city and go,
But I would have to go like a blind man
(For what difference if the eye dies or the sun?)
And stumble over rocks and fences.

Present me with a cross-roads clear,
That's easy; but today there's a full
360 degrees of possibility,
Like the fledgling in the nest has
Before he leaps out into space.

A sparrow flies from window ledge to ground;
A plane buzzes off westward;
A ship moves down the river to the sea;
The street says One-Way and the auto follows:
Each has a course to travel and a place to rest.
When I look for a sign there is none.

If I were naked I think my body
Would know where to go of its own accord;
In the spring mist compounded with soot, barefoot,
By the breeze on my skin and the feel of the stones
I would go, not in a straight line of course,
But this way and that, as human nature goes,
Finding, if not the place, the way there.

1956

THE FLOOR IS DIRTY:

Not only the soot from the city air
But a surprising amount of hair litters the room.
It is hard to keep up with. Even before
The room is all swept up it is dirty again.

We are shedding more than we realize.
The amount of hair I've shed so far
Could make sixty of those great rugs
The Duke of China killed his weavers for,
And strangle half the sons of Islam.

Time doesn't stop even while I scrub the floor
Though it seems that the mind empties like a bathtub,
That all the minds of the world go down the drain
Into the sewer; but hair keeps falling
And not for a moment can the floor be totally clean.

What is left of us after years of shitting and shedding?
Are we whom our mothers bore or some stranger now
With the name of son, but nameless,
Continually relearning the same words
That mean, with each retelling, less?

He whom you knew is a trail of leavings round the world.
Renewal is a lie: who I was has no more kisses.
Barbara's fierce eyes were long ago swept up from her floor.
A stranger goes by the name of Marianne; it is not she,
Nor for that matter was the Marianne I knew.

The floor having accumulated particles of myself
I call it dirty; dirty, the streets thick with the dead;
Dirty, the thick air I am used to breathing.
I am alive at least. Quick, who said that?
Give me the broom. The left-overs sweep the leavings away.

1957

KENNETH KOCH

MENDING SUMP

"Hiram, I think the sump is backing up.
The bathroom floor boards for above two weeks
Have seemed soaked through. A little bird, I think
Has wandered in the pipes, and all's gone wrong."
"Something there is that doesn't hump a sump,"
He said; and through his head she saw a cloud
That seemed to twinkle. "Hiram, well," she said,
"Smith is come home! I saw his face just now
While looking through your head. He's come to die
Or else to laugh, for hay is dried-up grass
When you're alone." He rose, and sniffed the air.
"We'd better leave him in the sump," he said.

1950

FRESH AIR

1

At the Poem Society a black-haired man stands up to say,
"You make me sick with all your talk about restraint and mature
  talent!
Haven't you ever looked out the window at a painting by Matisse,
Or did you always stay in hotels where there were too many
  spiders crawling on your visages?
Did you ever glance inside a bottle of sparkling pop,
Or see a citizen split in two by the lightning?
I am afraid you have never smiled at the hibernation
Of bear cubs except that you saw in it some deep relation
To human suffering and wishes, oh what a bunch of crackpots!"
The black-haired man sits down, and the others shoot arrows at
  him.

229

A blond man stands up and says,
"He is right! Why should we be organized to defend the kingdom
Of dullness? There are so many slimy people connected with
    poetry,
Too, and people who know nothing about it!
I am not recommending that poets like each other and organize
    to fight them,
But simply that lightning should strike them."
Then the assembled mediocrities shot arrows at the blond-haired
    man.
The chairman stood up on the platform, oh he was physically
    ugly!
He was small-limbed and -boned and thought he was quite se-
    ductive,
But he was bald with certain hideous black hairs,
And his voice had the sound of water leaving a vaseline bathtub,
And he said, "The subject for this evening's discussion is poetry
On the subject of love between swans." And everyone threw
    candy hearts
At the disgusting man, and they stuck to his bib and tucker,
And he danced up and down on the platform in terrific glee
And recited the poetry of his little friends — but the blond man
    stuck his head
Out of a cloud and recited poems about the east and thunder,
And the black-haired man moved through the stratosphere chant-
    ing
Poems of the relationships between terrific prehistoric charcoal
    whales,
And the slimy man with candy hearts sticking all over him
Wilted away like a cigarette paper on which the bumblebees
    have urinated,
And all the professors left the room to go back to their duty,
And all that were left in the room were five or six poets
And together they sang the new poem of the twentieth century
Which, though influenced by Mallarmé, Shelley, Byron, and
    Whitman,
Plus a million other poets, is still entirely original

And is so exciting that it cannot be here repeated.
You must go to the Poem Society and wait for it to happen.
Once you have heard this poem you will not love any other,
Once you have dreamed this dream you will be inconsolable,
Once you have loved this dream you will be as one dead,
Once you have visited the passages of this time's great art!

　　2
"Oh to be seventeen years old
Once again," sang the red-haired man, "and not know that poetry
Is ruled with sceptre of the dumb, the deaf, and the creepy!"
And the shouting persons battered his immortal body with stones
And threw his primitive comedy into the sea
From which it sang forth poems irrevocably blue.

Who are the great poets of our time, and what are their names?
Yeats of the baleful influence, Auden of the baleful influence,
　　Eliot of the baleful influence
(Is Eliot a great poet? no one knows), Hardy, Stevens, Williams
　　(is Hardy of our time?),
Hopkins (is Hopkins of our time?), Rilke (is Rilke of our time?),
　　Lorca (is Lorca of our time?), who is still of our time?
Mallarmé, Valéry, Apollinaire, Eluard, Reverdy, French poets are
　　still of our time,
Pasternak and Mayakovsky, is Jouve of our time?

Where are young poets in America, they are trembling in publish-
　　ing houses and universities,
Above all they are trembling in universities, they are bathing the
　　library steps with their spit,
They are gargling out innocuous (to whom?) poems about maple
　　trees and their children,
Sometimes they brave a subject like the Villa d'Este or a light-
　　house in Rhode Island,
Oh what worms they are! they wish to perfect their form.

Yet could not these young men, put in another profession,
Succeed admirably, say at sailing a ship? I do not doubt it, Sir,
　　and I wish we could try them.

(A plane flies over the ship holding a bomb but perhaps it will
  not drop the bomb,
The young poets from the universities are staring anxiously at the
  skies,
Oh they are remembering their days on the campus when they
  looked up to watch birds excrete,
They are remembering the days they spent making their elegant
  poems.)

Is there no voice to cry out from the wind and say what it is like
  to be the wind,
To be roughed up by the trees and to bring music from the scat-
  tered houses
And the stones, and to be in such intimate relationship with the
  sea
That you cannot understand it? Is there no one who feels like a
  pair of pants?

    3
Summer in the trees! "It is time to strangle several bad poets."
The yellow hobbyhorse rocks to and fro, and from the chimney
Drops the Strangler! The white and pink roses are slightly agitated
  by the struggle,
But afterwards beside the dead "poet" they cuddle up comfort-
  ingly against their vase. They are safer now, no one will com-
  pare them to the sea.

Here on the railroad train, one more time, is the Strangler.
He is going to get that one there, who is on his way to a poetry
  reading.
Agh! Biff! A body falls to the moving floor.

In the football stadium I also see him,
He leaps through the frosty air at the maker of comparisons
Between football and life and silently, silently strangles him!

Here is the Strangler dressed in a cowboy suit
Leaping from his horse to annihilate the students of myth!

The Strangler's ear is alert for the names of Orpheus,
Cuchulain, Gawain, and Odysseus,

And for poems addressed to Jane Austen, F. Scott Fitzgerald,
To Ezra Pound, and to personages no longer living
Even in anyone's thoughts — O Strangler the Strangler!

He lies on his back in the waves of the Pacific Ocean.

4

Supposing that one walks out into the air
On a fresh spring day and has the misfortune
To encounter an article on modern poetry
In *New World Writing,* or has the misfortune
To see some examples of some of the poetry
Written by the men with their eyes on the myth
And the Missus and the midterms, in the *Hudson Review,*
Or, if one is abroad, in *Botteghe Oscure,*
Or indeed in *Encounter,* what is one to do
With the rest of one's day that lies blasted to ruins
All bluely about one, what is one to do?
O surely one cannot complain to the President,
Nor even to the deans of Columbia College,
Nor to T. S. Eliot, nor to Ezra Pound,
And supposing one writes to the Princess Caetani,
"Your poets are awful!" what good would it do?
And supposing one goes to the *Hudson Review*
With a package of matches and sets fire to the building?
One ends up in prison with trial subscriptions
To the *Partisan, Sewanee,* and *Kenyon Review!*

5

Sun out! perhaps there is a reason for the lack of poetry
In these ill-contented souls, perhaps they need air!

Blue air, fresh air, come in, I welcome you, you are an art student,
Take off your cap and gown and sit down on the chair.
Together we shall paint the poets — but no, air! perhaps you
   should go to them, quickly,
Give them a little inspiration, they need it, perhaps they are out
   of breath,
Give them a little inhuman company before they freeze the Eng-
   lish language to death!

(And rust their typewriters a little, be sea air! be noxious! kill
   them, if you must, but stop their poetry!
I remember I saw you dancing on the surf on the Côte d'Azur,
And I stopped, taking my hat off, but you did not remember me,
Then afterwards, you came to my room bearing a handful of or-
   ange flowers
And we were together all through the summer night!)

That we might go away together, it is so beautiful on the sea,
   there are a few white clouds in the sky!

But no, air! you must go . . . Ah, stay!

But she has departed and . . . Ugh! what poisonous fumes and
   clouds! what a suffocating atmosphere!
Cough! whose are these hideous faces I see, what is this rigor
Infecting the mind? where are the green Azores,
Fond memories of childhood, and the pleasant orange trolleys,
A girl's face, red-white, and her breasts and calves, blue eyes,
   brown eyes, green eyes, fahrenheit
Temperatures, dandelions, and trains, O blue?!
Wind, wind, what is happening? Wind! I can't see any bird but
   the gull, and I feel it should symbolize . . .
Oh, pardon me, there's a swan, one two three swans, a great white
   swan, hahaha how pretty they are! Smack!
Oh! stop! help! yes, I see — disrespect to my superiors — forgive
   me, dear Zeus, nice Zeus, parabolic bird, O feathered excel-
   lence! white!
There is Achilles too, and there's Ulysses, I've always wanted to
   see them, hahaha!
And here is Helen of Troy, I suppose she is Zeus too, she's so ter-
   ribly pretty — hello, Zeus, my you are beautiful, Bang!
One more mistake and I get thrown out of the Modern Poetry
   Association, help! Why aren't there any adjectives around?
Oh there are, there's practically nothing else — look, here's *grey,
   utter, agonized, total, phenomenal, gracile, invidious, sundered,*
   and *fused,*
Elegant, absolute, pyramidal, and . . . Scream! but what can I
   describe with these words? States!

States symbolized and divided by two, complex states, magic
    states, states of consciousness governed by an aroused sincer-
    ity, cockadoodle doo!
Another bird! is it morning? Help! where am I? am I in the barn-
    yard? oink oink, scratch, moo! Splash!
My first lesson. "Look around you. What do you think and feel?"
    Uhhh . . . "Quickly!" *This Connecticut landscape would have
    pleased Vermeer.* Wham! A-Plus. "Congratulations!" I am pro-
    moted.
OOOhhhhh I wish I were dead, what a headache! My second
    lesson: "Rewrite your first lesson line six hundred times. Try
    to make it into a magnetic field." I can do it too. But my poor
    line! What a nightmare! Here comes a tremendous horse,
Trojan, I presume. No, it's my third lesson. "Look, look! Watch
    him, see what he's doing? That's what we want you to do. Of
    course it won't be the same as his at first, but . . ." I demur. Is
    there no other way to fertilize minds?
Bang! I give in . . . Already I see my name in two or three anthol-
    ogies, a serving girl comes into the barn bringing me the an-
    thologies,
She is very pretty and I smile at her a little sadly, perhaps it is
    my last smile! Perhaps she will hit me! But no, she smiles in
    return, and she takes my hand.
My hand, my hand! what is this strange thing I feel in my hand,
    on my arm, on my chest, my face — can it be . . . ? it is! AIR!
Air, air, you've come back! Did you have any success? "What do
    you think?" I don't know, air. You are so strong, air.
And she breaks my chains of straw, and we walk down the road,
    behind us the hideous fumes!
Soon we reach the seaside, she is a young art student who places
    her head on my shoulder,
I kiss her warm red lips, and here is the Strangler, reading the
    Kenyon Review! Good luck to you, Strangler!

Goodbye, Helen! goodbye, fumes! goodbye, abstracted dried-up
    boys! goodbye, dead trees! goodbye, skunks!
Goodbye, manure! goodbye, critical manicure! goodbye, you big
    fat men standing on the east coast as well as the west giving

poems the test! farewell, Valéry's stern dictum!

Until tomorrow, then, scum floating on the surface of poetry! goodbye for a moment, refuse that happens to land in poetry's boundaries! adieu, stale eggs teaching imbeciles poetry to bolster up your egos! adios, boring anomalies of these same stale eggs!

Ah, but the scum is deep! Come, let me help you! and soon we pass into the clear blue water. Oh GOODBYE, castrati of poetry! farewell, stale pale skunky pentameters (the only honest English meter, gloop gloop!)! until tomorrow, horrors! oh, farewell!

Hello, sea! good morning, sea! hello, clarity and excitement, you great expanse of green —

O green, beneath which all of them shall drown!

1955

THANK YOU

Oh thank you for giving me the chance
Of being ship's doctor! I am sorry that I shall have to refuse —
But, you see, the most I know of medicine is orange flowers
Tilted in the evening light against a cashmere red
Inside which breasts invent the laws of light
And of night, where cashmere moors itself across the sea.
And thank you for giving me these quintuplets
To rear and make happy . . . My mind was on something else.

Thank you for giving me this battleship to wash,
But I have a rash on my hands and my eyes hurt,
And I know so little about cleaning a ship
That I should rather clean an island.
There one knows what one is about — sponge those palm trees, sweep up the sand a little, polish those coconuts;
Then take a rest for a while and it's time to trim the grass as well as separate it from each other where gummy substances have made individual blades stick together, forming an ugly bunch;
And then take the dead bark off the trees, and perfume these islands a bit with a song . . . That's easy — but a battleship!

Where does one begin and how does one do? to batten the
hatches? I would rather clean a million palm trees.

Now here comes an offer of a job for setting up a levee
In Mississippi. No thanks. Here it says *Rape or Worse*. I think
they must want me to publicize this book.
On the jacket it says "Published in Boothbay Harbor, Maine" —
what a funny place to publish a book!

I suppose it is some provincial publishing house
Whose provincial pages emit the odor of sails
And the freshness of the sea
Breeze . . . But publicity!

The only thing I could publicize well would be my tooth,
Which I could say came with my mouth and in a most engaging
manner
With my whole self, my body and including my mind,
Spirits, emotions, spiritual essences, emotional substances, poetry,
dreams, and lords
Of my life, everything, all embraceleted with my tooth
In a way that makes one wish to open the windows and scream
"Hi!" to the heavens,
And "Oh, come and take me away before I die in a minute!"

It is possible that the dentist is smiling, that he dreams of extrac-
tion
Because he believes that the physical tooth and the spiritual
tooth are one.

Here is another letter, this one from a textbook advertiser;
He wants me to advertise a book on chopping down trees.
But how could I? I love trees! and I haven't the slightest sym-
pathy with chopping them down, even though I know
We need their products for wood-fires, some houses, and maple
syrup —
Still I like trees better
In their standing condition, where they sway at the beginning of
evening . . .

And thank you for the pile of driftwood.
Am I wanted at the sea?

And thank you for the chance to run a small hotel
In an elephant stopover in Zambezi,
But I do not know how to take care of guests, certainly they
would all leave soon
After seeing blue lights out the windows and rust on their iron
beds — I'd rather own a bird-house in Jamaica:
Those people come in, the birds, they do not care how things are
kept up . . .
It's true that Zambezi proprietorship would be exciting, with
people getting off elephants and coming into my hotel,
But as tempting as it is I cannot agree.
And thank you for this offer of the post of referee
For the Danish wrestling championship — I simply do not feel
qualified . . .

But the fresh spring air has been swabbing my mental decks
Until, although prepared for fight, still I sleep on land.
Thank you for the ostriches. I have not yet had time to pluck
them,
But I am sure they will be delicious, adorning my plate at sunset,
My tremendous plate, and the plate
Of the offers to all my days. But I cannot fasten my exhilaration
to the sun.

And thank you for the evening of the night on which I fell off my
horse in the shadows. That was really useful.

1958

FRANK O'HARA

CHEZ JANE

The white chocolate jar full of petals
swills odds and ends around in a dizzying eye
of four o'clocks now and to come. The tiger,
marvellously striped and irritable, leaps
on the table and without disturbing a hair
of the flowers' breathless attention, pisses
into the pot, right down its delicate spout.
A whisper of steam goes up from that porcelain
eurythra. "Saint-Saëns!" it seems to be whispering,
curling unerringly around the furry nuts
of the terrible puss, who is mentally flexing.
Ah be with me always, spirit of noisy
contemplation in the studio, the Garden
of Zoos, the eternally fixed afternoons!
There, while music scratches its scrofulous
stomach, the brute beast emerges and stands,
clear and careful, knowing always the exact peril
at this moment caressing his fangs with
a tongue given wholly to luxurious usages;
which only a moment before dropped aspirin
in this sunset of roses, and now throws a chair
in the air to aggravate the truly menacing.

1952

FOR JAMES DEAN

Welcome me, if you will,
as the ambassador of a hatred
who knows its cause

239

and does not envy you your whim
of ending him.

For a young actor I am begging
peace, gods. Alone
in the empty streets of New York
I am its dirty feet and head
and he is dead.

He has banged into your wall
of air, your hubris, racing
towards your heights and you
have cut him from your table
which is built, how unfairly
for us! not on trees, but on clouds.

I speak as one whose filth
is like his own, of pride
and speed and your terrible
example nearer than the siren's speech,
a spirit eager for the punishment
which is your only recognition.

Peace! to be true to a city
of rats and to love the envy
of the dreary, smudged mouthers
of an arcane dejection
smoldering quietly in the perception
of hopelessness and scandal
at unnatural vigor. Their dreams
are their own, as are the toilets
of a great railway terminal
and the sequins of a very small,
very fat eyelid.
             I take this
for myself, and you take up
the thread of my life between your teeth,
tin thread and tarnished with abuse,
you still shall hear
as long as the beast in me maintains

its taciturn power to close my lids
in tears, and my loins move yet
in the ennobling pursuit of all the worlds
you have left me alone in, and would be
the dolorous distraction from,
while you summon your army of anguishes
which is a million hooting blood vessels
on the eyes and in the ears
at the instant before death.

                                        And
the menials who surrounded him critically,
languorously waiting for a
final impertinence to rebel
and enslave him, starlets and other
glittering things in the hog-wallow,
lunging mireward in their inane
moth-like adoration of niggardly
cares and stagnant respects
paid themselves, you spared,
as a hospital preserves its orderlies.
Are these your latter-day saints,
these unctuous starers, muscular
somnambulists, these stages for which
no word's been written hollow
enough, these exhibitionists in
well-veiled booths, these navel-suckers?

Is it true that you high ones, celebrated
among amorous flies, hated the
prodigy and invention of his nerves?
To withhold your light
from painstaking paths!
your love
should be difficult, as his was hard.

Nostrils of pain down avenues
of luminous spit-globes breathe in
the fragrance of his innocent flesh
like smoke, the temporary lift,

the post-cancer excitement
of vile manners and veal-thin lips,
obscure in the carelessness of your scissors.

Men cry from the grave while they still live
and now I am this dead man's voice,
stammering, a little in the earth.
I take up
the nourishment of his pale green eyes,
out of which I shall prevent
flowers from growing, your flowers.

ODE

An idea of justice may be precious,
one vital gregarious amusement . . .

What are you amused by? a crisis
like a cow being put on the payroll
with the concomitant investigations and divinings?
Have you swept the dung from the tracks?
Am I a door?
If millions criticize you for drinking too much
the cow is going to look like Venus and you'll make a pass
yes, you and your friend from High School,
the basketball player whose black eyes exceed yours
as he picks up the ball with one hand.
But doesn't he doubt, too?

To be equal? it's the worst!
Are we just muddy instants?

No, you must treat me like a fox; or, being a child,
kill the oriole though it reminds you of me.
Thus you become the author of all being. Women
unite against you.

It's as if I were carrying a horse on my shoulders
and I couldn't see his face. His iron legs

hang down to the earth on either side of me
like the arch of triumph in Washington Square.
I would like to beat someone with him
but I can't get him off my shoulders, he's like evening.
Evening! your breeze is an obstacle,
    it changes me, I am being arrested,
    and if I mock you into a face
and, disgusted, throw down the horse — ah! there's his face!
and I am, sobbing, walking on my heart.

    I want to take your hands off my hips
    and put them on a statue's hips;

then I can thoughtfully regard the justice of your feelings
for me, and, changing, regard my own love for you
as beautiful. I'd never cheat you and say "It's inevitable!"
    It's just barely natural.
    But we do course together
like two battleships maneuvering away from the fleet.
I am moved by the multitudes of your intelligence
and sometimes, returning, I become the sea —
in love with your speed, your heaviness and breath.

1955

WHY I AM NOT A PAINTER

I am not a painter, I am a poet.
Why? I think I would rather be
a painter, but I am not. Well,

For instance, Mike Goldberg
is starting a painting. I drop in.
"Sit down and have a drink" he
says. I drink; we drink. I look
up. "You have SARDINES in it."
"Yes, it needed something there."
"Oh." I go and the days go by
and I drop in again. The painting

is going on, and I go, and the days
go by. I drop in. The painting is
finished. "Where's SARDINES?"
All that's left is just
letters, "It was too much," Mike says.

But me? One day I am thinking of
a color: orange. I write a line
about orange. Pretty soon it is a
whole page of words, not lines.
Then another page. There should be
so much more, not of orange, of
words, of how terrible orange is
and life. Days go by. It is even in
prose, I am a real poet. My poem
is finished and I haven't mentioned
orange yet. It's twelve poems, I call
it ORANGES. And one day in a gallery
I see Mike's painting, called SARDINES.

1956

IN MEMORY OF MY FEELINGS

to Grace Hartigan

1
My quietness has a man in it, he is transparent
and he carries me quietly, like a gondola, through the streets.
He has several likenesses, like stars and years, like numerals.

My quietness has a number of naked selves,
so many pistols I have borrowed to protect myselves
from creatures who too readily recognize my weapons
and have murder in their heart!
                            though in winter
they are warm as roses, in the desert
taste of chilled anisette.
                            At times, withdrawn,

I rise into the cool skies
and gaze on at the imponderable world with the simple identi-
    fication
of my colleagues, the mountains. Manfred climbs to my nape,
speaks, but I do not hear him,
                                    I'm too blue.
An elephant takes up his trumpet,
money flutters from the windows of cries, silk stretching its mirror
across shoulder blades. A gun is "fired."
                                    One of me rushes
to window #13 and one of me raises his whip and one of me
flutters up from the center of the track amidst the pink flamingoes,
and underneath their hooves as they round the last turn my lips
are scarred and brown, brushed by tails, masked in dirt's lust,
definition, open mouths gasping for the cries of the bettors for the
    lungs
of earth.

        So many of my transparencies could not resist the race!
Terror in earth, dried mushrooms, pink feathers, tickets,
a flaking moon drifting across the muddied teeth,
the imperceptible moan of covered breathing,
                                    love of the serpent!
I am underneath its leaves as the hunter crackles and pants
and bursts, as the barrage-balloon drifts behind a cloud
and animal death whips out its flashlight,
                                    whistling
and slipping the glove off the trigger hand. The serpent's eyes
redden at sight of those thorny fingernails, he is so smooth!
                                    My transparent selves
flail about like vipers in a pail, writhing and hissing
without panic, with a certain justice of response
and presently the aquiline serpent comes to resemble the Medusa.

    2

The dead hunting
and the alive, ahunted.
                    My father, my uncle,

my grand-uncle and the several aunts. My
grand-aunt dying for me, like a talisman, in the war,
before I had even gone to Borneo
her blood vessels rushed to the surface
and burst like rockets over the wrinkled
invasion of the Australians, her eyes aslant
like the invaded, but blue like mine.
An atmosphere of supreme lucidity,

                      humanism,

the mere existence of emphasis,

                      a rusted barge

painted orange against the sea
full of Marines reciting the Arabian ideas
which are a proof in themselves of seasickness
which is a proof in itself of being hunted.
A hit? *ergo* swim.

                My 10   my 19,

my 9,   and the several years. My
12 years since they all died, philosophically speaking.
And now the coolness of a mind
like a shuttered suite in the Grand Hotel
where mail arrives for my incognito,

                       whose façade

has been slipping into the Grand Canal for centuries;
rockets splay over a *sposalizio*,

                 fleeing into night

from their Chinese memories, and it is a celebration,
the trying desperately to count them as they die.
But who will stay to be these numbers
when all the lights are dead?

   3

The most arid stretch is often richest,
the hand lifting towards a fig tree from hunger

                      digging

and there is water, clear, supple, or there
deep in the sand where death sleeps, a murmurous bubbling
proclaims the blackness that will ease and burn.

You preferred the Arabs? but they didn't stay to count
their inventions, racing into sands, converting themselves into
so many,
            embracing, at Ramadan, the tenderest effigies of
themselves with penises shorn by the hundreds, like a camel
ravishing a goat.
                    And the mountainous-minded Greeks could speak
of time as a river and step across it into Persia, leaving the pain
at home to be converted into statuary. I adore the Roman copies.
And the stench of the camel's spit I swallow,
and the stench of the whole goat. For we have advanced, France,
together into a new land, like the Greeks, where one feels nostalgic
for mere ideas, where truth lies on its death-bed like an uncle
and one of me has a sentimental longing for number,
as has another for the ball gowns of the Directoire and yet
another for "Destiny, Paris, destiny!"
                            or "Only a king may kill a king."

How many selves are there in a war hero asleep in names? under
a blanket of platoon and fleet, orderly. For every seaman
with one eye closed in fear and twitching arm at a sigh for Lord
    Nelson,
he is all dead; and now a meek subaltern writhes in his bedclothes
with the fury of a thousand, violating an insane mistress
who has only herself to offer his multitudes.
                            Rising,
he wraps himself in the burnoose of memories against the heat of
    life
and over the sands he goes to take an algebraic position *in re*
a sun of fear shining not too bravely. He will ask himselves to
vote on fear before he feels a tremor,
                        as runners arrive from the mountains
bearing snow, proof that the mind's obsolescence is still capable
of intimacy. His mistress will follow him across the desert
like a goat, towards a mirage which is something familiar about
one of his innumerable wrists,
                        and lying in an oasis one day,
playing catch with coconuts, they suddenly smell oil.

4

Beneath these lives
the ardent lover of history hides,

                              tongue out
leaving a globe of spit on a taut spear of grass
and leaves off rattling his tail a moment
to admire this flag.

                    I'm looking for my Shanghai Lil.
Five years ago, enamored of fire-escapes, I went to Chicago,
an eventful trip: the fountains! the Art Institute, the Y
for both sexes, absent Christianity.

                              At 7, before Jane
was up, the copper lake stirred against the sides
of a Norwegian freighter; on the deck a few dirty men,
tired of night, watched themselves in the water
as years before the German prisoners on the *Prinz Eugen*
dappled the Pacific with their sores, painted purple
by a Naval doctor.

                    Beards growing, and the constant anxiety
over looks. I'll shave before she wakes up. Sam Goldwyn
spent $2,000,000 on Anna Sten, but Grushenka left America.
One of me is standing in the waves, an ocean bather,
or I am naked with a plate of devils at my hip.

                                        Grace
to be born and live as variously as possible. The conception
of the masque barely suggests the sordid identifications.
I am a Hittite in love with a horse. I don't know what blood's
in me I feel like an African prince I am a girl walking downstairs
in a red pleated dress with heels I am a champion taking a fall
I am a jockey with a sprained ass-hole I am the light mist
                              in which a face appears
and it is another face of blonde I am a baboon eating a banana
I am a dictator looking at his wife I am a doctor eating a child
and the child's mother smiling I am a Chinaman climbing a
    mountain
I am a child smelling his father's underwear I am an Indian
sleeping on a scalp

and my pony is stamping in the birches,
and I've just caught sight of the *Niña,* the *Pinta* and the *Santa Maria.*

What land is this, so free?

I watch
the sea at the back of my eyes, near the spot where I think
in solitude as pine trees groan and support the enormous winds,
they are humming *L'Oiseau de feu!*

They look like gods, these whitemen,
and they are bringing me the horse I fell in love with on the frieze.

5
And now it is the serpent's turn.
I am not quite you, but almost, the opposite of visionary.
You are coiled around the central figure,

the heart
that bubbles with red ghosts, since to move is to love
and the scrutiny of all things is syllogistic,
the startled eyes of the dikdik, the bush full of white flags
fleeing a hunter,

which is our democracy

but the prey
is always fragile and like something, as a seashell can be
a great Courbet, if it wishes. To bend the ear of the outer world.

When you turn your head
can you feel your heels, undulating? that's what it is
to be a serpent. I haven't told you of the most beautiful things
in my lives, and watching the ripple of their loss disappear
along the shore, underneath ferns,

face downward in the ferns
my body, the naked host to my many selves, shot
by a guerrilla warrior or dumped from a car into ferns
which are themselves *journalières.*

The hero, trying to unhitch his parachute,
stumbles over me. It is our last embrace.

And yet
I have forgotten my loves, and chiefly that one, the cancerous
statue which my body could no longer contain,

                                                    against my will
                                                    against my love
become art,
            I could not change it into history
and so remember it,
                    and I have lost what is always and everywhere
present, the scene of my selves, the occasion of these ruses,
which I myself and singly must now kill
                            and save the serpent in their midst.

                                            6/27 — 7/1/56

ODE TO JOY

We shall have everything we want and there'll be no more dying
        on the pretty plains or in the supper clubs
for our symbol we'll acknowledge vulgar materialistic laughter
        over an insatiable sexual appetite
and the streets will be filled with racing forms
and the photographs of murderers and narcissists and movie stars
        will swell from the walls and books alive in steaming rooms
        to press against our burning flesh not once but interminably
as water flows down hill into the full lipped basin
and the adder dives for the ultimate ostrich egg
and the feather cushion preens beneath a reclining monolith
        that's sweating with post-exertion visibility and sweetness
        near the grave of love
                                    No more dying

We shall see the grave of love as a lovely sight and temporary
        near the elm that spells the lovers' names in roots
and there'll be no more music but the ears in lips and no more wit
        but tongues in ears and no more drums but ears to thighs
as evening signals nudities unknown to ancestors' imaginations
and the imagination itself will stagger like a tired paramour of ivory
        under the sculptural necessities of lust that never falters
        like a six-mile runner from Sweden or Liberia covered with
        gold

as lava flows up and over the far-down somnolent city's abdication
and the hermit always wanting to be lone is lone at last
and the weight of external heat crushes the heat-hating Puritan
    who's self-defeating vice becomes a proper sepulchre at last
    that love may live

Buildings will go up into the dizzy air as love itself goes in
    and up the reeling life that it has chosen for once or all
while in the sky a feeling of intemperate fondness will excite the
    birds to swoop and veer like flies crawling across absorbèd
    limbs
that weep a pearly perspiration on the sheets of brief attention
and the hairs dry out that summon anxious declaration of the
    organs as they rise like buildings to the needs of temporary
    neighbors pouring hunger through the heart to feed desire in
    intravenous ways
like the ways of gods with humans in the innocent combination of
    light
and flesh or as the legends ride their heroes through the dark to
    found
great cities where all life is possible to maintain as long as time
    which wants us to remain for cocktails in a bar and after dinner
    lets us live with it

                      No more dying

                        11/13/57

TO HELL WITH IT

"Hungry winter, this winter"

                  meaningful hints at dismay
                    to be touched, to see labelled as such
perspicacious Colette and Vladimirovitch meet with sickness and
    distress,

      it is because of sunspots on the sun.

                    I clean it off with an old sock
and go on:

    And blonde Gregory dead in Fall Out on a highway with his

Broadway wife,
the last of the Lafayettes,
                              (How I hate subject matter! melancholy,
            intruding on the vigorous heart,
                                          the soul telling itself
you haven't suffered enough ((Hyalomiel))
                              and all things that don't change:
photographs,
                  monuments,
                        memories of Bunny and Gregory and me in
                                                      costume
bowing to each other and the audience, like jinxes)

            nothing now can be changed, as
                                    last crying, no tears will dry
and Bunny will never change her writing of
                                    the Bear, nor Greg bear me
any further gift, beyond liking my poems
                              (no new poems for him.) and
a big red railroad handkerchief from the country
                                          in his sportscar
so like another actor . . .

For sentiment is always intruding on form,
                              the immaculate disgust of the
                                                      mind
beaten down by pain and the vileness of life's flickering disap-
      proval,
      endless torment pretending to be the rose of
acknowledgement (courage)
                        and fruitless absolution (hence the word: "hip")
to be cool,
        decisive,
                  precise,
                        yes, while the barn door hits you in the face
each time you get up
                  because the wind, seeing you slim and gallant, rises
            to embrace its darling poet. (It thinks *I'm* mysterious!)

All diseases are exchangeable.

> Wind, you'll have a terrible time
> smothering my clarity, a void
> behind my eyes,
>   into which existence
> continues to stuff its wounded limbs
>
> as I make room for them, on one
> after another filthy page of poetry.

                                                        7/13/57

ODE:

SALUTE TO THE FRENCH NEGRO POETS

From near the sea, like Whitman my great predecessor, I call
to the spirits of other lands to make fecund my existence

do not spare your wrath upon our shores, that trees may grow
upon the sea, mirror of our total mankind in the weather

one who no longer remembers dancing in the heat of the moon
    may call
across the shifting sands, trying to live in the terrible western
    world

here where to love at all's to be a politician, as to love a poem
is pretentious, this may sound tendentious but it's lyrical

which shows what lyricism has been brought to by our fabled
    times
where cowards are shibboleths and one specific love's traduced

by shame for what you love more generally and never would avoid
where reticence is paid for by a poet in his blood or ceasing to be

blood! blood that we have mountains in our veins to stand off
    jackals

in the pillaging of our desires and allegiances, Aimé Césaire

for if there is fortuity it's in the love we bear each other's differ-
    ences
in race which is the poetic ground on which we rear our smiles

standing in the sun of marshes as we wade slowly toward the cul-
    mination
of a gift which is categorically the most difficult relationship

and should be sought as such because it is our nature, nothing
inspires us but the love we want upon the frozen face of earth

and utter disparagement turns into praise as generations read the
    message
of our hearts in adolescent closets who once shot at us in door-
    ways

or kept us from living freely because they were too young then
    to know
what they would ultimately need from a barren and heart-sore life

the beauty of America, neither cool jazz nor devoured Egyptian
    heroes, lies in
lives in the darkness I inhabit in the midst of sterile millions

the only truth is face to face, the poem whose words become your
    mouth
and dying in black and white we fight for what we love, not are

                                                            7/9/58

ODE TO MICHAEL GOLDBERG
('S BIRTH AND OTHER BIRTHS)

I don't remember anything of then, down there around the
    magnolias
            where I was no more comfortable than I've been since
            though aware of a certain neutrality called satisfaction
            sometimes

and there's never been an opportunity to think of it as an idyll
as if everyone'd been singing around me, or around a tulip tree

a faint stirring of that singing seems to come to me in heavy
    traffic
but I can't be sure that's it, it may be some more recent singing
from hours of dusk in bushes playing tag, being called in, walk-
    ing up onto the porch crying bitterly because it wasn't a
    veranda
"smell that honeysuckle?" or a door you can see through terribly
    clearly,
            even the mosquitoes saw through it
suffocating netting
or more often being put into a brown velvet suit and kicked
    around
perhaps that was my last real cry for myself
in a forest you think of birds, in traffic you think of tires,
            where are you?
in Baltimore you think of hats and shoes, like Daddy did

            I hardly ever think of June 27, 1926
            when I came moaning into my mother's world
            and tried to make it mine immediately
            by screaming, sucking, urinating
            and carrying on generally
            it was quite a day

I wasn't proud of my penis yet, how did I know how to act? it
    was 1936
"no excuses, now"

    Yellow morning
                silent, wet
                    blackness under the trees over stone walls
hay, smelling faintly of semen
                    a few sheltered flowers nodding and smiling
at the clattering cutter-bar
                    of the mower ridden by Jimmy Whitney
"I'd like to put my rolling-pin to her"   his brother Bailey

leaning on his pitch-fork, watching
                    "you shove it in and nine months later
it comes out a kid"
                    Ha ha   where those flowers would dry out
and never again be seen
                    except as cow-flaps, hushed noon drinking cold
water in the dusty field   "their curly throats"   big milk cans

    full of cold spring water, sandy hair, black hair

          I went to my first movie
          and the hero got his legs
          cut off by a steam engine
          in a freightyard, in my second

          Karen Morley got shot
          in the back by an arrow
          I think she was an heiress
          it came through her bathroom door

          there was nobody there
          there never was anybody
          there at any time
          in sweet-smelling summer

I'd like to stay
          in this field forever
                              and think of nothing
but these sounds,
                    these smells and the tickling grasses
                              "up your ass, Sport"

          Up on the mountainous hill
          behind the confusing house
          where I lived, I went each
          day after school and some nights
          with my various dogs, the
          terrier that bit people, Arno
          the shepherd (who used to
          be wild but had stopped), the

wire-haired that took fits
and finally the boring gentle
cocker, spotted brown and white,
named Freckles   there,

the wind sounded exactly like
Stravinsky
            I first recognized art
as wildness, and it seemed right,
            I mean rite, to me

climbing the water-tower I'd
look out for hours in wind
and the world seemed rounder
and fiercer and I was happier
because I wasn't scared of falling off

nor off the horses, the horses!
to hell with the horses, bay and black

It's odd to have secrets at an early age, trysts
whose thoughtfulness and sweetness are those of a very aggres-
sive person
            carried beneath your shirt like an amulet against your sire
                what one must do is done in a red twilight
                    on colossally old and dirty furniture with knobs,
                and on Sunday afternoons you meet in a high place
                watching the Sunday drivers and the symphonic
                sadness
            stopped, a man in a convertible put his hand up a girl's
            skirt
        and again the twitching odor of hay, like a minor irritation
that gives you a hardon, and again the roundness of horse noises

            "Je suis las de vivre au pays natal"
                    but unhappiness, like Mercury, transfixed me
            there, un repaire de vipères
                        and had I known the strength and durability
of those invisible bonds I would have leaped from rafters onto
prongs

then
　　and been carried shining and intact
　　to the Indian Cemetery near the lake

　　　　　　　　　　　　　　but there is a glistening
　　　　　　　　　　　　　　blackness in the center
　　　　　　　　　　　　　　if you seek it

here . . .　　　it's capable of bursting
　　　　　　　　into flame or merely
　　　　　　　　gleaming profoundly in

　　　　　　　　　　　　　　the platinum setting
　　　　　　　　　　　　　　of your ornamental
　　　　　　　　　　　　　　human ties and hates

hanging between breasts
　　　　　　　　　　　　or, cross-like, on a chest of hairs
the center of myself is never silent
　　　　　　　　　　　　　　the wind soars, keening overhead
and the vestments of unnatural safety
　　　　　　　　　　　　　　part to reveal a foreign land
toward whom I have been selected to bear
　　　　　　　　　　　　　　the gift of fire
　　　　　　　　　　　the temporary place of light, the land of air

down where a flame illumines gravity and means warmth and
　　insight,
　　where air is flesh, where speed is darkness

and
　　things can suddenly be reached, held, dropped and known

where a not totally imaginary ascent can begin all over again in
　　tears

　　A couple of specifically anguished days
　　make me now distrust sorrow, simple sorrow
　　especially, like sorrow over death

　　it makes you wonder who you are to be sorrowful
　　over death, death belonging to another
　　and suddenly inhabited by you without permission

you moved in impulsively and took it up
declaring your Squatters' Rights in howls
or screaming with rage, like a parvenu in a Chinese laundry

disbelieving your own feelings is the worst
and you suspect that you are jealous of this death

YIPPEE! I'm glad I'm alive

                              "I'm glad you're alive
too, baby, because I want to fuck you"

                              you are pink
and despicable in the warm breeze drifting in the window
and the rent
              is due, in honor of which you have borrowed $34.96
                  from Joe
and it's all over but the smoldering hatred of pleasure
      a gorgeous purple like somebody's favorite tie
          "Shit, that means you're getting kind of ascetic, doesn't
          it?"

              So I left, the stars were shining
              like the lights around a swimming pool

              you've seen a lot of anemones, too
              haven't you, Old Paint? through the
              Painted Desert to the orange covered
              slopes where a big hill was moving in
              on L A and other stars were strolling
              in shorts down palm-stacked horse-walks
              and I stared with my strained SP stare
              wearing a gun
                        the doubts
      of a life devoted to leaving rumors of love for new
from does she love me to do I love him,
                              sempiternal farewell to hearths
and the gods who don't live there

              in New Guinea a Sunday morning figure
              reclining outside his hut in Lamourish languor

and an atabrine-dyed hat like a sick sun
over his ebony land on your way to breakfast

he has had his balls sowed into his mouth
by the natives who bleach their hair in urine
and their will; a basketball game and a concert
later if you live to write, it's not all advancing
towards you, he had a killing desire for their women

but more killing still the absence of desire, which in religion
                              used to be called hope,
I don't just mean the lack of a hardon, which may be sincerity
            or the last-minute victory of the proud spirit over flesh,
    no: a tangerine-like sullenness in the face of sunrise
            or a dark sinking in the wind on the forecastle
    when someone you love hits your head and says "I'd sail with
    you any where, war or no war"

who was about
            to die a tough blond death
                              like a slender blighted palm
in the hurricane's curious hail
                        and the maelstrom of bull-dozers
            and metal sinkings,
                              churning the earth
even under the fathomless deaths
                  below, beneath
                              where the one special
                  went to be hidden, never to disappear
                              not spatial in that way

        Take me, I felt, into the future fear of saffron pleasures
crazy strangeness and steam
                  of seeing a (pearl) white whale, steam of
being high in the sky
                  opening fire on Corsairs,
                              kept moving in berths
where I trade someone *The Counterfeiters* (I thought it was

about personal freedom then!) for a pint of whiskey,
                              banana brandy in Manila, spidery
steps trailing down onto the rocks of the harbor
                              and up in the black fir, the
pyramidal whiteness, Genji on the Ginza,
                              a lavender-kimono-sized
loneliness,
                and drifting into my ears off Sendai in the snow Carl
T. Fischer's *Recollections of an Indian Boy*
                              this tiny over-decorated
rock garden bringing obviously heart-shaped
                              the Great Plains, as is
my way to be obvious as eight o'clock in the dining car
                              of the
20th Century Limited (express)
                              and its noisy blast passing buttes to be
Atchison-Topeka-Santa Fé, Baltimore and Ohio (Cumberland),
                              leaving
beds in Long Beach for beds in Boston, via C-(D,B,) 47 (6)
pretty girls in textile mills,
                drowsing on bales in a warehouse of cotton
listening to soft Southern truck talk

                              perhaps it is "your miraculous
low roar" on Ulithi as the sailors pee into funnels, ambassadors of
       green-beer-interests bigger than Standard Oil in the South
Pacific, where the beaches flower with cat-eyes and ear fungus
       warm as we never wanted to be warm, in an ammunition
dump, my foot again crushed (this time by a case of 40 milli-
    meters)

                              "the
        only thing you ever gave New Guinea was your toe-nail
        and now
     the Australians are taking over"   . . . the pony of war?

              to "return" safe who will never feel safe
              and loves to ride steaming in the autumn of
              centuries of useless aspiration towards artifice

are you feeling useless, too, Old Paint?
I am really an Indian at heart, knowing it is all
all over but my own ceaseless going, never
to be just a hill of dreams and flint for someone later
but a hull laved by the brilliant Celebes response,
empty of treasure to the explorers who sailed me not

King Philip's trail,
                    lachrymose highway of infantile regrets and cayuse
meannesses,
            Mendelssohn driving me mad in Carnegie Hall like greed
grasping
            Palisades Park smiling, you pull a pretty ring out of the
                    pineapple
and blow yourself up
                        contented to be a beautiful fan of blood
                            above the earth-empathic earth

            Now suddenly the fierce wind of disease and Venus, as
when a child
            you wonder if you're not a little crazy, laughing
because a horse
            is standing on your foot
                            and you're kicking his hock
with your sneaker, which is to him
                            a love-tap, baring big teeth
laughing . . .
            thrilling activities which confuse
                                too many, too loud
too often, crowds of intimacies and no distance
                                the various cries
and rounds
            and we are smiling in our confused way, darkly
in the back alcove
            of the Five Spot, devouring chicken-in-the-basket
and arguing,
            the four of us, about loyalty

wonderful stimulation of bitterness
to be young and to grow bigger
more and more cells, like germs
or a political conspiracy

and each reason for love always
a certain hostility, mistaken
for wisdom
                        exceptional excitement
which is finally simple blindness
(but not to be sneezed at!) like
a successful American satellite . . .

Yes, it does, it would still
keep me out of a monastery if
I were invited to attend one

                                from round the window, you can't
        see the street!
                        you let the cold wind course through
and let the heart pump and gurgle
                        in febrile astonishment,
                                        a cruel world
to which you've led it by your mind,
                        bicycling no-hands
                                        leaving it gasping
there, wondering where you are and how to get back,
                                although you'll never let
        it go

        while somewhere everything's dispersed
at five o'clock
        for Martinis a group of professional freshnesses meet
and the air's like a shrub — Rose o' Sharon? the others,
                                                it's not
a flickering light for us, but the glare of the dark
                                        too much endlessness
stored up, and in store:

"the exquisite prayer
to be new each day
brings to the artist
only a certain kneeness"

I am assuming that everything is all right and difficult,
                                                    where hordes
        of stars carry the burdens of the gentler animals like our-
        selves with wit and austerity beneath a hazardous settle-
        ment which we understand because we made
                                        and secretly admire
        because it moves
yes! for always, for it is our way, to pass the tea-house and the
        ceremony by and rather fall sobbing to the floor with joy
        and freezing than to spill the kid upon the table and then
        thank the blood

        for flowing
                as it must throughout the miserable, clear and willful
life we love beneath the blue,
                        a fleece of pure intention sailing like
a pinto in a barque of slaves
                        who soon will turn upon their captors
lower anchor, found a city riding there
                        of poverty and sweetness paralleled
        among the races without time,
                        and one alone will speak of being
        born in pain
                and he will be the wings of an extraordinary liberty

                                                            1958

THE DAY LADY DIED

It is 12:20 in New York a Friday
three days after Bastille Day, yes
it is 1959 and I go get a shoeshine
because I will get off the 4:19 in Easthampton

at 7:15 and then go straight to dinner
and I don't know the people who will feed me

I walk up the muggy street beginning to sun
and have a hamburger and a malted and buy
an ugly NEW WORLD WRITING to see what the poets
in Ghana are doing these days
                              I go on to the bank
and Miss Stillwagon (first name Linda I once heard)
doesn't even look up my balance for once in her life
and in the GOLDEN GRIFFIN I get a little Verlaine
for Patsy with drawings by Bonnard although I do
think of Hesiod, trans. Richmond Lattimore or
Brendan Behan's new play or *Le Balcon* or *Les Nègres*
of Genet, but I don't, I stick with Verlaine
after practically going to sleep with quandariness

and for Mike I just stroll into the PARK LANE
Liquor Store and ask for a bottle of Strega and
then I go back where I came from to 6th Avenue
and the tobacconist in the Ziegfeld Theatre and
casually ask for a carton of Gauloises and a carton
of Picayunes, and a NEW YORK POST with her face on it

and I am sweating a lot by now and thinking of
leaning on the john door in the FIVE SPOT
while she whispered a song along the keyboard
to Mal Waldron and everyone and I stopped breathing

7/17/59

YOU ARE GORGEOUS AND I'M COMING

Vaguely I hear the purple roar of the torn-down 3rd Avenue El
it sways slightly but firmly like a hand or a golden-downed thigh
normally I don't think of sounds as colored unless I'm feeling cor-
    rupt
concrete Rimbaud obscurity of emotion which is simple and very
    definite

even lasting, yes it may be that dark and purifying wave, the
  death of boredom
nearing the heights themselves may destroy you in the pure air
to be further complicated, confused, empty but refilling, exposed
  to light

With the past falling away as an acceleration of nerves thunder-
  ing and shaking
aims its aggregating force like the Métro towards a realm of en-
  circling travel
rending the sound of adventure and becoming ultimately local
  and intimate
repeating the phrases of an old romance which is constantly re-
  newed by the
endless originality of human loss the air the stumbling quiet of
  breathing
newly the heavens' stars all out we are all for the captured time
  of our being

8/11/59

POEM

Hate is only one of many responses
true, hurt and hate go hand in hand
but why be afraid of hate, it is only there

think of filth, is it really awesome
neither is hate
don't be shy of unkindness, either
it's cleansing and allows you to be direct
like an arrow that feels something

out and out meanness, too, lets love breathe
you don't have to fight off getting in too deep
you can always get out if you're not too scared

an ounce of prevention's
enough to poison the heart

don't think of others
until you have thought of yourself, are true

all of these things, if you feel them
will be graced by a certain reluctance
and turn into gold

if felt by me, will be smilingly deflected
by your mysterious concern

                                                                    8/24/59

POEM

Khrushchev is coming on the right day!
                                        the cool graced light
is pushed off the enormous glass piers by hard wind
and everything is tossing, hurrying on up
                                        this country
has everything but *politesse,* a Puerto Rican cab driver says
and five different girls I see
                            look like Piedie Gimbel
with her blonde hair tossing too,
                                    as she looked when I pushed
her little daughter on the swing on the lawn it was also windy

last night we went to a movie and came out,
                                        Ionesco is greater
than Beckett, Vincent said, that's what I think, blueberry blintzes
and Khrushchev was probably being carped at
                                    in Washington, no *politesse*
Vincent tells me about his mother's trip to Sweden
                                            Hans tells us
about his father's life in Sweden, it sounds like Grace Hartigan's
painting *Sweden*
            so I go home to bed and names drift through my head
Purgatorio Merchado, Gerhard Schwartz and Gaspar Gonzalez,
    all
            unknown figures of the early morning as I go to work

where does the evil of the year go
                              when September takes New York
and turns it into ozone stalagmites
                                    deposits of light
                                    so I get back up
make coffee, and read François Villon, his life, so dark
      New York seems blinding and my tie is blowing up the street
I wish it would blow off
                        though it is cold and somewhat warms my neck
as the train bears Khrushchev on to Pennsylvania Station
      and the light seems to be eternal
      and joy seems to be inexorable
      I am foolish enough always to find it in wind

                                                      9/17/59

IN FAVOR OF ONE'S TIME

The spent purpose of a perfectly marvellous
life suddenly glimmers and leaps into flame
it's more difficult than you think to make charcoal
it's also pretty hard to remember life's marvellous
but there it is guttering choking then soaring
in the mirrored room of this consciousness
it's practically a blaze of pure sensibility
and however exaggerated at least something's going on
and the quick oxygen in the air will not go neglected
will not sulk or fall into blackness and peat

an angel flying slowly, curiously singes its wings
and you diminish for a moment out of respect
for beauty then flare up after all that's the angel
that wrestled with Jacob and loves conflict
as an athlete loves the tape, and we're off into
an immortal contest of actuality and pride
which is love assuming the consciousness of itself
as sky over all, medium of finding and founding
not just resemblance but the magnetic otherness

that that that stands erect in the spirit's glare
and waits for the joining of an opposite force's breath

so come the winds into our lives and last
longer than despair's sharp snake, crushed before it conquered
so marvellous is not just a poet's greenish namesake
and we live outside his garden in our tempestuous rights

9/24/59

HOTEL TRANSYLVANIE

Shall we win at love or shall we lose
                                        can it be
that hurting and being hurt is a trick forcing the love
we want to appear, that the hurt is a card
and is it black? is it red? is it a paper, dry of tears
chevalier, change your expression! the wind is sweeping over
the gaming tables ruffling the cards/they are black and red
like a Futurist torture and how do you know it isn't always there
waiting while doubt is the father that has you kidnapped by
    friends

        yet you will always live in a jealous society of accident
you will never know how beautiful you are or how beautiful
the other is, you will continue to refuse to die for yourself
you will continue to sing on trying to cheer everyone up
and they will know as they listen with excessive pleasure that
    you're dead
        and they will not mind that they have let you entertain
at the expense of the only thing you want in the world/you are
    amusing
as a game is amusing when someone is forced to lose as in a game
    I must

            oh *hôtel*, you should be merely a bed
surrounded by walls where two souls meet and do nothing but
    breathe
breathe in breathe out fuse illuminate confuse *stick* dissemble

but not as cheaters at cards have something to win/you have only
   to be
as you are being, as you must be, as you always are, as you shall
   be forever
no matter what fate deals you or the imagination discards like a
   tyrant
as the drums descend and summon the hatchet over the tinselled
   realities

you know that I am not here to fool around, that I must win or die
I expect you to do everything because it is of no consequence/no
   duel
you must rig the deck you must make me win at whatever cost to
   the reputation
of the establishment/sublime moment of dishonest hope/I must
   win
for if the floods of tears arrive they will wash it all away
                                                      and then

you will know what it is to want something, but you may not be
   allowed
to die as I have died, you may only be allowed to drift down-
   stream
to another body of inimical attractions for which you will sub-
   stitute/distrust
and I will have had my revenge on the black bitch of my nature
   which you
                    love as I have never loved myself

but I hold on/I am lyrical to a fault/I do not despair being too
   foolish
where will you find me, projective verse, since I will be gone?
for six seconds of your beautiful face I will sell the hotel and
   commit
an uninteresting suicide in Louisiana where it will take them a
   long time
to know who I am/why I came there/what and why I am and
   made to happen

                                                    12/12/59

JOHN ASHBERY

A BOY

I'll do what the raids suggest,
Dad, and that other livid window,
But the tide pushes an awful lot of monsters
And I think it's my true fate.

It had been raining but
It had not been raining.

No one could begin to mop up this particular mess.
Thunder lay down in the heart.
"My child, I love any vast electrical disturbance."
Disturbance! Could the old man, face in the rainweed,

Ask more smuttily? By night it charged over plains,
Driven from Dallas and Oregon, always *whither,*
Why not now? The boy seemed to have fallen
From shelf to shelf of someone's rage.

That night it rained on the boxcars, explaining
The thought of the pensive cabbage roses near the boxcars.
My boy. Isn't there something I asked you once?
What happened? It's also farther to the corner
Aboard the maple furniture. *He*
Couldn't lie. He's tell 'em by their syntax.

But listen now in the flood.
They're throwing up behind the lines.
Dry fields of lightning rise to receive
The observer, the mincing flag. *An unendurable age.*

1952

THE INSTRUCTION MANUAL

As I sit looking out of a window of the building
I wish I did not have to write the instruction manual on
    the uses of a new metal.
I look down into the street and see people, each walking
    with an inner peace,
And envy them — they are so far away from me!
Not one of them has to worry about getting out this
    manual on schedule.
And, as my way is, I begin to dream, resting my elbows
    on the desk and leaning out of the window a little,
Of dim Guadalajara! City of rose-colored flowers!
City I wanted most to see, and most did not see, in
    Mexico!
But I fancy I see, under the press of having to write the
    instruction manual,
Your public square, city, with its elaborate little band-
    stand!
The band is playing *Scheherazade* by Rimsky-Korsakov.
Around stand the flower girls, handing out rose- and
    lemon-colored flowers,
Each attractive in her rose-and-blue striped dress (Oh!
    such shades of rose and blue),
And nearby is the little white booth where women in
    green serve you green and yellow fruit.
The couples are parading; everyone is in a holiday mood.
First, leading the parade, is a dapper fellow
Clothed in deep blue. On his head sits a white hat
And he wears a mustache, which has been trimmed for
    the occasion.
His dear one, his wife, is young and pretty; her shawl is
    rose, pink, and white.
Her slippers are patent leather, in the American fashion,
And she carries a fan, for she is modest, and does not want
    the crowd to see her face too often.

But everybody is so busy with his wife or loved one
I doubt they would notice the mustachioed man's wife.
Here come the boys! They are skipping and throwing
    little things on the sidewalk
Which is made of gray tile. One of them, a little older,
    has a toothpick in his teeth.
He is silenter than the rest, and affects not to notice the
    pretty young girls in white.
But his friends notice them, and shout their jeers at the
    laughing girls.
Yet soon all this will cease, with the deepening of their
    years,
And love bring each to the parade grounds for another
    reason.
But I have lost sight of the young fellow with the tooth-
    pick.
Wait — there he is — on the other side of the bandstand,
Secluded from his friends, in earnest talk with a young
    girl
Of fourteen or fifteen. I try to hear what they are saying
But it seems they are just mumbling something — shy
    words of love, probably.
She is slightly taller than he, and looks quietly down into
    his sincere eyes.
She is wearing white. The breeze ruffles her long fine
    black hair against her olive cheek.
Obviously she is in love. The boy, the young boy with the
    toothpick, he is in love too;
His eyes show it. Turning from this couple,
I see there is an intermission in the concert.
The paraders are resting and sipping drinks through
    straws
(The drinks are dispensed from a large glass crock by a
    lady in dark blue),
And the musicians mingle among them, in their creamy
    white uniforms, and talk
About the weather, perhaps, or how their kids are doing
    at school.

Let us take this opportunity to tiptoe into one of the side
   streets.
Here you may see one of those white houses with green
   trim
That are so popular here. Look — I told you!
It is cool and dim inside, but the patio is sunny.
An old woman in gray sits there, fanning herself with a
   palm leaf fan.
She welcomes us to her patio, and offers us a cooling
   drink.
"My son is in Mexico City," she says. "He would wel-
   come you too
If he were here. But his job is with a bank there.
Look, here is a photograph of him."
And a dark-skinned lad with pearly teeth grins out at us
   from the worn leather frame.
We thank her for her hospitality, for it is getting late
And we must catch a view of the city, before we leave,
   from a good high place.
That church tower will do — the faded pink one, there
   against the fierce blue of the sky. Slowly we enter.
The caretaker, an old man dressed in brown and gray,
   asks us how long we have been in the city, and how
   we like it here.
His daughter is scrubbing the steps — she nods to us as we
   pass into the tower.
Soon we have reached the top, and the whole network
   of the city extends before us.
There is the rich quarter, with its houses of pink and
   white, and its crumbling, leafy terraces.
There is the poorer quarter, its homes a deep blue.
There is the market, where men are selling hats and
   swatting flies
And there is the public library, painted several shades of
   pale green and beige.
Look! There is the square we just came from, with the
   promenaders.

There are fewer of them, now that the heat of the day has
    increased,
But the young boy and girl still lurk in the shadows of
    the bandstand.
And there is the home of the little old lady —
She is still sitting in the patio, fanning herself.
How limited, but how complete withal, has been our ex-
    perience of Guadalajara!
We have seen young love, married love, and the love of
    an aged mother for her son.
We have heard the music, tasted the drinks, and looked
    at colored houses.
What more is there to do, except stay? And that we can-
    not do.
And as a last breeze freshens the top of the weathered old
    tower, I turn my gaze
Back to the instruction manual which has made me dream
    of Guadalajara.

1955

"HOW MUCH LONGER WILL I BE ABLE TO INHABIT THE DIVINE SEPULCHER..."

How much longer will I be able to inhabit the divine sepulcher
Of life, my great love? Do dolphins plunge bottomward
To find the light? Or is it rock
That is searched? Unrelentingly? Huh. And if some day

Men with orange shovels come to break open the rock
Which encases me, what about the light that comes in then?
What about the smell of the light?
What about the moss?

In pilgrim times he wounded me
Since then I only lie
My bed of light is a furnace choking me
With hell (and sometimes I hear salt water dripping).

I mean it — because I'm one of the few
To have held my breath behind the house. I'll trade
One red sucker for two blue ones. I'm
Named Tom. The

Light bounces off mossy rocks down to me
In this glen (the neat villa! which
When he'd had he would not had he of
And jests smarting of privet

Which on hot spring nights perfumes the empty rooms
With the smell of sperm flushed down toilets
On hot summer afternoons within sight of the sea.
If you knew why then professor) reads

To his friends: What a marvel is ancient man!
Under the tulip roots he has figured out a way to be a religious
    animal
And would be a mathematician. But where in unsuitable heaven
Can he get the heat that will make him grow?

For he needs something or will forever remain a dwarf,
Though a perfect one, and possessing a normal sized brain
But he has got to be released by giants from things.
And as the plant grows older it realizes it will never be a tree,

Will probably always be haunted by a bee
And cultivates stupid impressions
So as not to become part of the dirt. The dirt
Is mounting like a sea. And we say goodbye

Shaking hands in front of the crashing of the waves
That give our words lonesomeness, and make these flabby hands
    seem ours —
Hands that are always writing things
On mirrors for people to see later —

Do you want them to water
Plant, tear listlessly among the exchangeable ivy —
Carrying food to mouth, touching genitals —
But no doubt you have understood

It all now and I am a fool. It remains
For me to get better, and to understand you so
Like a chair-sized man. Boots
Were heard on the floor above. In the garden the sunlight was
    still purple

But what buzzed in it had changed slightly
But not forever . . .   but casting its shadow
On sticks, and looking around for an opening in the air, was quite
    as if it had never refused to exist differently. Guys
In the yard handled the belt he had made

Stars
Painted the garage roof crimson and black.
He is not a man
Who can read these signs . . .   his bones were stays . . .

And even refused to live
In a world and refunded the hiss
Of all that exists terribly near us
Like you, my love, and light.

For what is obedience but the air around us
To the house? For which the federal men came
In a minute after the sidewalk
Had taken you home? ("Latin . . .   blossom . . .")

After which you led me to the water
And bade me drink, which I did, owing to your kindness.
You would not let me out for two days and three nights,
Bringing me books bound in wild thyme and scented wild grasses

As if reading had any interest for me, you . . .
Now you are laughing.
Darkness interrupts my story.
I turn on the light.

Meanwhile what am I going to do?
I am growing up again, in school, the crisis will be very soon.
And you twist the darkness in your fingers, you
Who are slightly older . . .

Who are you, anyway?
And it is the color of sand,
The darkness, as it sifts through your hand
Because what does anything mean,

The ivy and the sand? That boat
Pulled up on the shore? Am I wonder,
Strategically, and in the light
Of the long sepulcher that hid death and hides me?

1957

V

PHILIP WHALEN

MARTYRDOM OF TWO PAGANS

Out on a limb and frantically sawing
The saw teeth go dull and at last
Wear smooth
Leaving us here, still throned in the air
    Like the sage in the basket
    And the one in the jar
Either branch or tree will fall
Or we'll both drop, sleeping
A heavenly meal for the animal saints
Who march continuously round the bole

A distinction or a difference, I said
Either one a horn on Io's head
A giddy heifer chased by bees
All are immortal
Laugh and lie down

Discriminate or perish, he replied
    While all with one voice (about
      the space of two hours) cried out
    Great is Diana of the Ephesians!
Stay awake, he said, sleep is confusion
    My eyelids have grown tea-leaves for the pot
Brew it strong
Defy illusion
The weakened branch snaps off
We join the company of saints
Remaining conscious —
               though dismembered
To the last.

The sacred beasts all ate
And marched and sang:
  'Love is better than hate
  Love is better than hate
Love is better than hate
   and stronger than hell'
   For we took our shoes off
   As we fell.

Seattle, 18-24:III:55

2 VARIATIONS: ALL ABOUT LOVE

I

So much to tell you
Not just that I love
There is so much more
You must hear and see

If I came to explain
It would do no good
Wordlessly nibbling your ear
Burying my face in your belly

All I would tell is you
And love; I must tell
Me, that I am a world
Containing more than love

Holding you and all your other
Lovers wherein you
And I are free from each other
A world that anyone can walk alone

Music, coat-hangers, the sea
Mountains, ink, trashy novels
Trees, pancakes, the *Tokaido Road*
The desert — it is yours

Refuse to see me!
Don't answer the door or the telephone
Fly off in a dragon-chariot
Forget you ever knew me

But wherever you are
Is a corner of me, San Juan Letran
Or Montreal, Brooklyn
Or the Lion Gate

Under my skin at the Potala
Behind my eyes at Benares
Far in my shoulder at Port-au-Prince
Lifted in my palm among stars

Anywhere you must be you
Drugged, drunk or mad
As old, as young, whatever you are
Living or dying the place will be me

And I alone the car that carries you away.

    II (BIG HIGH SONG FOR SOMEBODY)

F
Train
Absolutely stoned
Rocking bug-eyed billboards *waff*:
No more bridge than adam's
     off ox
       Pouring over it 16 2/3 MPH sodium —
vapor light yellow light

LOVE YOU

Got *you* on
    like a coat of paint
Steamy girder tile

LOVE YOU

cutting — out blues

(Tlaxcala left me
        like stoned on the F train
whole week's load ready
        For that long stretch ahead
        Prisoners jailed
            shBAM
Train chained to this train boring
        through diamonds
                SQUALL!

            LOVE YOU

Barreling zero up Balcony Street
        Leaning from ladders
            Same angle of lean; different cars
        Route of the PHOEBE SNOW

            LOVE YOU

Blue-black baby
        16-foot gold buddha in your arms
        Taking you with me!
            Straight up Shattuck Avenue

Hay-burning train, bull chariot
        With bliss-bestowing hands

            LOVE YOU

And I'm the laughing man
        with a load of goodies for all

Bridge still stands, bulls may safely graze
        Bee-birds in the frangipani
                clock

            LOVE *YOU*

Berkeley, 1955

SOURDOUGH MOUNTAIN LOOKOUT

For Kenneth Rexroth

I always say I won't go back to the mountains
I am too old and fat there are bugs mean mules
And pancakes every morning of the world

Mr. Edward Wyman (63)
Steams along the trail ahead of us all
Moaning, "My poor old feet ache, my back
Is tired and I've got a stiff prick"
Uprooting alder shoots in the rain

Then I'm alone in a glass house on a ridge
Encircled by chiming mountains
With one sun roaring through the house all day
& the others crashing through the glass all night
Conscious even while sleeping

Morning fog in the southern gorge
Gleaming foam restoring the old sea-level
The lakes in two lights: green soap & indigo
The high cirque-lake black half-open eye.

Ptarmigan hunt for bugs in the snow
Bear peers through the wall at noon
Deer crowd up to see the lamp
A mouse nearly drowns in the honey
I see my bootprints mingle with deer-foot
Bear-paw mule-shoe in the dusty path to the privy

Much later I write down:
        "raging.   Viking sunrise
        The gorgeous death of summer in the east"
(Influence of a Byronic landscape
Bent pages exhibiting depravity of style.)

Outside the lookout I lay nude on the granite
Mountain hot September sun but inside my head
Calm dark night with all the other stars

HERACLITUS: "The waking have one common world
But the sleeping turn aside
Each into a world of his own."

I keep telling myself what I really like
Are music, books, certain land and sea-scapes
The way light falls across them, diffusion of
Light through agate, light itself . . .   I suppose
I'm still afraid of the dark

> "Remember smart-guy there's something
> Bigger something smarter than you."
> Ireland's fear of unknown holies drives
> My father's voice (a country neither he
> Nor his great-grandfather ever saw)

> A sparkly tomb a plated grave
> A holy thumb beneath a wave

Everything else they hauled across Atlantic
Scattered and lost in the buffalo plains
Among these trees and mountains

From Duns Scotus to this page
A thousand years
> (". . . a dog walking on his hind legs —
> not that he does it well but that he
> Does it at all.")

Virtually a blank except for the hypothesis
That there is more to a man
Than the contents of his jock-strap

EMPEDOCLES: "At one time all the limbs
Which are the body's portion are brought together
By love in blooming life's high season; at another
Severed by cruel Strife, they wander each alone
By the breakers of life's sea."

Fire and pressure from the sun bear down
Bear down centipede shadow of palm-frond
A limestone lithograph — oysters and clams of stone

Half a black rock bomb displaying brilliant crystals
Fire and pressure Love and Strife bear down
Brontosaurus, look away

My sweat runs down the rock

HERACLITUS: "The transformations of fire
are, first of all, sea; and half of the sea
is earth, half whirlwind . . . .
It scatters and it gathers; it advances
and retires."

I move out of a sweaty pool
          (The sea!)
And sit up higher on the rock

Is anything burning?

The sun itself!   Dying
Pooping out, exhausted
Having produced brontosaurus, Heraclitus
This rock, me,
To no purpose

I tell you anyway (as a kind of loving) . . .
Flies & other insects come from miles around
To listen
I also address the rock, the heather,
The alpine fir

BUDDHA: "All the constituents of being are
Transitory: Work out your salvation with diligence."

(And everything, as one eminent disciple of that master
Pointed out, has been tediously complex ever since.)

There was a bird
Lived in an egg
And by ingenious chemistry
Wrought molecules of albumen
To beak and eye
Gizzard and craw

Feather and claw

My grandmother said:
"Look at them poor *bed-*
raggled pigeons!"

And the sign in McAlister Street:

"IF YOU CAN'T COME IN
SMILE AS YOU GO BY

L♡VE
THE BUTCHER

I destroy myself, the universe (an egg)
And time — to get an answer:
There are a smiler, a sleeper and a dancer

We repeat our conversation in the glittering dark
Floating beside the sleeper.
The child remarks, "You knew it all the time."
I: "I keep forgetting that the smiler is
Sleeping; the sleeper, dancing."

From Sauk Lookout two years before
Some of the view was down the Skagit
To Puget Sound: From above the lower ranges,
Deep in forest — lighthouses on clear nights.

This year's rock is a spur from the main range
Cuts the valley in two and is broken
By the river;   Ross dam repairs the break,
Makes trolley buses run
Through the streets of dim Seattle far away.

I'm surrounded by mountains here
A circle of 108 beads, originally seeds
            of *ficus religiosa*
                  BO-Tree
A circle, continuous, one odd bead
Larger than the rest and bearing
A tassel (hair-tuft) (the man who sat

      under the tree)
In the center of the circle,
A void, an empty figure containing
All that's multiplied;
Each bead a repetition, a world
Of ignorance and sleep.

Today is the day the goose gets cooked
Day of liberation for the crumbling flower
Knobcone pinecone in the flames
Brandy in the sun

Which, as I said, will disappear
Anyway it'll be invisible soon
Exchanging places with stars now in my head
To be growing rice in China through the night.
Magnetic storms across the solar plains
Make aurora borealis shimmy bright
Beyond the mountains to the north.

Closing the lookout in the morning
Thick ice on the shutters
Coyote almost whistling on a nearby ridge

The mountain is THERE (between two lakes)
I brought back a piece of its rock
Heavy dark-honey-color
With a seam of crystal, some of the quartz
Stained by its matrix
Practically indestructible
A shift from opacity to brilliance
(The zenbos say, "Lightning-flash & flint-spark")
Like the mountains where it was made

What we see of the world is the mind's
Invention and the mind
Though stained by it, becoming
Rivers, sun, mule-dung, flies —
Can shift instantly
A dirty bird in a square time

Gone	Gate
Gone	Gate
Really gone	Paragate
Into the cool.	Parasamgate
Oh Mama!	Svaha!

Like they say, "Four times up,
Three times down."   I'm still on the mountain.

                                                    1955-56

DENUNCIATION: OR, UNFROCK'D AGAIN

The trouble with you is
That sitting on a bench in the backyard
You see an old plank in the fence become
A jeweled honeycomb of golden wires
Discoursing music, et cetera

The trouble is aggravated by the grass
Flashing alternately green
And invisible   green
And non-existent
While the piano in the house plays
THE STARS & STRIPES FOREVER!

The landlady's son has a tin ear

> "The trouble with you is you keep acting like a genius:
> Now, you're not a genius, you're nothing but a prick . . .
> In fact, you're not even *that*, you're nothing
> But a son of a bitch!
>   GET OUT OF MY HOUSE!"

"There you are, sitting in the sun too!
Have you noticed all the flowers?   There
Is an iris;   there are hyacinths;   these
Are tulip buds.   I thought that was a peach tree
In the neighbors' yard.   The landlady says it is
An *ammand,* but the *ammand* is always the first to flower . . ."

The trouble with you is
You neither take it nor leave it alone.

What plant puts out those
Tall thin stiff green leaves?   Lines
Drawn from the tip of each one would describe
The surface of what regular solid polyhedron?
You don't dare invent a name.
Nameless it threatens you with destruction —

To hell with it.   It's a sub-tropical lily.

The trouble is that you are backed up against a wall
Convinced that any instant you will fall right through it.
The real trouble with you really is
You don't think, you simply worry.

I sat down in my house and ate a carrot.

Berkeley, 11: III: 56

THE SAME OLD JAZZ

OK, it's imperishable or a world as Will
& Idea, a Hindu illusion that our habits continuously
Create.   Whatever I think, it
Keeps changing from bright to dark, from clear
To colored: Thus before I began to think and
So after I've stopped, as if it were real & I
Were its illusion

But as Jaime de Angulo said, "What's wrong with two?"

So Sunday morning I'm in bed with Cleo
She wants to sleep & I get up naked at the table
Writing
And it all snaps into focus
The world inside my head & the cat outside the window
A one-to-one relationship
While I imagine whatever I imagine

WEED

dry stalks of yarrow,
        repeated y-branching V's, a multiplication
Of antelope, deer-horns?   Umbels
Hairy brown stars at the tip of brown wires
A *menorah*, or more learnedly, "hand" written in Great Seal Script

Almost against the window, horns again
Reindeer colored (in the sun) branching
Bare young loquat tree

Next door on the right the neighbors are building
Something in the garage, sawing & whirly-grinding
On wood. Models of the NIÑA, the PINTA & the SANTA
  MARIA
Life-size with television sails

Bright sky & airplanes & bugs mixed with
Flying paper ashes, the lid's off somebody's incinerator

There all that is & the reflection of tatami-color
In the silver bowl of my hanging lamp.

What if I never told any of this?

White cat
Spooked in the grass, alert against satyrs
That pursue, she's full of kittens already
       . . . gone under the steps, under the porch

Cleo rises to bathe
& closes the bathroom door
My own bathtub becomes a mystery

Now that cat's on the window-ledge
Propped against the green sash, whiter
In the creamy light reflected off the kitchen door

What if I never said?

Singing & splashing in the bathtub
A mystery, a transformation, a different woman

Will emerge

      the birds have been pleased to show up
Bugs in the air won't last
And the chief satyr cat arrives
Ignores the birds, ascends the back stairs to spray the newel-post
A Message To The White Queen:
      "Sweet Papa is here."

He disappears and immediately
There she is, delicate pink nose reading:
      "Sweet Papa!   The same old jazz."

Water glugs in the drain
A strange girl scours herself with my tired old towels
I think of her body & stop writing
To admire my own, some of her beauty rubbed off on me
Now some of my ugliness, some of my age
Whirls down the bathroom drain.

She'll go away.   I'll go away.   The world will go away.
      ("The idea of emptiness engenders compassion
      Compassion does away with the distinction
            between Self & Other . . .")
But through her everything else is real to me & I have
No other self.
"What's wrong with two?"

FORTY-FIVE YEARS SINCE THE FALL
OF THE CH'ING DYNASTY

The Summer Palace burnt, the Winter Palace, wherever it was
"Ordre, ordre, Je suis une maniaque pour l'ordre!"
(Meaning that all those sheets are promptly sent to the wooden
   laundries of the Seine,
That all the shoes and sox are lined up in rows
That the words follow each other in ecstatic parentheses, NOT
That you and me are lined up against the innocent wall, torn

By the bullets of righteousness)

I am hid, as William Blake puts it, where nobody can see me not
Even those sad angels who busted the slippery membrane across
My stifled face so I could breathe the incense coming in
From the pavilion under Coal Hill, my brocade sleeves ravelling
Among the chips of jade and the withered peony blossoms and
The night of the boat-light Dragonboat orgies on the River
In pious memory of Whosis that first made the water scene
With an ingenious system of *canali* and Nationally Federated
  Dams

             where nobody can see me

                    I read all about James Dean with 16 photographs
                    and more than a hundred pages of vulgar prose

Nobody can find me, I came here with that purpose, of being
  alone

          X . . . . . says we have all these self-destructive impulses
                    and it BUGS him

(He says it is like he went to the neighborhood soda-fountain for
A coca-cola and everybody [all these monster teen-age hoods]
Jumped on him at once)

Not unlike the United States Marines building teakwood camp-
  fires
out of the Empress's bedroom furniture on the Phoenix-Viewing
Terrace toasting their wienies.

                                        Newport: 10 October, 1957

FOR C.

I wanted to bring you this Jap iris
Orchid-white with yellow blazons
But I couldn't face carrying it down the street
Afraid everyone would laugh
And now they're dying of my cowardice.

Abstract beauty in the garden,
In my hand, in the street it is a sign
A whole procession of ithyphallic satyrs
Through a town whose people like to believe:
"I was made like Jesus, out of Love; my daddy was a spook."

The upright flower would scare them. "What's shot,"
They think, "From the big flesh cannon will decay."
Not being there I can't say that being born is a chance
To learn, to love and to save each other from ourselves:
Live ignorance rots us worse than any grave.

And lacking the courage to tell you, "I'm here,
Such as I am; I need you and you need me"
Planning to give you this flower instead —
Intending it to mean "This is really I, tall, slender,
Perfectly formed —" is uglier than their holy fantasies,

Worse to look at than my own gross shape.
After all this fuss about flowers I walked out,
Just to walk, not going to see you (I had nothing to bring —
This poem wasn't finished, didn't say
What was on my mind; I'd given up)

I saw bushes of crimson rhododendron, sparkling wet,
Beside the hospital walk — I had to see you.
If you were out, I'd leave these flowers.
Even if I couldn't write or speak
At least I broke and stole that branch with love.

1957

TAKE I, 4 : II : 58

What I need is lots of money
No
What I need is somebody to love with unparalleled energy and
    devotion for 24 hours & then goodbye

I can escape too easily from this time & this place
That isn't the reason I'm here

What I need is where am I

Sometimes a bed of nails is really necessary to any man
Or a wall (Olson, in conversation, 'That wall, it *has* to be there!')

Where are my hands.
Where are my lungs.
All the lights are on in here I don't see nothing.

I don't admit that this is personality disintegration
My personality has a half-life of 10^∞ years besides

I can put my toe in my mouth
If (CENSORED), then (CENSORED), something like
Plato his vision of the archetypal human being

Or the Gnostic Worm.

People see me; they like that . . .
I try to warn them that it's really me

They don't listen; afterwards they complain
About how I had no right to really be just that:
Invisible & in complete control of everything.

GILBERT SORRENTINO

A CLASSIC CASE

The moon's a little arch
pasted on black cardboard
just outside his bedroom
window,
   lovely Major Hoople.

I swear the room is warm,
the night is cold, the bedspread
turned down has a comfortable
feel,
   lovely Major Hoople.

Tomorrow he'll get up, put on
his fez, and stand behind
his gut. The sagging furniture
his friends,
   lovely Major Hoople.

Yow! That world
of yours is crumbling away,
the rotary lawn sprayers and The
Neighbors,
   lovely Major Hoople,

when will they possess
your useless yard and send
you out to work, to
work!
   lovely Major Hoople.

1958

296

THE ZOO

Goliathus goliathus, the one banana
peeling beetle in the U S A, brighter
than a comicstrip, is dead.

"Wrapped in his native grasses," left
on the doorstep of the museum
and a favorite of the visitors,

4 and 1 half inches long with an
8 inch wingspread, bigger than
Skeezix, with a life more full,

peeling his bananas for survival,
unlike Mamie Mullins, unlike Moon,
who would be Skeezix but for

the environment, ah! Who cares
or believes in them at all, at all,
goliathus was better and he

not a native.

1959

STUART Z. PERKOFF

FLOWERS FOR LUIS BUNUEL

What is the word for 'death'
in French?   What word triggers
laughter at slit eyes and guttered
cripples?
        What is the word for
the language of eye, the montage of
blood?

        Bunuel, Bunuel,
the musicians in the buildings play no tune
comparable to the whirring lens
of hideous glare of light and blood.
The knives and dwarfs and round firm tits
say death in French for a language too
strong to hold in the gut.

        Bunuel, Bunuel,
is the world?   A place?
            such dirty
cunts and open flies! an unwiped ass
editing the noise of the city,
the wind an instrument of long black hair,
all the mothers dying.

Let us go to the cinema.
Let us go
      to the sinema.
Every rock depends for life upon
the spilling of blood, and torn flesh.
Every death creates a small quiver,
a hatred of mirrors.
        Who knew guilt
before this?   The eye, the eye,
burning too steadily through the ugly night
in the theatre dark with the smells

298

of all our hatred.   The cinema of
the slit, the wound, the crawling ants.
Bunuel, did you do it?   Did you?
Have you built the handless queer,
the only sighted murderer?   Have you
built them?

                    Let the misshapen dance
around the rock.   Only a priest can eat
this shit and not vomit.   This is the
cross made of bones.   Prayers?   Never!

                    Bunuel, Bunuel,
is the world?   Did you?

                                                        1955

THE RECLUSES

They paper the walls of their world
with their strange rhythms,
visions of this, their sighted dreams.
They have within their deepest eardooms
fragments of freshest wildness.

                    That of a woman
never feeling breastingly through their eyes,
they have no sin.   But on their walls
of rhythmed visioned scenes
they often have lines about a mountain.

That black which is the greedy of the mind,
that reaches up and grasps from
the perceiving eye
all of the memoric stanzas brought on by the world
is their fine house.

They live there.
They have their own dark lines.
They are always

inside

                                                        1956

FEASTS OF DEATH, FEASTS OF LOVE

ONE

1.

down the Wolf river
backs to the sun thru water shallow & flat
beautiful girls & boys

> the birds wing tip to tip
> swinging thru & around
> calling calling

we carried city eyes
over the rushing water
the stunned vision of scene after changing
scene
expanding & including
as our shouts & grunts & songs
wailed outward

(i had to get out, once, & push the canoe from behind, my
body from the ankles up was hot, sweaty, sun gleaming, my feet
cool in the river, lifting & pushing the heavy canoe.

i thought the others wd get too far ahead, & we wd be lost, off
in the wisconsin woods, where there were neither jews nor cities,
a world hot & in winter my feet wd be like encased in the cement
of the river, & the canoe wd never be pushed over the flat scrapey
sand.)

the river movement
coiled around our eyes
the quiet sound of the breathing of work
set the beat
of our songs

2.

the next year we took a different trip, out lake tomahawk & an
adjacent lake, i dont remember which one. in that part of wis-
consin the lakes lay on the land like a thousand eyes, peering

into & thru each other.

from lake to lake
between two mountains
all blue green quiet movement water
in the air & eye
the huge walls rising

a great grass field
covered the inlet
& the canoe went thru
as over land, it looked

so quiet

   rustling of grass

      the soft voices

          hot beautiful girls & boys

               hot beautiful summer day

TWO

   1.
wake up!   to a morning
sun shining thru even newspaper
headlines
sun on
men in sand wading thru
blood

        "woe, woe unto
        the bloody city of litchfield"
        he cried with his bare feet
        in the gutters of blood

naked feet
naked legs
naked eyes

        into the market place howling
        along the streets howling

         in the living rooms howling

the sun!   shining shining
in our eyes

    2.
at the edge of the water
the glass house eye of God
embraced us, pure
in white

           clean after communal showers
& communal food

"boruch ataw Adaonai
Elohenu melech ha'olam
ha'motzi lechem
min ha'awritz"

reverberating thru the food
the eyes
the air out out into many rhythms
& tongues

sitting on the benches, bodies warm & throats filled with joy & love
we offered worship
sitting warm to warm, our eyes & skins touching, love flowing
we offered worship

       we sang
& spoke languages & poems
offered worship & love
mixing the birds of passion & the swords of God
in our beautiful young eyes

   it wd always be dark by the time the services were over. &
secure, in the glass house, lit by the God that shined all our faces,
the burning candles of love in our bodies, sharing the glow out-
ward to trees & wind.   & the younger kids went to their cabins
while the older ones had ·a dance, & carried on intrigues & polit-

ical arguments & love affairs until 11:30, when the boys walked the joyous road back to their portion of the camp, singing & shouting, clean & alive.

by the time the saturday morning services were over, we were so full & whole that anything was possible.

3. *political song*

the people circle the room
coming together

the blood circles the body
coming together

the earth circles the sun
coming together

> hangon, man
> as it
> wobbles around
>
> hand to hand
> as it
> wobbles around

o living communities
men & women who love & are loved
o living bodies
men & women who love & are loved
o loving cities
men & women who live & are lived

eat
drink
embrace
each
other
inner
face

THREE

1.

i see clothes piled in great heaps
against grey sky
with the smoke & sun in the air
of human flesh
& in the pockets of those beasts
who wear my name
things of value jingle & clank
in those black pockets
teeth & eyes & skulls & skin
in those black pockets

> there are bodies
> naked
> not talking of love
>
> in their last waters
> naked
> not talking of love

naked hunger
naked hatred
naked minds

> howling in the crowded boxcars
> howling in the dark barracks
> howling in the hot showers
> howling & whimpering in the final chambers
>
> silent
> in the furnaces

2.

such visions
wove their shroudeyes
thru our songs

such knowledge
blackened the edge
of every flame

each kiss
bittered with the salt
of their blood

(many summers later i hitchhiked over a thousand miles back
to the wisconsin holy lakes, to speak anguish to a wise man, seek-
ing seeking peace.

& we sat outside under a fat moon, at the edge of an open field
of grass, scenes of love & myth echoing in my mind.

i asked him why the six million had died.   i thought somehow,
this man, an aronin, descendant of the first & holiest priests of
israel, humble seeker & generous fountain of love, wd have an
insight, a knowledge, a hope.

God's plan?   if there had not been such blood & terror in his
mouth, he wd have laughed.   & told me he had no answer, no
peace.   & told me of the many nites & days he had fasted &
prayed.

& found nothing?

found only hope that came from the realisation of the cleansing
& purification of pain.

whose? i so young, so bitter, so needing an answer, sd, whose?
good for their souls?   or ours!
                              so bitter, so young
such needs)

even now
it is difficult for me to fix
in my mind's eye, the image
of the God/Priest
lifting sin from the souls of the people

                    my soul, my sin

clothing these six million in my sins
& thrusting them in their foreign wrappings
into the flaming mouths of agony.

FOUR

when the sun dies
many other suns will still flame

all things contain the seeds
of their own completion.
all seeds contain the things
of their own destruction.

the sun
makes a morning
bright descending on hooded eyes

the sun's morning
floods into the sands
of war
    wake up
    hangon

coming together

coming together

coming together

1957

GARY SNYDER

PRAISE FOR SICK WOMEN

1

The female is fertile, and discipline
(contra naturam) only
          confuses her
Who has, head held sideways
Arm out softly, touching,
A difficult dance to do, but not in mind.

Hand on sleeve: she holds leaf turning
            in sunlight on spiderweb;
Makes him flick like trout through shallows
Builds into ducks & cold marshes
Sucks out the quiet: bone rushes in
Behind the cool pupil a knot grows
Sudden roots sod him and solid him
Rain falls from skull-roof mouth is awash
            with small creeks
Hair grows, tongue tenses out — and she

Quick turn of the head: back glancing, one hand
Fingers smoothing the thigh, and he sees.

2

Apples will sour at your sight.
Blossoms fail the bough,
Soil turn bone-white: wet rice,
Dry rice, die on the hillslope.
           all women are wounded
Who gather berries, dibble in mottled light,
Turn white roots from humus, crack nuts on stone —
High upland with squinted eye
           or rest in cedar shade.

Are wounded
In yurt or frame or mothers
Shopping at the outskirts in fresh clothes.

Whose sick eye bleeds the land,
Fast it!   thick throat shields from evil,
                    you young girls
First caught with the gut-cramp
Gather punk wood and sour leaf
Keep out of our kitchen.
Your garden plots, your bright fabrics,
Clever ways to carry children
Hide
        a beauty like season or tide
                        sea cries

Sick women
Dreaming of long-legged dancing in light

No, our Mother Eve: slung on a shoulder
Lugged off to hell.
                    kali/shakti
Where's hell then?
In the moon.
In the change of the moon:
In a bark shack
Crouched from sun, five days,
Blood dripping through crusted thighs.

1954

RIPRAP

Lay down these words
Before your mind like rocks.
                    placed solid, by hands
In choice of place, set
Before the body of the mind
                    in space and time:

Solidity of bark, leaf, or wall
          riprap of things:
Cobble of milky way,
          straying planets,
These poems, people,
          lost ponies with
Dragging saddles —
          and rocky sure-foot trails.
The worlds like an endless
          four-dimensional
Game of *Go*.
          ants and pebbles
In the thin loam, each rock a word
          a creek-washed stone
Granite; ingrained
          with torment of fire and weight
Crystal and sediment linked hot
          all change, in thoughts,
As well as things.

FOR A FAR-OUT FRIEND

Because I once beat you up
Drunk, stung with weeks of torment
And saw you no more,
And you had calm talk for me today
          I now suppose
I was less sane than you,
You hung on dago red,
          me hooked on books.
You once ran naked toward me
Knee deep in cold March surf
On a tricky beach between two
          pounding seastacks —
I saw you as a Hindu Deva-girl
Light legs dancing in the waves,

Breasts like dream breasts
Of sea, and child, and astral
            Venus-spurting milk.
And traded our salt lips.

Visions of your body
Kept me high for weeks, I even had
            a sort of trance for you
A day in a dentist's chair.
I found you again, gone stone,
In Zimmer's book of Indian Art:
Dancing in that life with
Grace and love, with rings and
A little golden belt, just above
            your naked snatch,
And I thought — more grace and love
In that wild Deva life where you belong,
Than in this dress-and-girdle life
You'll ever give
Or get.

1955

THIS TOKYO

Peace, war, religion,
Revolution, will not help.
This horror seeds in the agile
Thumb and greedy little brain
That learned to catch bananas
With a stick.
            The millions of us worthless
To each other or the world
Or selves, the sufferers of the real
Or of the mind — this world
Is but a dream?   Or human life
A nightmare grafted on solidity
Of planet — mental, mental,

Shudder of the sun — praise
Evil submind freedom with De Sade
Or highest Dantean radiance of the God
Or endless Light or Life or Love
Or simple tinsel angel in the
Candy heaven of the poor —
Mental divinity or beauty, all,
Plato, Aquinas, Buddha,
Dionysius of the Cross, all
Pains or pleasures hells or
What in sense or flesh
Logic, eye, music, or
Concoction of all faculties
& thought tend — tend — to this:
      This gaudy apartment of the rich.
The comfort of the U.S. For its own.
The shy shivering pair of girls
Who dyked each other for a show
A thousand yen before us men
— In an icy room — to buy their relatives
A meal.   This scramble spawn of
Wire dirt rails tin boards blocks
Babies, students, crookt old men.
      We live
On the meeting of sun and earth.
We live — we live — and all our lives
Have led to this, this city,
Which is soon the world, this
Hopelessness where love of man
Or hate of man could matter
None, love if you will or
Contemplate or write or teach
But know in your human marrow you
Who read, that all you tread
Is earthquake rot and matter mental
Trembling, freedom is a void,
Peace war religion revolution
Will not help.

27 December 1956

MYTHS & TEXTS, PART III

BURNING

 1 *second shaman song*

Squat in swamp shadows.
            mosquitoes sting;
            high light in cedar above.
Crouched in a dry vain frame
            — thirst for cold snow
            — green slime of bone marrow
Seawater fills each eye.

Quivering in nerve and muscle
Hung in the pelvic cradle
Bones propped against roots
A blind flicker of nerve

Still hand moves out alone
Flowering and leafing
            turning to quartz
Streaked rock   congestion of karma
The long body of the swamp.
A mud-streaked thigh.

Dying carp biting air
            in the damp grass,
River recedes.   No matter.

Limp fish sleep in the weeds
The sun dries me as I dance

 2

One moves continually with the consciousness
Of that other, totally alien, non-human:
Humming inside like a taut drum,
Carefully avoiding any direct thought of it,
Attentive to the real-world flesh and stone.

Intricate layers of emptiness
This only world, juggling forms
            a hand, a breast, two clasped
Human tenderness scuttles
Down dry endless cycles
Forms within forms falling
                        clinging
Loosely, what's gone away?
                        — love

In Spring the Avocado sheds dead leaves
Soft rattling through the Cherry greens

Bird at this moment
All these books
    wearing a thin sweater
    & no brassiere
    in failing light
One glance, miles below
Bones & flesh knit in the rock
    "have no regret —
chip chip
            (sparrows)
& not a word about the void
To which one hand diddling
Cling

        3 *Maudgalyâyana saw hell*

Under the shuddering eyelid
Dreams gnawing the nerve-strings,
The mind grabs and the shut eye sees:
Down dimensions floating below sunlight,
Worlds of the dead, Bardo, mind-worlds
& horror of sunless cave-ritual
Meeting conscious monk bums
Blown on winds of karma from hell
To endless changing hell,
Life and death whipped

On this froth of reality (wind & rain
Realms human and full of desire) over the cold
Hanging enormous unknown, below
Art and History and all mankind living thoughts,
Occult & witchcraft evils each all true.
The thin edge of nature rising fragile
And helpless with its love and sentient stone
And flesh, above dark drug-death dreams.

Clouds I cannot lose, we cannot leave.
We learn to love, horror accepted.
Beyond, within, all normal beauties
Of the science-conscious sex and love-receiving
Day-to-day got vision of this sick
Sparkling person at the inturned dreaming
Blooming human mind
Dropping it all, and opening the eyes.

4 *Maitreya the future Buddha*

He's out stuck in a bird's craw
                 last night
Wildcat vomited his pattern on the snow.

Who refused to learn to dance, refused
To kiss you long ago.   You fed him berries
But fled, the red stain on his teeth;
And when he cried, finding the world a Wheel —
         you only stole his rice,
Being so small and gray.   He will not go,
But wait through fish scale, shale dust, bone
         of hawk and marmot,
         caught leaves in ice,
Til flung on a new net of atoms:
Snagged in flight
Leave you hang and quiver like a gong

Your empty happy body
Swarming in the light

7

Face in the crook of her neck
                    felt throb of vein
Smooth skin, her cool breasts
All naked in the dawn
                    "byrdes
sing forth from every bough"
                    where are they now
And dreamt I saw the Duke of Chou

The Mother whose body is the Universe
Whose breasts are Sun and Moon,
                    the statue of Prajna
From Java: the quiet smile,
The naked breasts.

"Will you still love me when my
        breasts get big?"
the little girl said —

"Earthly Mothers and those who suck
the breasts of earthly mothers are mortal —
but deathless are those who have fed
at the breast of the Mother of the Universe."

8

John Muir on Mt. Ritter:

After scanning its face again and again,
I began to scale it, picking my holds
With intense caution.   About half-way
To the top, I was suddenly brought to
A dead stop, with arms outspread
Clinging close to the face of the rock
Unable to move hand or foot
Either up or down.   My doom
Appeared fixed.   I MUST fall.
There would be a moment of

Bewilderment, and then,
A lifeless rumble down the cliff
To the glacier below.
My mind seemed to fill with a
Stifling smoke.   This terrible eclipse
Lasted only a moment, when life blazed
Forth again with preternatural clearness.
I seemed suddenly to become possessed
Of a new sense.   My trembling muscles
Became firm again, every rift and flaw in
The rock was seen as through a microscope,
My limbs moved with a positiveness and precision
With which I seemed to have
Nothing at all to do.

9

Night here,   a covert
All spun, webs in one
            how without grabbing hold it?
— Get into the bird-cage
            without starting them singing.

"Forming the New Society
            Within the shell of the Old"
The motto in the Wobbly Hall
Some old Finns and Swedes playing cards
Fourth and Yesler in Seattle.
O you modest, retiring, virtuous young ladies
            pick the watercress, pluck the yarrow
"Kwan kwan" goes the crane in the field,
            I'll meet you tomorrow;
A million workers dressed in black and buried,
We make love in leafy shade.

Bodhidharma sailing the Yangtze on a reed
Lenin in a sealed train through Germany
Hsüan Tsang, crossing the Pamirs
Joseph, Crazy Horse, living the last free

starving high-country winter of their tribes.
Surrender into freedom, revolt into slavery —
Confucius no better —
      (with Lao-tzu to keep him in check)
"Walking about the countryside
        all one fall
To a heart's content beating on stumps."

   10 *Amitabha's vow*

"If, after obtaining Buddhahood, anyone in my land
   gets tossed in jail on a vagrancy rap, may I
   not attain highest perfect enlightenment.

   wild geese in the orchard
   frost on the new grass

"If, after obtaining Buddhahood, anyone in my land
   loses a finger coupling boxcars, may I
   not attain highest perfect enlightenment.

   mare's eye flutters
   jerked by the lead-rope
   stone-bright shoes flick back
   ankles trembling: down steep rock

"If, after obtaining Buddhahood, anyone in my land
   can't get a ride hitch-hiking all directions, may I
   not attain highest perfect enlightenment.

   wet rocks buzzing
   rain and thunder southwest
   hair, beard, tingle
   wind whips bare legs
   we should go back
   we don't

   11

      Floating of vapour from brazier
Who hold emptiness

Whose bundle is broken, blank spot in creation
    still gong in a long-empty hall
        perceptions at idle play

    Q.   What is the way of non-activity?
    A.   It is activity
Ingather limbs, tighten the fingers
Press tongue to the roof
Roll the eyes
    dried & salted in the sun
In the dry, hard chrysalis, a pure bug waits hatching

Sudden flares: rush of water and bone
Netted, fitted
Flicker of action, nerves burnt in patterns
    fields of cabbages
    yet to consume
Imprint of flexible mouth-sounds,
Seared in the mind, on things.

Coyote: "I guess there never was a world anywhere"
Earthmaker: "I think if we find a little world,
        I can fix it up."

    13

Spikes of new smell driven up nostrils
Expanding & deepening, ear-muscles
Straining and grasping the sounds
Mouth filled with bright fluid coldness
Tongue crushed by the weight of its flavours
    — the Nootka sold out for lemon drops
(What's this talk about not understanding!
    you're just a person who refuses to see.)

Poetry a riprap on the slick rock of metaphysics
"Put a Spanish halter on that whore of a mare
& I'll lead the bitch up any trail"

(how gentle!   He should have whipped her first)

the wind turns.
a cold rain blows over the shale
we sleep in the belly of a cloud.
(You think sex art and travel are enough?
            you're a skinful of cowdung)

South of the Yellow River the Emperor Wu
Set the army horses free in the mountain pastures,
Set the Buffalo free on the Plain of the Peach Grove.
Chariots and armor were smeared with blood
            and put away.   They locked up
            the Arrows bag.
Smell of crushed spruce and burned snag-wood.
            remains of men,
Bone-chopped foul remains, thick stew
Food for crows —
            (blind, deaf, and dumb!
            shall we give him another chance?)
At Nyahaim-kuvara
Night has gone
Travelling to my land
            — that's a Mohave night
Our night too, you think brotherhood
Humanity & good intentions will stop it?
As long as you hesitate, no place to go.

Bluejay, out at the world's end
            perched, looked, & dashed
Through the crashing: his head is squashed.
            symplegades, the *mumonkwan,*
It's all vagina dentata
            (Jump!)
"Leap through an Eagle's snapping beak"

Actaeon saw Dhyana in the Spring.

            it was nothing special,
      misty rain on Mt. Baker,
            Neah Bay at low tide.

14

A skin-bound bundle of clutchings
        unborn and with no place to go
Balanced on the boundless compassion
Of diatoms, lava, and chipmunks.

Love, let it be,
Is a sacrifice
                knees, the cornered eyes
Tea on a primus stove after a cold swim
Intricate doors and clocks, the clothes
        we stand in —
Gaps between seedings, the right year,
Green shoots in the marshes
Creeks in the proper directions
Hills in proportion,
Astrologers, go-betweens present,
                a marriage has been.

Walked all day through live oak and manzanita,
Scrabbling through dust down Tamalpais —
Thought of high mountains;
Looked out on a sea of fog.
Two of us, carrying packs.

15

Stone-flake and salmon.
The pure, sweet, straight-splitting
                with a ping
Red cedar of the thick coast valleys
Shake-blanks on the mashed ferns
                the charred logs
Fireweed and bees
An old burn, by new alder
Creek on smooth stones,
Back there a Tarheel logger farm.
(High country fir still hunched in snow)

From Siwash strawberry-pickers in the Skagit
Down to the boys at Sac,
Living by the river
                riding flatcars to Fresno,
Across the whole country
Steep towns, flat towns, even New York,
And oceans and Europe & libraries & galleries
And the factories they make rubbers in
This whole spinning show
                (among others)
Watched by the Mt. Sumeru L.O.
From the middle of the universe
& them with no radio.
"What is imperfect is best"
                silver scum on the trout's belly
                rubs off on your hand.
It's all falling or burning —
                rattle of boulders
                steady dribbling of rocks down cliffs
                bark chips in creeks
Porcupine chawed here —
                                Smoke
From Tillamook a thousand miles
Soot and hot ashes.   Forest fires.
Upper Skagit burned I think 1919
Smoke covered all northern Washington.
                lightning strikes, flares,
Blossoms a fire on the hill.
Smoke like clouds.   Blotting the sun
Stinging the eyes.
The hot seeds steam underground
                still alive.

17

                        the text

Sourdough mountain called a fire in:
Up Thunder Creek, high on a ridge.

Hiked eighteen hours, finally found
A snag and a hundred feet around on fire:
All afternoon and into night
Digging the fire line
Falling the burning snag
It fanned sparks down like shooting stars
Over the dry woods, starting spot-fires
Flaring in wind up Skagit valley
From the Sound.
Toward morning it rained.
We slept in mud and ashes,
Woke at dawn, the fire was out,
The sky was clear, we saw
The last glimmer of the morning star.

the myth

Fire up Thunder Creek and the mountain —
                         troy's burning!
The cloud mutters

The mountains are your mind.
The woods bristle there,
Dogs barking and children shrieking
Rise from below.

Rain falls for centuries
Soaking the loose rocks in space
Sweet rain, the fire's out
The black snag glistens in the rain
& the last wisp of smoke floats up
Into the absolute cold
Into the spiral whorls of fire
The storms of the Milky Way
"Buddha incense in an empty world"
Black pit cold and light-year
Flame tongue of the dragon
Licks the sun

The sun is but a morning star

Crater Mt. L. O. 1952 — Marin-an 1956

EDWARD MARSHALL

LEAVE THE WORD ALONE

Leave the word alone it is dangerous.
    Leave the Bible alone   it is dangerous.
        Leave all barbed wires alone   they are
                    dangerous.
When you go in the country   au campagne   watch for
                the cows . . . beware of moo-
                her- moo-her.
There aren't too many bulls, but there are harsh
              fathers who still insist on
              impregnation at 35 while he is 41.

That was twenty three years age and now she is in an
              insane asylum because she wanted
                to read the Bible   and her
                    health book.
She reads nothing, for she is   catatonic, dementia-
              praecox among the wolverine
                gang of girls who   couldn't
                  get what they wanted in   the
                  29 crash.

Lena went to the asylum   at the age of 35   having just   had
              a child   and when the baby came to
              visit her   she   said: pretty
                baby;   you have a
                a very   beautiful
              baby and that baby   is now I.

If   I can finish   this poem   without   cracking up ‾ and
            becoming victorious — onslaught resurrection.
              It was the first of August that   she couldn't

take it any longer — pressure
and she ran   away.
The neighbors came and Papa Harry as   I   called him later
invited   all the neighbors   to take part   in
a hunting search — ordered a lot of bread   and
made sandwiches.
On the farm   Harry got   fat and no longer was called Edward
I am Edward Junior   and always knew of   my own father
as Papa Harry   and it was not healthy
either for I did not   know that he was
the stocky   guy that gave
the sperm to my mother,
still in the asylum.
Yes, she is still in the asylum   not too far from my   Concord
N.H. residence — and I stayed in
the same asylum nineteen years later
and I   remained there for five
months.
Harry —   He almost had her there after my second sister
was   born,
But Lena did not go to the hospital.

When   I   was   six the boy   out back said my mother   was
crazy   and I thought he   didn't like my mother
(present) who is my aunt
by marriage
Vernon — he heard loose talk from his
mother but I   always thought Vernon's
mother odd and his Sister   Irene
liked to play around with me before I
understood   sex   and
Vernon   used to get pleasure   sticking
paper up my ass and he was   Greek
American —   Father worked at St. Clair's
ice cream shop
David, my cousin asked when I was going back to
live with my mother and father (I   thought I
was living with them) (they were my aunt and
uncle)

You naughty boy if you don't watch out I shall send
you back to the farm with Papa   Harry.
You must appreciate what I do and I was
confused
for   I didn't know   I came from a fertile
process and I didn't understand
how babies came until I was 12.
Honte! Shame!
I didn't understand how I was born until a smart Greek   boy
a few blocks over got to talking about
it one night when we were
sleeping in a pup tent.
You are dumb!   It wasn't long before
I knew more about the subject than he did and he
was dumb about Greek love but when I
said I didn't know about babies he said
his younger sister did.
Never shall that be anymore.   And that same
year   I was adopted —
My father let his sister-in-law adopt me — he was broke,
It was World   War 2 and he wasn't   living

on the farm.
I was adopted then he got involved with some   women.
And   when one   woman found he didn't have any
money she withdrew alienation of affections   suit
against him.
And Harry visited   the hospital to see my
mother — faint recognition
She was gone — knew no one — no more Bible.
Lena was once a school teacher after she graduated from
Normal School.
Then she was a teacher down in the Hollow
when she met Harry thru robust Eva
who afterwards kept house for
sister Lena.
With   a little honey-moon   at Rye Beach they   came to the

farm   in Chichester
where   she slaved   til   35.
"Get   these potatoes ready for the working men" but
she kept reading the Bible and
Harry wasn't good in   taking
her to Church and   she
enjoyed church   so.
The religion   was in the dining room where all the tramps
would come in and sit down and when
she felt injured   there was   the
health book nearby
and no relatives from up country   understood
and the sister in Boston was getting ready
for the mental hospital.

She (Olive) died three years   ago of tuberculosis
and while I was a patient at
NHSH
I met Dr. Quimby from Sandwich who tended my grandmother
or Lena and Olive's
mother.
Dr. Quimby, manic depressive and yet he
always went up-country to
practice.
In his last years Papa Harry went with Bertha   whom
my adopted mother couldn't stomach —
immoral — living together!
Immoral!
But the kind relatives would answer but a man
is entitled to a house-keeper who housekeeps for
him — It is the property   she wants. So it was but
Bertha never got   the property —
not one cent when Harry died —
(*passed on* to Christian-Science-
Bertha).
Sister Margie had the chance to buy some of the estate-
woodlot   to help pay off the

                    funeral bill to that funeral
                    parlor in Gloucester where
                  they tried to make my father   alive
                    after he died — blasphemy!
        And he died a year before my grandmother died.
          And when my grandmother died she got the same
                    treatment — to make her alive?
      My grandmother was a Saint and she would have been horrified
            to have them make her alive when she is alive
                        in some of our memories.
                  Blasphemy!   Burn down that funeral home and
                    to the pyre!   And to the pyre and the
                    funeral home still sends bills.
                          And not because of fire.
      They send bills because they said   they did a lot to make
                    both of them alive and an   in-law
                        (by marriage who eats water-melon
                            in the summer to his ears)
                  kissed her (my grandmother) and he is a
                  Presbyterian from New Jersey.   And he went
                    by the bier and kissed her and I
                    thought it disgusting but he never sent
                        anything for her bill.
      W. C. Williams as the Irish would say —   I dig you —   Come and
              show us how to perform a funeral.   And show
              us Congregationalists the way.
        In the house in West Gloucester I used to love to go up
                  the back stairs and smell the home-made
                  soap   and working men's bread but that
                  dynasty is over and went after my
                        grandfather died.

  Gloucester and Chichester — two kingdoms gone!
                  one by the ocean —   Cole's Island

                                near large estates — non
                                    occupada
                    Chichester where even Harry Kelley   has

given up.

Chichester — an inland cranberry marsh and swamp and
sweet-smelling hay brings back

Antipus, George and Moses Marshall

And they were truly Georgians, indeed!

And if I wish   to use sweet-smelling hay — that is all
right!   sweet peas   are a fact in
Chichester and Gloucester.

Are you to take anything from man's collected
experience?   If you do — you are

a traducer and I shall stamp on you. And what   business
did you have   giving me a Rorschach?

Me?   Child   destined   to take a Rorschach, no, damn it!

No, professor Bowers you gave me a Rorschach and
yet a year later I saw you   with a cute
number with shorts on   on Main
Street Concord.

Children destined to take a Rorschach   get back to your
parents — never leave
them — know their
sex organs, if
possible.

Children   to take a Rorschach get back to your parents —
Antipus, Moses, George what do you think —
an insult to thee who gave us and you
were healthy too

Lena, child, grand-child of Rhoda Straw that one
Indian — whatever happened to you!

Did the grand-son of Antipus expect too much of
you?

The Marshalls and Warsons and Harrises are the healthy
types but there is a bad clot —
the Pitmans.

Who will ever know?

I visited the fool

— daughter of Marjorie Webster, my great-Aunt, a Pitman.

And the daughter is mentally wrong (understatement)

and when I asked my other great aunt what
this was all about said the insanity is
in your immediate family but I
knew   better.
And at the death of my great-Aunt Bell   I met my great Uncle
John who spent some time at NHSH.
and great-uncle Sam who wanted to
become a minister — got struck by a
baseball bat
And that affected his mentality so he had a
chicken farm.
Great-Uncle   Sam   is supposed   to have   a couple
nice looking children.
The Pitmans from the Straws, no doubt
the cause of that insanity when Rhoda
waked   at morn on   the lake
and saw the black cloud over head.
And she cursed the lake as Kierkegaard's
father felt the curse of God
on   a hill in Denmark.
Rhoda   you have a long line of descendants — too much to
carry, indeed too much?
I don't believe my own mother ever thought of Rhoda
but Rhoda is a fact because I traced
her back in the Tappan genealogy under the guise of
Miss Tappan, a librarian with an Indian
poker-face.   And in the
genealogies there were some free-will Baptists
with   MA degrees   but the tree
looked rather bad on the
whole.
I have   that Nova-Scotian blueblood and that is
what saves me and through   that I
get butch at times.   And that is why
I can survive under Steve   and the cock-
roach society (Steve not to be
confused with cockroach society)

No guilt   by association   I cry and I   suppose
that was my father's argument about   Bertha
but he was limited in the
provoked image.
Rhoda Straw was never limited in images they were too heavy
and the dust was under their feet
and between her toes   and the
milkweed in her hair but that   is
the story of one girl.
And is she thankful for someone of hers to bang on the
typewriter   as my mother banged on   the
asylum wall   until Catatonia
came in?
I am rigid and will often curl up on my bed
and   if my backbone was ever snapped — to
the ward of geriatrics!
My sister did visit her and she said it was   a pitiful
sight   and not to be seen
again.
And I   have never seen her — tho'
I lived near her in my home-town.
Well I am here writing on blue paper and I must watch
myself for I hear
a spoken word telling
me to read this and that —
Williams and Olson
I   suppose   that is the punishment of all who
have stepped over the crescent and
stepped   on the hot of the
grit.   There   was no
fireplace   where I was born and that was
because   I was born in a
put-up house originally
to house summer boarders   for the well-
to-do Shaws   next door.
Wood — no stoves — yes —   And when I was born was in June
and when winter came I was not on the farm

but I was living with my Aunt and uncle in
the Congregational   town of
Pittsfield.
I never stayed over on the farm in winter until
I was in my teens and then I spent
my time — looking over the parsing
and the McDuffy readers of my mother
and I found out that she was a member
of the German Club and could   speak
a little and that was when   girls were
allowed at New Hampshire (New Hampton)
but after World War I boys got more sexy
after hearing rumors about France
and the ex-patriates.
A tract for the age was coming (End of an Age)
W. R. Inge.
I don't know whether my mother read Eliot or Joyce but
I found Longfellow and a rather
nice copy at that.
O, I found her wedding dress and it tore easy and
the brides-maid clothes were
there   what   Olive   wore
and   Eva played some old stringed
instrument
When   I was in high school   I was talking with a neigh-
bor down the farm road: And my
daughter went with your uncle when he
was in high school and you look just like
him.
I couldn't say for I had never seen Uncle
Arthur. He was my mother's
little brother — tall
dark as an Indian — swarthy
to an extent.
When I go to that town —

Chichester —
I find out about myself and when I hear

the   moo-her I shiver and I say
is it my mother?
And when I dream, I dream of riding on a bicycle
from Concord to Durham
where I went to college
for   a year.
And when I got half way — Chichester a
valve leaks in my tube and it
is just   to annoy   me.
Chichester will not let   me alone and I haven't
let it alone.
Sometimes I hear cries and cries when I   go
through the center road to the far
farm where the blueberry
bushes are high
and the upper pasture   and
fields —   the sheep
nose apples wither and the pears rot —
the ice-house turned about and no barn
with cupola
The barn burned down to get fire insurance —
never proven.
And there was an attempt to get a veteran
who was to get farm machinery   from   the
government to cultivate the land and it never worked.
My soul   is   Chichester and my origin is a womb whether
one likes it or not.
And the womb is Lena's who read the Bible and health book
and no one cared and she couldn't get to
church   and she ran down   the
Center   Road
where one thought that she   was going
to run to the quicksand —
suicide?
She read the Bible and she did go out   and work in   the
garden   and the daughters weren't
scrubbed   and all   was scurvy

She was fed well   in the asylum
                        and the strength   of nervous energy
                              was manifested:
                                 Down on   a heavy table!
And don't think this mere journalism for when the child was
              brought: "You have a beautiful child,
                                    Ella."
And this   is the most painful   process   that I have had
                        to go through for a long while
                  And I am a Christian because I know how deep
                              is the sore and womb from
                                    which I came,
      And I know that   the wages of sin is death   and that the
                        sins of the fathers are visited upon the
            children
And I know that the gift of God is eternal life through   Jesus
                        Christ, Our Lord.
                  for the one who could go through the trauma
                        and write of it.   And it is not my fingers
                              that writes this.
                  It is Lena; it is Rhoda Straw —
                              It   is the sore womb and that is
                                    fertility.
It is a painful process but it is a process I must go   through
              to stay out of the asylum — perhaps the bear cave by
                        Newfound   Lake where animals —
                        bears, lynx have made their
                              imprint on Rhoda's   paths.

                                                      1955

MICHAEL McCLURE

THE BREECH

              — A barricade — a wall — a stronghold,
      Sinister and joyous, of indigo and saffron —
                  To hurl myself against!
                    To crush or
             To be a part of the wall . . .
          Spattered brains or the imprint
              of a violent foot —
     To crumble loose some brilliant masonry
             Or knock it down —
            To send pieces flying
               Like stars!

        To be the chalice of the hunt,
           To handspring
      Through a barrier of white trees!

At work — 3:00 in the morning — In the produce market
  Moving crates of lettuce and cauliflower — Predawn
  A vision — The rats become chinchillas — I stand
At the base of a cliff — sweating — flaming — in terror and joy
  Surrounded in the mist — by whirling circles of dark
  Chattering animals — a black lynx stares from the hole
              In the cliff.

Rotten lettuce — perfume — The damp carroty street.

     It is my head — These are my hands.
          I don't will it.
     Out in the light — Noon — the City.
       A Wall — a stronghold.

1954

334

THE RUG

I'd draw all this into a fine element, — a color.
Rosy, rust-red, Orange white.

It's love; I bring it, hair-on-end.
A reflection in my eyes — part of this still room,

our strange shape — and I put my hands

to you — like cool jazz coming.
Seeing these designs we make in pure air.
I'm half-man, half-snake — and you
A BURROW
There are no words but color and muscled form
AND THIS IS NOT IT
I can't remember that instant
and I alter it to elegance
to flowers and animals — and no speech
covers the blankness.
I'm filled perfectly, giving your gift to me.
AND THIS IS NOT IT
This is failure, no trick, no end
but speech for those who'll listen.
I cry 'Love, Love, Love, Love Love,'
but this is not my voice —
these are enormous forms
Rosy, rust-red, Orange, white!

                                                              1955

HYMN TO ST. GERYON, I

THE GESTURE THE GESTURE THE GESTURE THE GESTURE
                                              [THE GESTURE THE
        GESTURE THE GESTURE   to make fists of it.

Clyfford Still: "We are committed to an unqualified act,
not illustrating outworn myths or contemporary alibis. One must
accept total responsibility for what he executes.
And the measure of his greatness will be the depth of his

insight and courage in realizing
his own vision. Demands for communication are pre-
sumptuous and irrelevant."

To hit with the thing. To make a robe of it
TO WEAR.
To fill out the thing as we see it!
To clothe ourselves in the action,
to remove from the precious to the full swing.
To hit the object over the head. To step
into what we conjecture.
Name it the *stance*. Not politics

but ourselves — is the question.
HERE I SEE IT WITH FLOWERS ENTERING INTO IT
that way.
Not caring except for my greatness, caring
only for my size I would enter it.

THE SELFS FREE HERO

THOREAU is there, LAWRENCE, BLAKE and GOYA
ST. POLLOCK is there and KLINE whom I imagine
in a world of nerves and nightsweats.
To hit it again. 'The foot is to kick with.'
If I do violence to myself I am beautiful, blood is red
on the face and bruises are not without . . .

But the thing I say!! Is to see

Or as one says: Not to lie about goodness.
Even Geryon (as Geryon) is beautiful but not if you look
only at the head or body. BUT

BACK TO IT . . . it is a robe
that I want. The gestures that we make are
our clothing. Small gestures
are like smoke, a slight breeze causes a drifting
and we are bare again . . . uneternal.
Say it! What a small thing to want, it is not
noble. Shelley wanted to save the Irish.

But I love my body my face only
first and then others'.
To fill out a vision until I become
one with it. Or perhaps both happen together. But
I must be an animal. Shelley had
no gods either.   . . . .
an impetuous man — he was mostly
Gesture ! ! ! ! ! ! ! ! ! ! ! !
There are so few poems
but so much of him.
ID I COULD BE FORCED BY SOMEONE TO CHANGE THIS
IEY WOULD KNOW THAT WHAT I SAY IS NOT MEANT AS HUMOR

Or to
STRIKE THEM
with the
GESTURE.
I mean that I love myself which is an act of pride
and I would decorate myself with what is beautiful.
The tigers of wrath are wiser than the horses of instruction. —
means that the belief of something is necessary to its beauty.
Size, numbers are part of any esthetic. I must
believe my gesture. Beauty fades so quickly

that it does not matter. Belief, pride, — remain.
AND   AND   AND   AND   AND   AND   AND   AND

the gesture.
The mark of the strong shoulder and hand.

·

Yes, confuses. The whole thing.
Sometimes intentional and sometimes out of my hands.
Robe Gesture   ROBE/GESTURE   Robe Gesture

The poem like painting is black and white.

•

And I am still not swinging it — there is still confusion
I PICK IT UP BY THE TAIL AND HIT
YOU OVER THE HEAD WITH IT.

WHAP WHAP WHAP WHAP WHAP WHAP WHAP WHAP WHAP
DO YOU BELIEVE ME NOW?

No. But if I started huge paragraphs moving toward you
or enormous stanzas, simple things, part of
a gesture, then, you would get out of the way.
You would see them coming at you,
rapidly, determined, indifferent. But this
is really not to attack you.
I mean only to move words. To set
something into motion toward a goal. Not
to invent new confusions.

It is hard to avoid some issues.
The poem could easily become a body,
with elbows, lymph systems, muscles.
But how ugly! How much better for it

to be a body of words.
A POEM — NO MORE
(Not a body of words but a poem)

I am the body, the animal, the poem
is a gesture of mine.

A confusion is avoided here,

Beauty: How beautiful I move
and make gestures. How
beautiful that sometimes I believe in them.
Sometimes I make a strong gesture — a poem
and I record it.

CANTICLE

The sharks tooth is perfect for biting. The intent
matters./ I am sick of beautiful things
/ and I would make a robe of gestures

without beauty except for the beauty inherent
in words and motion.

Listen/ Listen/ listen/ Listen/ Listen

to the words as waves/ pressures
all is destruction — without it there is
no strength.   The muscle builds
itself double   by destruction of cells.

The tendons whisper to the skeleton

Listen/ Listen/ listen/ Listen/ Listen
and only the nerves hear.
The field and seed are one thing destroying
the other. Intent, enwrapped with one another

Erethism is love. Love

Inventing a thing of leaves and flowers

'retractions devour' the thing burgeoning
is the thing intent/ Love/ Strength/ Light
and Dark/ spring to blossoms.

                                                    1957

PEYOTE POEM, PART I

Clear — the senses bright — sitting in the black chair — Rocker —
       the white walls reflecting the color of clouds
              moving over the sun. Intimacies! The rooms

   not important — but like divisions of all space
          of all hideousness and beauty. I hear
       the music of myself and write it down

   for no one to read. I pass fantasies as they

sing to me with Circe-Voices. I visit
among the peoples of myself and know all
                I need to know.
I KNOW EVERYTHING! I PASS INTO THE ROOM

    there is a golden bed radiating all light

the air is full of silver hangings and sheathes

            I smile to myself. I know

    all that there is to know. I see all there

        is to feel. I am friendly with the ache
        in my belly. The answer

        to love is my voice. There is no Time!
No answers. The answer to feeling is my feeling.

        The answer to joy is joy without feeling.

        The room is a multicolored cherub
of air and bright colors. The pain in my stomach

        is warm and tender. I am smiling. The pain
        is many pointed, without anguish.

        Light changes the room from yellows to violet!

The dark brown space behind the door is precious
        intimate, silent and still. The birthplace
                of Brahms. I know

        all that I need to know. There is no hurry.

I read the meanings of scratched walls and cracked ceilings.

    I am separate. I close my eyes in divinity and pain.

    I blink in solemnity and unsolemn joy.

            I smile at myself in my movements. Walking
            I step higher in carefulness. I fill

        space with myself. I see the secret and distinct
        patterns of smoke from my mouth

I am without care part of all. Distinct.
I am separate from gloom and beauty. I see all.

(SPACIOUSNESS

And grim intensity — close within myself. No longer
                    a cloud
        but flesh real as rock. Like Herakles
              of primordial substance and vitality.
        And not even afraid of the thing shorn of glamor

              but accepting.
The beautiful things are not of ourselves

        but I watch them. Among them.

        And the Indian thing. It is true!
    Here in my Apartment I think tribal thoughts.)

        STOMACHE!!!

There is no time. I am visited by a man
              who is the god of foxes
        there is dirt under the nails of his paw
                    fresh from his den.
We smile at one another in recognition.

I am free from Time. I accept it without triumph

              — a fact.

Closing my eyes there are flashes of light.

My eyes won't focus but leap. I see that I have three feet.
        I see seven places at once!
    The floor slants — the room slopes
              things melt
        into each other. Flashes
              of light

and meldings. I wait

  seeing the physical thing pass.

    I am on a mesa of time and space.

        ! STOM – ACHE!

      Writing the music of life
          in words.
      Hearing the round sounds of the guitar
              as colors.
      Feeling the touch of flesh.

      Seeing the loose chaos of words
            on the page.
          (ultimate grace)
(Sweet Yeats and his ball of hashish.)

My belly and I are two individuals
      joined together
          in life.

    THIS IS THE POWERFUL KNOWLEDGE

      we smile with it.

At the window I look into the blue-gray
        gloom of dreariness.
I am warm. Into the dragon of space.
  I stare into clouds seeing
        their misty convolutions.

        The whirls of vapor

I will small clouds out of existence.

They become fish devouring each other.

And change like Dante's holy spirits

becoming an osprey frozen skyhigh

      to challenge me.

ODE FOR SOFT VOICE

for Jo Ann

And sometimes in the cool night I see you are an animal
LIKE NO OTHER AND HAVE AS STRANGE A SCENT AS
[ANY AND MY BREATH AND
energy go out to you.
And see love as an invention and play it extemporaneously.

And I who cannot love can love you.
OH THIS THIS THIS IS THE HURT / THAT WE DO
[NOT KICK
down the walls and do not see them.
And I do not ache until I scent you. And I
do not scent you. Breathing moves us. Breath is . . .

And more than this that we are huge and clear
and open — locked inside
and moving out and we make outlines in the air the shapes
they are. And we shift so. We move and never keep our forms
[but stare
at them address them as if they were there. This is my hand with
5 fingers, my heart nerves lungs
are there and part of me
and I move.
I have no form but lies and drop them from me.

I am a shape and meet you
at our skins edge.
We change and speak and make our histories. I am all I feel
and what you see and what you touch.
There are no walls but ones we make.
I AM SICK CONFUSED AND DROP IT FROM ME
The nerves are dead that feel no hunger or pain theres no tri-
umph but failure. This is the last speech of seraphim or beast sick
in need for change and chaos. The room of banished love for
beauty. The tooth in our breast. What we see is real and able to
our hand, what we feel is beauty (BEAUTY   ) what we strike
is hatred, what we scent is odorous. This about me is my bride if

I kick aside the forms of it for woman world and mineral for air
for earth for fire and water for table chair and blood.

FOR ARTAUD

1

The nets are real — heroin (sniffed) clears them. Peyote
                                                    [(5 buttons)

    dispels them forever perhaps. Or until we come out
  and smear ourselves upon all we see or touch. It is real!!

They are real! We are black interiors. Are battlegrounds
        of what is petty and heroic. Projecting
        out all that is base and slack from us. But
           not far enough!
And not all — but part / of all / a minute quantity to foul
        the air.

  And not base and petty but the struggle (heroic)
      and its opposite. As we writhe to see
        they cohere and cannot
          see it.
OH BEAUTY BEAUTY BEAUTY BEAUTY BEAUTY BEAUTY
                [IS HIDEOUS
    We are black within and sealed from light.
      And cannot know it. To move
out from / there / where it is black and mysterious
      thru desire and reaching.
AND NOT TO PROJECT THE BASE AND SLACK!

2

(OH HERAKLES OH UNKNOWING MAN I WILL BE LIKE
                    [YOU AND ACT
        and not know myself.
    Not to question love or hate and to suffer
        for my mistakes.

No webs about my seeing no doubt about my feeling.

Let my hand be as strong as the soul (the interior)
I know is there.
I am free and open from the blackness.
I am so strong I can say there is loveliness and not be touched

by it.
Let me feel great pain and strength of suffering.
My eyes are clear and my voice shakes from joy.
I am strong in my crying. Strong in my blackness
for a lady I love.
Strong for my child in the world.
Let me see out from my seal into the colors and shapes.

Let me know the blackness to see from. What is real
occurs within and moves out.)

3

YES YES THIS IS THE CHAIR THIS IS THE TABLE
[THIS IS THE AIR
I breathe.
But I am not here. I know I am within   and all outward
are acts.
I move from my skin grasping out in desire.
OR MY WILL MOVES ME TO THIS

and I fail,
there are webs about my feeling and clouds about my touch.
And I am out upon all I see and nothing
can return me.
THERE IS NOTHING TO KNOW. I KNOW ALL FROM
[MY BLACKNESS
All that I see is real all that I touch.
I am here within and know it.
My skin is the cliff of my being and I
have fallen from it.

Love will not help and not simply truth.
This is the edge (of my being) and I peer from it.

I have returned to the souls
STOMACH AND BRAIN.

/ AND ALL ALL ALL

4

The face is love — the head is clouded by the smoke we make
of it. Shows. madness.
Swirling burning and vacant. A superhuman
devotion to make it tell its lies. Do not
LIE TO ME IT MAKES ME SUFFER TOO TO SEE
your face.
I CANNOT STAND THE PAIN WE MAKE BETWEEN US
and I cannot sleep at night.
And I cannot stand the touch of your projections

on my cheeks and arms. The real nets
that lie within the fact of seeing. The sick

signs we cast on all things. Don't throw
them in my face. I am weak
and they gather about me / too . / The genitals
are purity and make
the shapes (like hands) of love.

The nerves are weak or strong and pass from interior
to exterior and join
us at our edges.

5

MY BRAIN MY BRAIN MY BRAIN THAT I STUMBLE
[WHEN I WALK
I do not see the table. My stomach when I talk

that all I feel is hatred
for myself. And I am proud. Without pride. I stand
leaned on myself. I hear myself mumble.
When (I know) I am black inside and sealed from light.

And I spread   in the open air
am myselfs protagonist.
There's no pain from it but sickness smoke
and vacancy.
Where is my error? In my cells? Protein, acid chains?

What is my sickness and my vacancy? / I care
for love and will not
serve it. And it will not move to serve me.
In my chest (dull ache) and knee
(twitching).
And I do not act from spirit or
from individuality
from my black and inner animal and being.

6

This is the ache (remembered) of my present being
that I do not desire and move from it
BUT ACT AND SWINGING LOATHE MYSELF FOR IN-
[SINCERITY

and throw poisons
(that do not matter) in the air and breathe
them in again. And
hate myself for acting and for
breathing.
I WILL NOT BE SICK BUT BLACK STRONG AND REACH
[FROM IT
I don't have love but what is turned from within.
There's no love for me to ask for. But what
is turned out to me. I am sick and weak from sick —
ness and I hate it. Here is love turned
from me.
Poison thrown outward to make a radiance
and not a net or web.
These are two lines drawn from me and pulled
to me   from myself.

7 ──────────────────────────

That we are animals — this is my paw — my eyes see out!
I love you from deep inside from my very edge.
THE TRUTH IS VIRTUAL. LOVE LOVE APPROXIMATES
[TO MAKE
its manner known.
Bone teeth nail and cheeks ankle (and) vein.
I cannot (can) swing to you thru body and pain.
Is nothing! A song.
I am not virtual and speak alone.
Is a song lost in lack of feeling and comes from the edge.
I am sealed in light and spread to my
outer skin. Where only blindness keeps my cells
from being eyes.
STOMACH BRAIN AND BODY ARE THE ROOMS OF OUR
[LIVES
and they are filled with blackness

for we need no light
except about us. If skin is eyes and fingers
and there is no virtual speech
or acts or
love.

8

AND ALL HUGE AND ALL /

I am a flask sealed and nothing is happening!
I am black and I do not move out. See
nothing. Or for an instant I am tall look down
on all as it is fit
for seeing. That all is water clear and running,
solid and wavering,
that all is real and I walk in it. Among it.

And see in a face or breast an animal
loveliness.
And feel my chest and stomach beat for it.
AND IT IS NOT LOVELINESS! BUT CLARITY BUT PURE
responding. When I see
a breast I love. Or face of suffering.
In the cold water black worms (planarians)
move and dart or crawl unseen.
And all is clear holy and not beautiful
to them.
But icy light icy dark and green wet leaves
above.

1958

THE FLOWERS OF POLITICS, I

THIS IS THE HUGE DREAM OF US THAT WE ARE HEROS
[THAT THERE IS COURAGE
in our blood! That we are live!
That we do not perpetrate the lie of vision
forced upon ourselves
by ourselves. That we have made the nets of vision real!
AND SNARED THEM

OH I AM BLIND AS A FLOWER AND SENSE LESS
we see nothing but banality.
Break in the forms and take real postures!

This is the real world clear and open.
The flower moves and motion is its sense,
and transference of ions
all that it does is perception
and vision.
OH BREAK UP THE FORMS AND FEEL NEW THINGS
I declare that I am love who have never known
it and I make new love.
My hand is pink and white and blue and great
to me. My eyes are bright

and I know that love is air. An act
and nothing more. That we are seraphs,
cherubim and heros, chieftans and gods.
This is the blind senseless thing of knowing
that unconscious we walk in it, and strive
among all things. This is
A CANDLE
and shape of light.
The hand and arm annunciate all things

and draw the eye upon the speaking face

declaring from the inner body.
We are wrought on a bending shaft of air and light
and make an animal around it

and spread a radiance from ourselves that melts
in light.

THE FLOWERS OF POLITICS, II

ONLY WHAT IS HEROIC AND COURAGEIOUS MOVES
[OUR BLOOD
we are lost within ourselves and tangles
of a narrow room and world if we do not speak out, reach out
and strive from individuality. This is

WHAT I HEAR IN HEART NERVES LUNGS, NOT ELEGIES.
I am a black beast and clear man in one. With no
split or division. But from one without.
AND WALK IN IT FREE
as flowers or blood
and hate the forms of it you make
destroying it to take it from my touch
and sight. I hate
you in the night when I am whole and free.

And I know you will be stamped out by your forms
and invisible revolutions and I

do what I will and can to speed them on.
THOSE LEFT WILL BE GODS AND SERAPHIM
and need no memory of you —
only this is more than beauty
without holiness and self-conceit.

Your sickness poisons you and you
are dying. No aid
or speed can save you. And I
am free!

Free of politics. Liberty and pride to guide you. You pass
from ancestral myths to myth of self. And make
the giant bright stroke like that madman Van Gogh.

1959

RAY BREMSER

POEM OF HOLY MADNESS, PART IV

let me lay it to you gently, Mr. Gone!
fed up is what I'M!
your heaps of slick and apathetic succor
transvestite my human animal until I walk
with knuckles on the ground, my Einstein essence
split by prehistoric gobs of eyed typography

— the world and papers never
                              never meant
to furnish mankind substitute_for ghostwriting
on the cavern's corner's vague museum walls!
it is a little
              let us say
                        too much
man,
     too much!
                too much
the white unbloodly Cadillac caught
cryptic on the air to lure another
netherman with California Rugolo
and too much the rigid enterprising
     caterwauling!

too much the cross
that fries its nigger-toast south of a drawn
out isolation line, whereon approaches two
hostilities — magnificent isomorphic white,
and poor enpaupered isomorphic black!

too much
          the weight of gangs
                                and people running

sure-shot ex-marine police force
coming down with pride in prejudice
to break the jewish high empiracies
and beat the butcher, steal his pork to poison
maybe blind but living hearts, whose black base
reveals the urge of nevertheless and sudden light!

too much
the roving flood of moraine clay out of the high
and Adirondack ice — unsleeping hollow!
Catskill Peekskill League for Prevention of Bogus
Pinball Machines!

                is it your life,
New Jersey? yours, New York?
                         freaks of nature,
giant, and the dwarf with the blowed-up head —
east and north and westerly and south
and hallelujah Alabamy mammy jubilee
prophetic anti-nigger-lumbee-semitist!

praise to you, my country!
praises, America!
I would bequeath
your whole to another blazer,
Charlie Starkweather!
                    he would know how to handle the infinite
putrid scumbags somebody's mother manufactures —
he would annul your vast vagina
into a finer
              better business bureau box of the mange!

but enough of these corners —
                  let me begin
to level with you here — I'm unafraid, and finally
proficient in decision —
                I am a traitor fascist
to your face!

call me a communist, or this and that —

I am a traitor traitor traitor
                              traitor
traitor!
        you will investigate me finally,
along with my mother, who furnished change
for lunch knowing my reputation as a thief!
I am a traitor,
                weigh this evidence
however you want it on your Italian little-bit
cheating scale —
                but I love
the visionary journey out of jail,
that spectral escape that screws the federal
                                        government!
I would prefer to run around with tramps,
and homosexual cats in drag rather than suck
the tinfoil tits of brittle broads
born in Nebraska!
                I'm a myth
whose roustabout's prevarication!
I am a nonbeliever too — neither your giftless
painted gooddesses of Cash — of Tax,
nor Silver Certificate!

if you can face it,
I love a luke-warm Jew,
thirsty with lips that barely slobber
over the kosher Mogan David wine!
                            give me a black
and miserable hide — and I will un-tar it!
                            and I dig jazz,
and hipsters, and prevail over the tiny nurses of the park
minding your children, beautiful long with ten minutes
sexual pleasure, letting your little Mary and Joey watch,
drooling to turn you, Mother America, back into
the one-time-great Shoshonee magnanimous squaw
to the decadent indian-poet — lost god of the plains
whose whistling arrows still echo the hungering lust

over the mountains and into the bellicose brawn of the white
pretender to Father!
                              tomorrow their buffalo-dead
will arise
              and embrace the beating breathing religion
no longer shouting nor questioning who may be right,
only digging the sky,
                              and the clouds,
bringing acres of free for the Negro —
offering Jews their Elohim repast!

listen!
        they're revving those millioning motors!
war is declared!
                        without bombs!
the Apache uprising is here
                              and the scores
of apostle-like
              lances of Thomas,
                              and hatchets of Matthew,
and bladed Bartholomew,
                        Paul-sword,
                              and Matthias's
battle-axe!
              really comes finities black with avenge
and the multiple roaring —
                              cloven and halo-ed,
come hordes of white justice
                              come rain
on the leprous forty-eight states
                              come moan of new mornings,
murder and blinding swift light,
                              come prong to the virgin
whose rip-sawed vagina gnaws gnats for the hell,
                              come weight
that will crush every judgment
                              those hooves
                              come all
galloping headlong into the soft-spoken kiss

of the poets
          whose sad skinny banners
were long-ago verbs
               that had long-ago moved
so much more than mere mankind
                    to gestures,
and love!

Bordentown, 1958

BLOOD

I have this deal of death about my hands
whose silent espionage of half a thousand
days ago still carries your stigma
in the palms . . .

my knuckles love you readily, forgetfully,
my fingertips are able to caress & instigate
while heaving on the carapace of chest
a crimson countenance is wrung
because of cisterns in those paraqueets,
your simple rosy tears of rosy breast . . .

build temples where I touch!
create a sodium monologue on your gut,
convict the maps & scapings of my geld,
that terrible old hold around those thighs
whose wooded areas are fortunate complaints
against misfortunate & clitoral delights . . .

& resining my sharpest flagrancies,
denoun my tongue from its own hotel of mouth
that I shall lick this dying death with spittle,
spy upon intolerable spying agents of the void
gone suddenly vision —
gone to womb & over flesh,
gone suddenly straight beyond this blood
of our deaths . . .

1959

LEROI JONES

IN MEMORY OF RADIO

Who has ever stopped to think of the divinity of Lamont Cranston?
(Only Jack Kerouac, that I know of; & me.
The rest of you probably had on WCBS and Kate Smith,
Or something equally unattractive.)

What can I say?
It is better to have loved and lost
Than to put linoleum in your living rooms?

Am I a sage or something?
Mandrake's hypnotic gesture of the week?
(Remember, I do not have the healing powers of Oral Roberts . . .
I cannot, like F. J. Sheen, tell you how to get saved & *rich*!
I cannot even order you to gaschamber satori like Hitler or Goody
    Knight.

& Love is an evil word.
Turn it backwards/ see, see what I mean?
An evol word. & besides
who understands it?
I certainly wouldn't like to go out on that kind of limb.

Saturday mornings we listened to *Red Lantern* & his undersea folk.
At 11, *Let's Pretend*/ & we did/ & I, the poet, still do, Thank God!

What was it he used to say (after the transformation, when he
    was safe
& invisible, & the unbelievers couldn't throw stones?) "Heh, Heh,
    Heh,
Who knows what evil lurks in the hearts of men? The Shadow
    knows!"

O, yes he does
O, yes he does

357

LeRoi Jones

An evil word it is,
This love.

FOR HETTIE

My wife is left-handed.
Which implies a fierce de-
termination. A complete other
worldliness. IT'S WEIRD BABY
The way some folks
are always trying to be different.
A sin & a shame.

But then, she's been a bohemian
all her life . . . black stockings,
refusing to take orders. I sit
patiently, trying to tell her
what's right. TAKE THAT DAMM
PENCIL OUTTA THAT HAND. YOU'RE
RITING BACKWARDS. & such. But
to no avail. & it shows
in her work. Left-handed coffee,
left-handed eggs: when she comes
in at night . . . it's her left hand
offered for me to kiss. DAMM.

& now her belly droops over the seat.
They say it's a child. But
I ain't quite so sure.

1958

WAY OUT WEST

for Gary Snyder

As simple an act
as opening the eyes. Merely
coming into things by degrees.

Morning: some tear is broken
on the wooden stairs
of my lady's eyes. Profusions
of green. The leaves. Their
constant prehensions. Like old
junkies on Sheridan Square, eyes
cold and round. There is a song
Nat Cole sings . . . This city
& the intricate disorder
of the seasons.

Unable to mention
something as abstract as time.

Even so (bowing low in thick
smoke from cheap incense; all
kinds of questions filling the mouth,
till you suffocate & fall dead
to opulent carpet). Even so,

shadows will creep over your flesh
& hide your disorder, your lies.

There are unattractive wild ferns
outside the window
where the cats hide. They yowl
from there at nights. In heat
& bleeding on my tulips.

Steel bells, like the evil
unwashed Sphinx, towing in the twilight.
Childless old murderers, for centuries
with musty eyes.

I am distressed. Thinking
of the seasons, how they pass,
how I pass, my very youth, the
ripe sweet of my life; drained off . . .

Like giant rhesus monkeys,
picking their skulls,

with ingenious cruelty
sucking out the brains.

No use   for beauty
collapsed, with moldy breath
done in. Insidious weight
of cankered dreams. Tiresias'
weathered cock.

Walking into the sea, shells
caught in the hair. Coarse
waves tearing the tongue.

Closing the eyes. As
simple an act. You float

ONE NIGHT STAND

We entered the city at noon! High bells. The radio on.
Some kind of Prokovieff; snaring the violent remains of the day
in sharp webs of dissonance.

We roared through the old gates. Iron doors hanging
all grey, with bricks mossed over and gone into chips
dogs walked through.

The river also roared. And what sun we had
disappeared into the water, or buried itself
in the badly pitched tents of the wounded soldiers.

There, also, at the river, blue steel hats glinted
on the sparse grass, and brown showed through
where the grass was trampled.

We came in, with our incredulousness, from the south.
On steely highways from the marble entrails of noon.
We had olives, and the green buds locked on our lutes.

Twisted albion-horns, rusted in warm rain, peasant carts,
loud black bond-servants dazed and out of their wool heads,
Wild shrubs impecuniously sheltered along the concrete,

Rumble of the wheels over cobblestones, The green knocked out.
The old houses dusty seeming & old men watching us slyly
as we come in: all of us laughing too loud.

We *are* foreign seeming persons. Hats flopped so the sun
can't scald our beards; odd shoes, bags of books & chicken.
We have come a long way, & are uncertain which of the masks

is cool.

TO A PUBLISHER...cut-out

The blight rests in your face.
For your unknown musiks. The care & trust
Undeliberate. Like an axe-murder
Or flat pancake. The night cold and asexual
A long sterile moon lapping at the dank Hudson.
The end of a star. The water more than any
Other thing. We are dibbled here. Seurat's
Madness. That kind of joke. Isolate
Land creatures in a wet unfriendly world.

We must be strong. (smoke Balkan Sobranie)
People will think you have the taste
In this hyar family. Some will stroke your face.
Better posture is another thing. Watch out for Peanuts.
He's gonna turn out bad/ A J.D./ A Beatnik/ A
Typical wise-ass N.Y. kid. "X" wanted to bet me
That Charlie Brown spent most of his time
whacking his doodle, or having wierd relations
with that dopey hound of his (though that's
a definite improvement over "Arf Arf" & that
filthy little lesbian he's hung up with).

As if any care could see us through. Could defend us.
Save us from you, Little Darling. Or me, which is worse.
"A far far worser thing I do/ than I has ever done."
Put that in your pipe & watch out for the gendarmes.
They arresses people for less than that. For less

Than we are ever capable of. Any kind of sincerity
Guarantees complete disregard. Complete abnegation.
"Must dig with my fingers/ as nobody will lend me
or sell me a pick axe" Axe the man who owns one.
Hellzapoppin. The stars might not come on tonight . . .
& who the hell can do anything about that?? Eh,
Milord/ Milady/ The kind Dubarry wasn't. Tres slick.

But who am I to love anybody? I ride the 14th St. bus
everyday . . . reading Hui neng/Raymond Chandler/ Olson . . .
I have slept with almost every mediocre colored woman
On 23rd St . . . At any rate, talked a good match. And
Frightened by the lack of any real communication
I've addressed several perfumed notes to Uncle Don
& stuffed them into the radio. In the notes,
Of course, crude assignations, off-color suggestions,
Diagrams of new methods for pederasts, lewd poems
That rime. IF ONLY HE WOULD READ THESE ON THE AIR.
(There are other things could take my mind from
this childe's play . . . but none nearly as interesting.)

I long to be a mountain climber
& wave my hands up 8,000 feet.
Out of sight & snow blind/ the tattered
Stars and Stripes poked in the new peak.

& come down later, Clipper by my side,
To new wealth & eternal fame. That
Kind of care. I could wear
Green corduroy coats & felt tyroleans
For the rest of my days; & belong to clubs.

Grandeur in boldness. Big & stupid as the wind.
But so lovely. Who's to understand that kind of con?
As if each day, after breakfast, someone asked you,
"What do you want to be when you grow up??" &
Day in, Day out, you just kept belching.

OSTRICHES & GRANDMOTHERS!

All meet here with us, finally: the
uptown, way-west, den of inconstant
moralities.
Faces up: all
my faces turned up
to the sun.

1.

Summer's mist nods against the trees
till distance grows in my head
like an antique armada
dangled motionless from the horizon.

Unbelievable changes. Restorations.
Each day like my niña's fan
tweaking the flat air
back and forth till the room
is a blur of flowers.

Intimacy takes on human form
& sheds it like a hide.
                              Lips, eyes,
tiny lace coughs
reflected on night's stealth.

2.

Tonight, one star.
eye of the dragon.
                    The Void
signaling.
Reminding someone
it's still there.

3.

It's these empty seconds
I fill with myself. Each
a recognition. A complete
utterance.

Here, it is color; motions:
the feeling of dazzling beauty
Flight.

As
the trapeze rider
leans
with arms spread

wondering
at the bar's
delay

THE TURNCOAT

The steel fibrous slant & ribboned glint
of water. The Sea. Even my secret speech is moist
with it. When I am alone & brooding, locked in
with dull memories & self hate, & the terrible disorder
of a young man.

I move slowly. My cape spread stiff & pressing cautiously
in the first night wind off the Hudson. I glide down
onto my own roof, peering in at the pitiful shadow of myself.

How can it mean anything? The stop & spout, the
wind's dumb shift. Creak of the house & wet smells
coming in. Night forms on my left. The blind still
up to admit a sun that no longer exists. Sea move.

I dream long bays & towers . . . & soft steps on moist sand.
I become them, sometimes. Pure flight. Pure fantasy. Lean.

1959

JOHN WIENERS

A POEM FOR PAINTERS

Our age bereft of nobility
How can our faces show it?
I look for love.
    My lips stand out
dry and cracked with want
               of it.
               Oh it is well.

Again we go driven by forces
we have no control over. Only
               in the poem
comes an image — that we rule
    the line by the pen
in the painter's hand one foot
            away from me.
Drawing the face
    and its torture.
That is why no one dares tackle it.
Held as they are in the hands
        of forces
they cannot understand.
           That despair
is on my face and shall show
in the fine lines of any man.

I held love once in the palm of my hand.
    See the lines there.
          How we played
its game, are playing now
in the bounds of white and heartless fields.
    Fall down on my head,

365

love, drench my flesh in the streams
                of fine sprays. Like
                        French perfume
    so that I light up as
                morning glorys and
I am showered by the scent
    of the finished line.

                    No circles
but that two parallels do cross
      And carry our souls and
bodies together as the planets
      Showing light on the surface
              of our skin, knowing
    that so much flows through
              the veins underneath.
The cheeks puffed with it.
    Our pockets full.

        2
Pushed on by the incompletion
    of what goes before me
I hesitate before this paper
    scratching for the right words.
Paul Klee scratched for seven years
    on smoked glass to develop
    his line, Lavigne says: Look
at his face!   he who has spent
    all night drawing mine.

The sun
also rises on the rooftops
    beginning with violet.
I begin in blue knowing what's cool.

        3
My middle name is Joseph and I
walk beside an ass on the way to

what Bethlehem, where a new babe is born.
          Not the second hand of Yeats but
first prints on a cloudy windowpane.

                    4
America, you boil over

The cauldron scalds.
Flesh is scarred.
Eyes shot.

The street aswarm with
vipers and heavy armed bandits.
There are bandages on the wounds
but blood flows unabated.
                              Oh stop
                       up the drains.
          We are run over.

                    5
Let us stay with what we know.
That love is my strength, that
I am overpowered by it:
                    Desire
                         that too
is on the face: gone stale.
When green was the bed my love
and I laid down upon.
Such it is, heart's complaint,
You hear upon a day in June.
And I see no end in view
when summer goes, as it will,
upon the roads, like singing
companions across the land.

South of Mission, Seattle,
over the Sierra Mountains,
the Middle West and Michigan,
moving east again, easy
coming into Chicago and

the cattle country, calling
to each other over canyons,
careful not to be caught
at night, they are still out,
the destroyers, and down
into the South, familiar land,
lush places, blue mountains
of Carolina, into Black Mountain
and you can sleep out, or
straight across into states

I cannot think of their names
this nation is so large, like
our hands, our love it lives
with no lover, looking only
for the beloved, back home
into the heart, New York,
New England, Vermont, green
mountains and Massachusetts
my city, Boston and the sea
again to smell what this calm
ocean cannot tell us. The seasons.
Only the heart remembers
and records in the words

6

At last. I come to the last defense.

My poems contain no
wilde beestes, no
lady of the lake, music
of the spheres, or organ chants.

Only the score of a man's
struggle to stay with
what is his own, what
lies within him to do.

Without which is nothing.
And I come to this
knowing the waste,

leaving the rest up to love
and its twisted faces,
my hands claw out at
only to draw back from the
blood already running there.

                                             6.18.58

A POEM FOR THE OLD MAN

God love you
    Dana my lover
lost in the horde
on this Friday night
500 men are moving up
& down from the bath
room to the bar
Remove this desire
from the man I love.
Who has opened
    the savagery
of the sea to me.

See to it that
his wants are filled
on California Street
Bestow on him lar-
gesse that allows him
peace in his loins.

Leave him not
to the moths.
Make him out a lion
so that all who see him
hero worship his
thick chest as I did
moving my mouth
over his back bringing
our hearts to heights

I never hike over
   anymore.

Let blond hair
burn on the back of his
neck, let no ache
screw his face
up in pain, his soul
   is so hooked.

Not heroin
Rather fix these
hundred men as his
lovers & lift him
with the enormous bale
of their desire.

Strip from him
hunger and the hungry
ones who eat in the night.
The needy & the new
found ones who would weight him down.
Weight him w/ pride and —
pushing the love I put
   in his eyes.

Overflow the 500 with it
Strike them dumb,
on their knees, let them
bow down before it,
this dumb human
who has become
   my beloved
who picked me up
at 18 & put love
so that my pockets
will never be empty,
cherished as they are
against the inside flesh
   of his leg.

I occupy that space
as the boys around me
choke out desire and
drive us both back
home in the hands
      of strangers

                                                    6.20.58

A POEM FOR MUSEUM GOERS

I walk down a long
passageway with a
red door waiting for me.
It is Edward Munch.

Turn right turn
right. And I see my
                              sister
hanging on the wall,
heavy breasts and hair

Tied to a tree in the garden
with the full moon
are the ladies of the street.
Whipped for whoring.
Their long hair binds them,

They have lain long
hours in bed, blood
on their mouths, arms
reaching down for
ground not given them.

They are enveloped
in pain. Bah.
There is none. Munch

knew it. Put the
Shriek in their ears

to remove it from his own.

Open thy mouth, tell us
the landscape you have
escaped from, Fishing
boats are in the bay, no
outgoing tides for you
who he anchored to
                    Hell.

Even here the young lovers
cast black shadows.

The nets are down.
Huge seasnakes
squirm on shore
taking away even
the beach from us.
Move on. Moonlight

I see the garden women
in their gravy days
when hair hung golden or
black to the
floor & the walls
were velvet.

An old sailor his face like wood
his chin splintered
by many shipwrecks
keeps their story
in his eyes. How the house
at the top of the drive
held them all, and their lovers,
with Munch the most
obsessed. His face
carved by knife blades.

Lover leaves lover,
1896, 62 years

            later, the men
            sit, paws and
            jagged depths
            under their heads,

            Now the season of
            the furnished room. Gone
            the Grecian walls & the
            cypress trees,
            plain planks and spider
            webs, a bed
            only big enough for one,
            it looks like a
            casket. Death
            death on every
            wall, guillotined
            and streaming in
            flames.

                                                    6.21.58

A POEM FOR THE INSANE

            The 2nd afternoon I come
            back to the women of Munch.
            Models with god over

            their shoulders, vampires,
            the heads are down and
            blood is the water —
            color they use to turn on.
            The story is not done.
            There is one wall
            left to walk. Yeah

            Afterwards — Nathan
            gone, big Eric busted,
            Swanson down. It is
            right, the Melancholy

on the Beach. I do not
split

I hold on to the demon
tree, while shadows drift
around me. Until at last
there is only left the
Death Chamber. Family Reunion
in it. Rocking chairs and

who is the young man
who sneaks out thru
the black curtain, away
from the bad bed.

Yeah stand now
on the new road, with the
huge mountain on your
right out of the mist

the bridge before me,
the woman waiting
with no mouth, waiting
for me to kiss it on.

I will. I will walk with
my eyes up on you for
ever. We step into
the Kiss, 1897.
The light streams.

Melancholy carries
a red sky and our dreams
are blue boats
no one can bust or
blow out to sea.
We ride them
and Tingel-Tangel
in the afternoon.

1958

A POEM FOR TRAPPED THINGS

This morning with a blue flame burning
this thing wings its way in.
Wind shakes the edges of its yellow being.
Gasping for breath.
Living for the instant
Climbing up the black border of the window.
Why do you want out.
I sit in pain
A red robe amid debris,
You bend and climb, extending antennae.

I know the butterfly is my soul
and weak from battle.

A giant fan on the back of
                    a beetle.
A caterpillar, chrysalis that seeks
a new home apart from this room.

And will disappear from sight
at the pulling of invisible strings.
Yet so tenuous, so fine
this thing is, I am
sitting on the hard bed, we could
          vanish from sight like the puff
               off an invisible cigarette.
Furred chest, ragged silk under
          wings beating against the glass

               no one will open.

The blue diamonds on your back
are too beautiful to do
          away with.
I watch you
          all morning
                    long
With my hand over my mouth.

1959

RON LOEWINSOHN

PASTORAL

Death.
The death of a million
        honeydew melons
festering in the fields
east of Tracy.
        The scent of death
narcotic in its sweetness
which we mistook for the smell
        of fresh-churned butter
until I ran across the road
into the field
& was attacked by flies,
                        Later
on another road, I smelled myself
the fetor of the living
like locker rooms & loving beds.
& thought about the mutilated melons
which from a distance looked like
a field of wild buttercups.

INSOMNIAC POEM

. . . awake, alone, aware
& afraid of my own hands
which have begun to replace my personal mirage
green-eyed oasis in the wilderness
where we wander, thirsty prisoners in our skins
fettered by our will,
            to be liberated

376

only by love into the green mountains
watered by the warming snows of previous winters
— hillsides resplendent with Shasta Daisies
preternatural color & brilliance of God
God whom I've seen in the Alleghenies
in the sensuous mountains
     lining the Sacramento Valley
in the snowflowers
     on the Cloud's Rest Trail
in my own body in the shower.

God whom I resemble but am not
any more than I'm the Alleghenies
     or Lake Michigan
any more than I'm more or less than
     my own consciousness
thirsting for love, to love
realizing only now that
     I've got to surrender
myself to others
     some other consciousness
as thirsty as myself
before I can enter the flower.

— Merely being awake, alone & aware
of our own absurdity
we can begin to love & to give
to clothe ourselves in the color
     of the Shasta Daisy
which is never idle, even in death:
the face of God! Two & a half billion Gods
crowning the crazy world with sainthood
a supernatural patch of Shasta Daisies
blazing in the light of all-year eternal
     holy August.

1956

THE THING MADE REAL

The thing made real by
a sudden twist of the mind:
relate the darkness to a face
rather than
impose a face on the darkness
which has no face, in reality.

The Daisy made recognisable
suddenly
by a flash of
magic light, the tongue
of fire, Pentecost.

The ox made real
in its own essence
without change or pollution . . .
waking up in the cellar to find
him, rusty & contemplative, staring
me in the face
. . . the thing in its own essence
outside the confines of those
perfunctory fields, in the unlimited
environment of the imagination —

till it thunders into
the consciousness
in all its pure & beautiful
absurdity,
like a White Rhinoceros.

THE STILLNESS OF THE POEM

The stillness of the jungle
a clearing amid the vines
which distant bird sounds enter,

timidly. The overpowering silence
of the jungle clearing
into which Rhinoceri &
other wild beasts are always
charging suddenly from the canebrake
to reveal themselves
one instant
in all their natural savagery
or fear,
their nature made known to us
out of the jungle's quiet.

The stillness of the poem
a moment full of silence &
portent, like
the sudden halt of great machines.
Silence that becomes a fabric
to clothe the consciousness
. . . the events & observations of
a walk up Market Street
are admitted, as if
from a great distance,
the White Rhinoceros
charging
suddenly, in the form of a sailor
with a shopping bag
whom nobody notices.

1957

MRS. LOEWINSOHN &c

How can a girl with such a big belly be so desirable?
— Venus of Düsseldorf, curvilinear, oviform.
More — the *made* Thing, the idea Realised
the thing made real — the idea, but in Things:
fulfillment of promises, purposes —
Out of sweat labor & glazed eye DESIRE
— Invention out of all that!

. . . I think of Mozart, his father returning him
the ms of the symphony he'd dashed off
years earlier; forgotten. Now, hearing it again
— HEARING the made notes issuing
as if for the first time from his consciousness
: A Joy to make the heart sing! SING, & DANCE
even to our daily jobs.
      We haven't forgotten
the glazed eye sweat & labor, Sue,
DESIRE of the first invention.
Yes, invention. A made idea:
Eli Whitney's cotton gin,
kept under padlock in the barn out back.
Stolen later, the whole door off its pins
gaping open to the world, its vital issue gone
only the horses left, stepping around &
swatting flies absently in the halfdark.
— Stolen: their insatiable yen for the best,
leisure, the best of everything,
the beauty their loot'd buy . . .
The beauty we'll all buy
& sweat toward in field or factory,
under lampshade after long casings, nervousness,
fear of apprehension, at night, in sneakers & crowbar
tiptoe thru the garden, its vine-perch hazards
to steal a machine, a box full of toothed cylinders.
— To corner the cotton market.
But it clothed the world, for profit, yes
— but it clothed the world.

. . .

& we still remember Whitney's bleary nights
in the barn with his life's desire.
. & you, big bellied little girl,
think of our further sweats & pains
the night we come all masked & gloved
to take your oviform invention from you, for the world.

Ron Loewinsohn

MY SONS

I'll teach my sons
　　　　the same as me — LOOK
at those girls on the bus to work
　　　　intimations of real
warm bloodgiving flesh,
　　　　comfortable, moving
beneath the cloth . . .
. . . to fill our days with beauty
from whatever faucet's available.

1958

DAVID MELTZER

REVELATION

It comes to this:
my teacup filled with steaming green tea.
Basho sits beside me with ohashi,
waiting for Reiko to bring out
the Nikku Nabe, the sake, some Kirin Beer.

The haiku will come later.
After dinner &
a Havatampa cigar.

12th RAGA / FOR JOHN WIENERS

An overdose of beautiful words
keeps rushing inside my mind
but won't relate to thought or talk.
Like balloons, they will not last long
& insist on flying out of the hand
to die in the sky — released.

I want to assure you
that all the blues we've compiled
& sung, all the nigger-yelling
pumped out of our neon loins,
all the silent, tentative touch —
strokes we've made upon public wounds

I want to assure you
that they, too,
dream thru the mind
like the beautiful words.

15th RAGA / FOR BELA LUGOSI

Sir, when you say
Transylvania or wolfbane
or
I am Count Dracula,
your eyes become wide
&, for the moment, pure
white marble.

It is no wonder that
you were so long a junkie.

It's in the smile. The way
you drifted into Victorian bedrooms
holding up your cape like skirts,

then covering her face
as you bent over her to kiss
into her neck & sup.

It is no wonder & it was
in good taste too.

PRAYERWHEEL / 2

for John Wieners

Don't worry about growing old.
When we talk
it is the sea I see from your mouth.
The winds, the wee fish (silver
parasites) feeding on the whale's white hide.
Why not die alone? Roar
of the fake waterfall, chewing down
the steel slides & braces of
the gone Bond sign — once high
above Broadway. That's it.
What I mean, when I talk about poetry.

Neon over the big street.
Plaster statues of Man & Woman,
cut off by the mock waterfall.
Lights — B.O.N.D.
As if the mind needed the eye
when writing a poem.
As if a poem was in the mind
when reading a poem. Don't
worry about a single thing.
When we talk, the worry's behind us.
Steel rods & strictures propping up
the Man, the Woman, the monster
electrical words.

Gone is the giant Bond sign.
Is anything ever gone
to the poet who works up everything
eventually? Somewhere, without mind,
Love begins. The poet begins
to examine the dissolution of Love.
The sea continues. We continue
talking, growing nervous, drinking
too much coffee.

1959

VI

STATEMENTS ON POETICS

CHARLES OLSON:

PROJECTIVE   VERSE

   (projectile   (percussive   (prospective

           vs.

      The NON-Projective

(or what a French critic calls "closed" verse, that verse which print bred and which is pretty much what we have had, in English & American, and have still got, despite the work of Pound & Williams:

it led Keats, already a hundred years ago, to see it (Wordsworth's, Milton's) in the light of "the Egotistical Sublime"; and it persists, at this latter day, as what you might call the private-soul-at-any-public-wall)

Verse now, 1950, if it is to go ahead, if it is to be of *essential* use, must, I take it, catch up and put into itself certain laws and possibilities of the breath, of the breathing of the man who writes as well as of his listenings. (The revolution of the ear, 1910, the trochee's heave, asks it of the younger poets.)

I want to do two things: first, try to show what projective or OPEN verse is, what it involves, in its act of composition, how, in distinction from the non-projective, it is accomplished; and II, suggest a few ideas about what stance toward reality brings such verse into being, what that stance does, both to the poet and to his reader. (The stance involves, for example, a change beyond, and larger than, the technical, and may, the way things look, lead to new poetics and to new concepts from which some sort of drama, say, or of epic, perhaps, may emerge.)

I

First, some simplicities that a man learns, if he works in OPEN, or what can also be called COMPOSITION BY FIELD, as opposed to inherited line, stanza, over-all form, what is the "old" base of the non-projective.

(1) the *kinetics* of the thing. A poem is energy transferred from where the poet got it (he will have some several causations), by way of the poem itself to, all the way over to, the reader. Okay. Then the poem itself must, at all points, be a high energy-construct and, at all points, an energy-discharge. So: how is the poet to accomplish same energy, how is he, what is the process by which a poet gets in, at all points energy at least the equivalent of the energy which propelled him in the first place, yet an energy which is peculiar to verse alone and which will be, obviously, also different from the energy which the reader, because he is a third term, will take away?

This is the problem which any poet who departs from closed form is specially confronted by. And it involves a whole series of new recognitions. From the moment he ventures into FIELD COMPOSITION — puts himself in the open — he can go by no track other than the one the poem under hand declares, for itself. Thus he has to behave, and be, instant by instant, aware of some several forces just now beginning to be examined. (It is much more, for example, this push, than simply such a one as Pound put, so wisely, to get us started: "the musical phrase," go by it, boys, rather than by, the metronome.)

(2) is the *principle*, the law which presides conspicuously over such composition, and, when obeyed, is the reason why a projective poem can come into being. It is this: FORM IS NEVER MORE THAN AN EXTENSION OF CONTENT. (Or so it got phrased by one, R. Creeley, and it makes absolute sense to me, with this possible corollary, that right form, in any given poem, is the only and exclusively possible extension of content under hand.) There it is, brothers, sitting there, for USE.

Now (3) the *process* of the thing, how the principle can be made so to shape the energies that the form is accomplished. And I think it can be boiled down to one statement (first pounded into my head by Edward Dahlberg): ONE PERCEPTION

MUST IMMEDIATELY AND DIRECTLY LEAD TO A FUR-
THER PERCEPTION. It means exactly what it says, is a matter
of, at *all* points (even, I should say, of our management of daily
reality as of the daily work) get on with it, keep moving, keep in,
speed, the nerves, their speed, the perceptions, theirs, the acts,
the split second acts, the whole business, keep it moving as fast
as you can, citizen. And if you also set up as a poet, USE USE
USE the process at all points, in any given poem always, always
one perception must must must MOVE, INSTANTER, ON
ANOTHER!

So there we are, fast, there's the dogma. And its excuse, its
usableness, in practice. Which gets us, it ought to get us, inside
the machinery, now, 1950, of how projective verse is made.

If I hammer, if I recall in, and keep calling in, the breath, the
breathing as distinguished from the hearing, it is for cause, it is to
insist upon a part that breath plays in verse which has not (due,
I think, to the smothering of the power of the line by too set a
concept of foot) has not been sufficiently observed or practiced,
but which has to be if verse is to advance to its proper force and
place in the day, now, and ahead. I take it that PROJECTIVE
VERSE teaches, is, this lesson, that that verse will only do in
which a poet manages to register both the acquisitions of his ear
and the pressures of his breath.

Let's start from the smallest particle of all, the syllable. It is
the king and pin of versification, what rules and holds together
the lines, the larger forms, of a poem. I would suggest that verse
here and in England dropped this secret from the late Eliza-
bethans to Ezra Pound, lost it, in the sweetness of meter and
rime, in a honey-head. (The syllable is one way to distinguish the
original success of blank verse, and its falling off, with Milton.)

It is by their syllables that words juxtapose in beauty, by
these particles of sound as clearly as by the sense of the words
which they compose. In any given instance, because there is a
choice of words, the choice, if a man is in there, will be, spon-
taneously, the obedience of his ear to the syllables. The fineness,
and the practice, lie here, at the minimum and source of speech.

> O western wynd, when wilt thou blow
> And the small rain down shall rain
> O Christ that my love were in my arms
> And I in my bed again

It would do no harm, as an act of correction to both prose and verse as now written, if both rime and meter, and, in the quantity words, both sense and sound, were less in the forefront of the mind than the syllable, if the syllable, that fine creature, were more allowed to lead the harmony on. With this warning, to those who would try: to step back here to this place of the elements and minims of language, is to engage speech where it is least careless — and least logical. Listening for the syllables must be so constant and so scrupulous, the exaction must be so complete, that the assurance of the ear is purchased at the highest — 40 hours a day — price. For from the root out, from all over the place, the syllable comes, the figures of, the dance:

> "Is" comes from the Aryan root, *as*, to breathe. The English "not" equals the Sanscrit *na*, which may come from the root *na*, to be lost, to perish. "Be" is from *bhu*, to grow.

I say the syllable, king, and that it is spontaneous, this way: the ear, the ear which has collected, which has listened, the ear, which is so close to the mind that it is the mind's, that it has the mind's speed . . .

it is close, another way: the mind is brother to this sister and is, because it is so close, is the drying force, the incest, the sharpener . . .

it is from the union of the mind and the ear that the syllable is born.

But the syllable is only the first child of the incest of verse (always, that Egyptian thing, it produces twins!). The other child is the LINE. And together, these two, the syllable *and* the line, they make a poem, they make that thing, the — what shall we call it, the Boss of all, the "Single Intelligence." And the line comes (I swear it) from the breath, from the breathing of the man who writes, at the moment that he writes, and thus is, it is here that, the daily work, the WORK, gets in, for only he, the man who writes, can declare, at every moment, the line its metric and its ending — where its breathing, shall come to, termination.

The trouble with most work, to my taking, since the breaking away from traditional lines and stanzas, and from such wholes as, say, Chaucer's *Troilus* or S's *Lear*, is: contemporary workers go lazy RIGHT HERE WHERE THE LINE IS BORN.

Let me put it baldly. The two halves are:
       the HEAD, by way of the EAR, to the SYLLABLE
       the HEART, by way of the BREATH, to the LINE
And the joker? that it is in the 1st half of the proposition that, in composing, one lets-it-rip; and that it is in the 2nd half, surprise, it is the LINE that's the baby that gets, as the poem is getting made, the attention, the control, that it is right here, in the line, that the shaping takes place, each moment of the going.

I am dogmatic, that the head shows in the syllable. The dance of the intellect is there, among them, prose or verse. Consider the best minds you know in this here business: where does the head show, is it not, precise, here, in the swift currents of the syllable? can't you tell a brain when you see what it does, just there? It is true, what the master says he picked up from Confusion: all the thots men are capable of can be entered on the back of a postage stamp. So, is it not the PLAY of a mind we are after, is not that that shows whether a mind is there at all?

And the threshing floor for the dance? Is it anything but the LINE? And when the line has, is, a deadness, is it not a heart which has gone lazy, is it not, suddenly, slow things, similes, say, adjectives, or such, that we are bored by?

For there is a whole flock of rhetorical devices which have now to be brought under a new bead, now that we sight with the line. Simile is only one bird who comes down, too easily. The descriptive functions generally have to be watched, every second, in projective verse, because of their easiness, and thus their drain on the energy which composition by field allows into a poem. *Any* slackness takes off attention, that crucial thing, from the job in hand, from the *push* of the line under hand at the moment, under the reader's eye, in his moment. Observation of any kind is, like argument in prose, properly previous to the act of the poem, and, if allowed in, must be so juxtaposed, apposed, set in, that it does not, for an instant, sap the going energy of the content toward its form.

It comes to this, this whole aspect of the newer problems. (We now enter, actually, the large area of the whole poem, into the FIELD, if you like, where all the syllables and all the lines must be managed in their relations to each other.) It is a matter, finally, of OBJECTS, what they are, what they are inside a poem, how they got there, and, once there, how they are to be used. This is something I want to get to in another way in Part II, but, for the moment, let me indicate this, that every element in an open poem (the syllable, the line, as well as the image, the sound, the sense) must be taken up as participants in the kinetic of the poem just as solidly as we are accustomed to take what we call the objects of reality; and that these elements are to be seen as creating the tensions of a poem just as totally as do those other objects create what we know as the world.

The objects which occur at every given moment of composition (of recognition, we can call it) are, can be, must be treated exactly as they do occur therein and not by any ideas or preconceptions from outside the poem, must be handled as a series of objects in field in such a way that a series of tensions (which they also are) are made to *hold*, and to hold exactly inside the content and the context of the poem which has forced itself, through the poet and them, into being.

Because breath allows *all* the speech-force of language back in (speech is the "solid" of verse, is the secret of a poem's energy), because, now, a poem has, by speech, solidity, everything in it can now be treated as solids, objects, things; and, though insisting upon the absolute difference of the reality of verse from that other dispersed and distributed thing, yet each of these elements of a poem can be allowed to have the play of their separate energies and can be allowed, once the poem is well composed, to keep, as those other objects do, their proper confusions.

Which brings us up, immediately, bang, against tenses, in fact against syntax, in fact against grammar generally, that is, as we have inherited it. Do not tenses, must they not also be kicked around anew, in order that time, that other governing absolute, may be kept, as must the space-tensions of a poem, immediate, contemporary to the acting-on-you of the poem? I would argue that here, too, the LAW OF THE LINE, which projective verse creates, must be hewn to, obeyed, and that the conventions which logic has forced on syntax must be broken open as quietly as must the too set feet of the old line. But an analysis of how far a new poet can stretch the very conventions on which communication by language rests, is too big for these notes, which are meant, I hope it is obvious, merely to get things started.

Let me just throw in this. It is my impression that *all* parts of speech suddenly, in composition by field, are fresh for both sound and percussive use, spring up like unknown, unnamed vegetables in the patch, when you work it, come spring. Now take Hart Crane. What strikes me in him is the singleness of the push to the nominative, his push along that one arc of freshness, the attempt to get back to word as handle. (If logos is word as thought, what is word as noun, as, pass me that, as Newman Shea used to ask, at the galley table, put a jib on the blood, will ya.) But there is a loss in Crane of what Fenollosa is so right about, in syntax, the sentence as first act of nature, as lightning, as passage of force from subject to object, quick, in this case, from Hart to me, in every case, from me to you, the VERB, between two nouns. Does not Hart miss the advantages, by such an isolated push, miss the point of the whole front of syllable, line, field, and what happened to all language, and to the poem, as a result?

I return you now to London, to beginnings, to the syllable, for the pleasures of it, to intermit:

> If music be the food of love, play on,
> give me excess of it, that, surfeiting,
> the appetite may sicken, and so die.
> That strain again. It had a dying fall,
> o, it came over my ear like the sweet sound
> that breathes upon a bank of violets,
> stealing and giving odour.

What we have suffered from, is manuscript, press, the removal of verse from its producer and its reproducer, the voice, a removal by one, by two removes from its place of origin *and* its destination. For the breath has a double meaning which latin had not yet lost.

The irony is, from the machine has come one gain not yet sufficiently observed or used, but which leads directly on toward projective verse and its consequences. It is the advantage of the typewriter that, due to its rigidity and its space precisions, it can, for a poet, indicate exactly the breath, the pauses, the suspensions even of syllables, the juxtapositions even of parts of phrases, which he intends. For the first time the poet has the stave and the bar a musician has had. For the first time he can, without the convention of rime and meter, record the listening he has done to his own speech and by that one act indicate how he would want any reader, silently or otherwise, to voice his work.

It is time we picked the fruits of the experiments of Cummings, Pound, Williams, each of whom has, after his way, already used the machine as a scoring to his composing, as a script to its vocalization. It is now only a matter of the recognition of the conventions of composition by field for us to bring into being an open verse as formal as the closed, with all its traditional advantages.

If a contemporary poet leaves a space as long as the phrase before it, he means that space to be held, by the breath, an equal length of time. If he suspends a word or syllable at the end of a line (this was most Cummings' addition) he means that time to pass that it takes the eye — that hair of time suspended — to pick up the next line. If he wishes a pause so light it hardly separates the words, yet does not want a comma — which is an interruption of the meaning rather than the sounding of the line — follow him when he uses a symbol the typewriter has ready to hand:

"What does not change / is the will to change"

Observe him, when he takes advantage of the machine's multiple margins, to juxtapose:

"Sd he:
          to dream takes no effort
            to think is easy
                to act is more difficult

>   but for a man to act after he has taken thought, this!
>   is the most difficult thing of all"

Each of these lines is a progressing of both the meaning and the
breathing forward, and then a backing up, without a progress or
any kind of movement outside the unit of time local to the idea.

There is more to be said in order that this convention be rec-
ognized, especially in order that the revolution out of which it
came may be so forwarded that work will get published to offset
the reaction now afoot to return verse to inherited forms of
cadence and rime. But what I want to emphasize here, by this
emphasis on the typewriter as the personal and instantaneous
recorder of the poet's work, is the already projective nature of
verse as the sons of Pound and Williams are practicing it. Already
they are composing as though verse was to have the reading its
writing involved, as though not the eye but the ear was to be its
measurer, as though the intervals of its composition could be so
carefully put down as to be precisely the intervals of its regis-
tration. For the ear, which once had the burden of memory to
quicken it (rime & regular cadence were its aids and have merely
lived on in print after the oral necessities were ended) can now
again, that the poet has his means, be the threshold of projective
verse.

II

Which gets us to what I promised, the degree to which the
projective involves a stance toward reality outside a poem as well
as a new stance towards the reality of a poem itself. It is a matter
of content, the content of Homer or of Euripedes or of Seami as
distinct from that which I might call the more "literary" masters.
From the moment the projective purpose of the act of verse is
recognized, the content does — it will — change. If the beginning
and the end is breath, voice in its largest sense, then the material
of verse shifts. It has to. It starts with the composer. The dimen-
sion of his line itself changes, not to speak of the change in his
conceiving, of the matter he will turn to, of the scale in which he
imagines that matter's use. I myself would pose the difference by
a physical image. It is no accident that Pound and Williams both

were involved variously in a movement which got called "objectivism." But that word was then used in some sort of a necessary quarrel, I take it, with "subjectivism." It is now too late to be bothered with the latter. It has excellently done itself to death, even though we are all caught in its dying. What seems to me a more valid formulation for present use is "objectism," a word to be taken to stand for the kind of relation of man to experience which a poet might state as the necessity of a line or a work to be as wood is, to be as clean as wood is as it issues from the hand of nature, to be shaped as wood can be when a man has had his hand to it. Objectism is the getting rid of the lyrical interference of the individual as ego, of the "subject" and his soul, that peculiar presumption by which western man has interposed himself between what he is as a creature of nature (with certain instructions to carry out) and those other creations of nature which we may, with no derogation, call objects. For a man is himself an object, whatever he may take to be his advantages, the more likely to recognize himself as such the greater his advantages, particularly at that moment that he achieves an humilitas sufficient to make him of use.

It comes to this: the use of a man, by himself and thus by others, lies in how he conceives his relation to nature, that force to which he owes his somewhat small existence. If he sprawl, he shall find little to sing but himself, and shall sing, nature has such paradoxical ways, by way of artificial forms outside himself. But if he stays inside himself, if he is contained within his nature as he is participant in the larger force, he will be able to listen, and his hearing through himself will give him secrets objects share. And by an inverse law his shapes will make their own way. It is in this sense that the projective act, which is the artist's act in the larger field of objects, leads to dimensions larger than the man. For a man's problem, the moment he takes speech up in all its fullness, is to give his work his seriousness, a seriousness sufficient to cause the thing he makes to try to take its place alongside the things of nature. This is not easy. Nature works from reverence, even in her destructions (species go down with a crash). But breath is man's special qualification as animal. Sound is a dimension he has extended. Language is one of his proudest acts. And when a poet rests in these as they are in himself (in his physiology, if you like, but the life in him, for all that) then he, if he chooses to speak from these roots, works in that area where nature has given him size, projective size.

It is projective size that the play, *The Trojan Women*, possesses, for it is able to stand, is it not, as its people do, beside the Aegean — and neither Andromache or the sea suffer diminution. In a less "heroic" but equally "natural" dimension Seami causes the Fisherman and the Angel to stand clear in *Hagoromo*. And Homer, who is such an unexamined cliche that I do not think I need to press home in what scale Nausicaa's girls wash their clothes.

Such works, I should argue — and I use them simply because their equivalents are yet to be done — could not issue from men who conceived verse without the full relevance of human voice, without reference to where lines come from, in the individual who writes. Nor do I think it accident that, at this end point of the argument, I should use, for examples, two dramatists and an epic poet. For I would hazard the guess that, if projective verse is practiced long enough, is driven ahead hard enough along the course I think it dictates, verse again can carry much larger material than it has carried in our language since the Elizabethans. But it can't be jumped. We are only at its beginnings, and if I think that the *Cantos* make more "dramatic" sense than do the plays of Mr. Eliot, it is not because I think they have solved the problem but because the methodology of the verse in them points a way by which, one day, the problem of larger content and of larger forms may be solved. Eliot is, in fact, a proof of a present danger, of "too easy" a going on the practice of verse as it has been, rather than as it must be, practiced. There is no question, for example, that Eliot's line, from "Prufrock" on down, has speech-force, is "dramatic," is, in fact, one of the most notable lines since Dryden. I suppose it stemmed immediately to him from Browning, as did so many of Pound's early things. In any case Eliot's line has obvious relations backward to the Elizabethans, especially to the soliloquy. Yet O. M. Eliot is *not* projective. It could even be argued (and I say this carefully, as I

have said all things about the non-projective, having considered
how each of us must save himself after his own fashion and how
much, for that matter, each of us owes to the non-projective, and
will continue to owe, as both go alongside each other) but it
could be argued that it is because Eliot has stayed inside the
non-projective that he fails as a dramatist — that his root is the
mind alone, and a scholastic mind at that (no high *intelletto*
despite his apparent clarities) — and that, in his listenings he has
stayed there where the ear and the mind are, has only gone from
his fine ear outward rather than, as I say a projective poet will,
down through the workings of his own throat to that place where
breath comes from, where breath has its beginnings, where drama
has to come from, where, the coincidence is, all act springs.
(*Poetry New York* No. 3, 1950)

CHARLES OLSON: Letter to Elaine Feinstein

May, 1959

DEAR E. B. FEINSTEIN,

   Your questions catch me athwart any new sense I might
have of a 'poetics.' The best previous throw I made on it was
in *Poetry NY* some years ago on Projective Open or Field verse
versus Closed, with much on the *line* and the *syllable*.

   The basic idea anyway for me is that one, that form is never
any more than an extension of content — a non-literary sense,
certainly. I believe in Truth! (Wahrheit) My sense is that beauty
(Schönheit) better stay in the thingitself: das Ding — Ja! — macht
ring (the attack, I suppose, on the 'completed thought,' or, the
Idea, yes? Thus the syntax question: what is the sentence?)

   The only advantage of speech rhythms (to take your 2nd
question 1st) is illiteracy: the non-literary, exactly in Dante's
sense of the value of the vernacular over grammar — that speech
as a communicator is prior to the individual and is picked up as
soon as and with ma's milk . . . he said nurse's tit. In other words,
speech rhythm only as anyone of us has it, if we come on from the
line of force as piped in as well as from piping we very much have

done up to this moment — if we have, from, that 'common' not grammatical source. The 'source' question is damned interesting today — as Shelley saw, like Dante, that, if it comes in, that way, primary, from Ma there is then a double line of chromosomic giving (A) the inherent speech (thought, power) the 'species,' that is; and (B) the etymological: this is where I find 'foreign' languages so wild, especially the Indo-European line with the advantage now that we have Hittite to back up to. I couldn't stress enough on this speech rhythm question the pay-off in *traction* that a non-literate, non-commercial and non-historical constant daily experience of tracking *any* word, practically, one finds oneself using, back along its line of force to Anglo-Saxon, Latin, Greek, and out to Sanskrit, or now, if someone wld do it, some 'dictionary' of roots which wld include Hittite at least.

I'll give in a minute the connection of this to form if capturable in the poem, that is, the usual 'poetics' biz, but excuse me if I hammer shortly the immense help archaeology, and some specific linguistic scholarship — actually, from my experience mainly of such completely different 'grammars' as North American Indians present, in the present syntax hangup: like Hopi. But also Trobriand space-Time premises. And a couple of North California tongues, like Yani. But it is the archaeology *behind* our own history proper, Hittite, for the above reason, but now that Canaanite is known (Ugaritic) and Sumerian, and the direct connection of the Celts to the Aryans and so to the Achaean-Trojan forbears which has *slowed* and opened the speech language thing as we got it, now, in our hands, to make it do more form than how form got set by Sappho & Homer, and hasn't changed much since.

I am talking from a new 'double axis': the replacement of the Classical-representational by the *primitive-abstract* ((if this all sounds bloody German, excuse the weather, it's from the east today, and wet)). I mean of course not at all primitive in that stupid use of it as opposed to civilized. One means it now as 'primary,' as how one finds anything, pick it up as one does new — fresh/first. Thus one is equal across history forward and back, and it's all levy, as present is, but sd that way, one states . . . a different space-time. Content, in other words, is also shifted

— at least from humanism, as we've had it since the Indo-Europeans got their fid in there (circum 1500 BC) ((Note: I'm for 'em on the muse level, and agin 'em on the content, or 'Psyche' side.

Which gets me to yr 1st question — "the use of the Image." "the Image" (wow, that you capitalize it makes *sense*: it is *all* we had (post-circum *The Two Noble Kinsmen*), as we had a sterile grammar (an insufficient 'sentence') we had analogy only: images, no matter how learned or how simple: even Burns say, allowing etc and including Frost! Comparison. Thus representation was never off the dead-spot of description. Nothing was *happening* as of the poem itself — ding and zing or something. It was referential to reality. And that a p. poor crawling actuarial 'real' — good enough to keep banks and insurance companies, plus mediocre governments etc. But not Poetry's *Truth* like my friends from the American Underground cry and spit in the face of 'Time.'

The Image also has to be taken by a double: that is, if you bisect a parabola you get an enantiomorph (The Hopi say what goes on over there isn't happening here therefore it isn't the same: pure 'localism' of space-time, but such localism can now be called: what you find out for yrself (*'istorin*) keeps all accompanying circumstance.

The basic trio wld seem to be: topos/typos/tropos, 3 in 1. The 'blow' hits here, and me, 'bent' as born and of sd one's own decisions for better or worse (allowing clearly, by Jesus Christ, that you do love or go down)
if this sounds 'mystical' I plead so. Wahrheit: I find the contemporary substitution of society for the cosmos captive and deathly.

Image, therefore, is vector. It carries the trinity via the double to the single form which one makes oneself able, if so, to issue from the 'content' (multiplicity: originally, and repetitively, chaos — Tiamat: wot the Hindo-Europeans knocked out by giving the Old Man (Juice himself) all the lightning.

The Double, then, (the 'home'/heartland/of the post-Mesopotamians AND the post-Hindo Eees:

At the moment it comes out   the Muse ('world'
                             ——————————————
                             the Psyche (the 'life'

You wld know already I'm buggy on say the Proper Noun, so much so I wld take it Pun is Rime, all from tope/type/trope, that built in is the connection, in each of us, to Cosmos, and if one taps, via psyche, plus a 'true' adherence of Muse, one does reveal 'Form'

in other words the 'right' (wahr-) proper noun, however apparently idiosyncratic, if 'tested' by one's own experience (out plus in) ought to yield along this phylo-line (as the speech thing, above) because — *decently* what one oneself can know, as well as what the word *means* — ontogenetic.

The other part is certainly 'landscape' — the other part of the double of Image to 'noun.' By Landscape I mean what 'narrative'; scene; event; climax; crisis; hero; development; posture; all that *meant* — all the substantive of what we call literary. To animate the scene today: wow: You say "orientate me." Yessir. Place it!

again

I drag it back: Place (topos, plus one's own bent plus what one *can* know, makes it possible to name.

O.K. I'm running out of appetite. Let this swirl — a bit like Crab Nebula — do for now. And please come back on me if you are interested. *Yrs.*

CHARLES OLSON

ROBERT DUNCAN: Pages from a Notebook

1.

ON REVISIONS. In one way or another to live in the swarm of human speech. This is not to seek perfection but to draw honey or poetry out of all things. After Freud, we are aware that unwittingly we achieve our form. It is, whatever our mastery, the inevitable use we make of the speech that betrays to ourselves and to our hunters (our readers) the spore of what we are becoming.

I study what I write as I study out any mystery. A poem, mine or anothers, is an occult document, a body awaiting vivisection, analysis, X-rays.

My revisions are my new works, each poem a revision of what

has gone before. In-sight. Re-vision.

I have learned to mistrust my judgment upon what I have done. Too often what I thot inadequate proved later richer than I knew; what I thot slavishly derivative proved to be "mine."

ON QUALITY AND POEMS. A longing grows to return to the open composition in which the accidents and imperfections of speech might awake intimations of human being.

He searches for quality like a jeweler — and he is dependent one suspects on whether his emotion (which he polishes) is a diamond or not. That is, he would attempt to cut any stone diamond-wise, to force his emotion to the test. He would discover much if he also would cut paper-crowns or scatter the pebbles and litter of a mind wherever he goes.

ON THE SECRET DOCTRINE. There are neglected, even scornd, books in which one begins to find the Gnosis of the modern world. These stories (Macdonald called his early novel *Phantastes*), fantasies, disclose for the explorer the thread of wisdom. The world of childhood created by Hans Christian Andersen, George Macdonald or L. Frank Baum. The power of these works lies not solely in their images of the subconscious, in their being our inherited dreams. But there is another source of mystery, of true "magic" — for these hold a kernel, a secret of the soul. These phantasies are re-inventions of the soul.

Where there is soul, all the world and body become the soul's adventure or trial. The body is real and all real things perish. But realities give birth to unrealities. As Plato discovered, or St Augustine discoverd in the City of God, unrealities, fantasies, mere ideas, can never be destroyd. Soul is the body's dream of its continuity in eternity — a wraith of mind. Poetry is the very life of the soul: the body's discovery that it can dream. And perish into its own imagination.

Why should one's art then be an achievement? Why not, more, an adventure? On one hand one produces only what one knows. Well, what else can one accomplish. The thrill is just that one did not know one knew it. But now I like to wander about in my work, writing so rapidly that I might overlook manipulations and design; the poetic experience advancing as far as one can (as far as one dares) toward an adventure. All design here is a recovery if it belongs to ones art; a discovery if it belongs to ones adventuring courage. Courage? Courage to travel on roads of no glory; to dwell in the storm which Shakespeare saw in the idiot's mind; a poor boob; to be even inarticulately simple.

ON PUBLISHING. Could it be that when poetry no longer has any cultural value; when poetry no longer furnishes the gentleman's library with its elegance or the English professor with his livelihood; that a poetry will remain, cherished only by unimportant people who love or adventure.

Poems are now, when they are "ours," fountains: as in Oz, of life or of forgetfulness of self-life. What we expected poetry to be when we were children. A world of our own marvels. Doors of language. Adoration. We dreamed not originally of publishing. What a paltry concern. No child of imagination would center there. But we dreamd of song and the reality of romance.

It is the marvellous of the *Pisan Cantos* that reassures me. Even after a lifetime of the struggle for publication and importance, because of his love for poetry, for song and for Romance, Pound dwells in the innermost enchantment of mind. He has been initiated into a world transformd and inhabited by spirits.

ON SUFFERING. I once dreaded happiness, for I thot that to be happy was to be contented. Coleridge writes in his *Table Talk* on the great evil of too entire domestication.

The domestic world might have been our achievement. The poet, the adventurer, dreads achievements, eschews rest. But for the imagination all "achievements" are unreally worlds; apparent entireties of domestication are in themselves undomesticated Africas. Our love is both the storm and the hearth of our emotional being.

I once dreaded happiness, for I thot that ones being, ones art, sprang full grown from suffering. But I found that one suffers happiness in that sense. There is no magic of poetry that will not remain magic because one has sought wisdom. The wisdom of the hearth is, one finds, an other magic. It was the disappearance of dread itself that made suffering unessential — as, indeed, happiness had become unessential.

And then (I am not domestic by nature) the home is the sheerest product of my imagination, a triumph of soul — at every point magically imaginary. I mean, of course, that happiness itself is a forest in which we are bewilderd, run wild, or dwell, like Robin Hood, outlawd and at home.

ON SCIENCE. Croce thinks with Vico that poetry is a kind of thot primitive to science, and that the imagination creates in poetry an inarticulate ground from which particulars and exactitudes are distinguishd. But poetry is not primitive to anything but poetry. Only ideas of poetry develop from the ideas of poetry. For the poet, science seems like poetry itself a primitive conceiving of things.

Medicine can cure the body. But soul, poetry, is capable of living in, longing for, choosing illness. Only the most fanatic researcher upon cancer could share with the poet the concept that cancer is a flower, an adventure, an intrigue with life.

The magnificence of Freud is that he never seeks to cure an individual of being himself. He seeks only that the individual may come to know himself, to be aware. It is an underlying faith in Freud that every "patient" is Man Himself, and that every "disease" is his revelation.

ON CHRISTIANITY. It is true that our salvation lies in Christ. That is, in the god who is crucified (lost) and then resurrected (saved). The outrage of the Christians upon humanity is that they sought to impose salvation as the sole adventure of life. Christian fury loosed upon those who do not desire to be saved thru Christ is the very hell, exactly the hell, which they condemn all non-Christians to. At times I would rather be burnd or physically tortured for my disinterest in or disavowal of salvation than to be subjected to Xtian argument. "It is not my intention to enter the city of man's salvation."

Yet one must honor Christ as one honors salvation. This non-Christian's view is just that he would not, in honoring Christ, dishonor or displace any of the other gods, dreams, goddesses, eternities of human vision. If one views all religions as human inventions, projections and pageants of the imagination, then Christ may be included, adored; one may even, seeking salvation there, come into heaven without casting a world into hell.

But if Christ, heaven or hell are real, in the sense that Christian belief demands, then we are all damnd. And I should knowingly choose an eternity of hell fire. For I find many gods more loveable than Jehovah, and I find Lao-Tse and Buddha more wise; and Confucius more reasonable than Christ.

ON CHILDREN ART AND LOVE. Created by the imagination, the parent's love might well have gone along with the child, but the parent, we notice, more often refuses love there; holds out in loving. Parental love goes only as the child goes along with the parent.

This is the crippling of the imagination or rather its starvation. The world of wonders is limited at last to the parent's will (for will prospers where imagination is thwarted); intellectual appetites become no more than ambitions; curious minds become consciences; love, hatred, affection and cruelty cease to be responses and become convictions. And the adventure of life becomes a self-improvement course.

It is the key to our own inner being that the child offers us in his self-absorption. He would eagerly share himself with us, were we not so determined that he be heir to our achievement.

Human learning is not a fulfillment but a process, not a development but an activity. Andersen, Macdonald, Baum tell us that wisdom belongs to the child as well as to us. But we have turned from, and indeed "willingly" forsaken, wisdom for what we might acquire.

Every moment of life is an attempt to come to life. Poetry is a "participation," a oneness. Can the ambitious artist who seeks success, perfection, mastery, ever get nearer to the universe, can he ever know "more" or feel "more" than a child may?

To be a child is not an affair of how old one is. "Child" like "angel" is a concept, a realm of possible being. Many children have never been allowed to stray into childhood. Sometimes I dream of at last becoming a child.

A child can be an artist, he can be a poet. But can a child be a banker? It is in such an affair as running a bank or managing a store or directing a war that adulthood counts, an experienced mind. It is in the world of these pursuits that "experience" counts. One, two, three, times and divided by. The secret of genius lies in this: that here experience is not made to count. Where experience knows nothing of counting, it creates only itself out of itself.

ON LIONS. The Christians thot of the lion as Christ the King: because the lion was a terrible power and at the same time a beast of great beauty.

For me, the Lion is the Child, the unfetterd intellect that knows in his nobility none of the convictions and dogmas which human mind inflicts itself with — what is the human desire to humiliate even its own being?

For me, the Lion is sexual appetite that knows no contradiction within itself. The dream of myself as Emperor of the World. Laura Riding suggests that in Story one is Emperor of the World, creator of all things; that wisdom comes in abdicating. The freedom of the individual lies in his institution of anarchy where before he was sole ruler.

2.

NOTES MIDWAY ON MY FAUST

Faust is right when he sez everything is Truth. But each of us finds everything beyond his conception. And even of the everything with which we compose our minds we have constructed designs of which we knew nothing, edifices of much that we had named lies we have fitted, ourselves, into monuments of eternal truth.

The malice of churches, the malice of witches: how can they exceed each other? The wisdom of the parent, the wisdom of the child: how can they exceed each other?

The only thing a student can learn from a teacher is what he can teach his teacher. What can a teacher learn from a student?

My *Faust* is not a very divine Comedy. At times in writing it I am dismayd by the cheap turns that seem to suffice: but if one must have revelation, one must accept that what is reveald may not be disgraceful in any glamorous sense.

Writing is compounded of wisdom and intuition. Faust seeks to wrench himself free from the world of wisdom and to achieve pure intuition. My lot is not Faust's lot, but the play's lot: this conflict unresolved. But then the trouble of the soul is not in this carcass a tug of war or a choice of two worlds. Everywhere dissenting, contradictory voices speak up, I find. I don't seek a synthesis, but a melee. It is only as I have somewhat accepted my inconsequential necessities that I have been able to undertake a play. But a play is a play here — a prolongd charged aimless, constantly aimd, play ground. Only play for me did not mean slides, games, teeter-totters and tots; but moods, cities and desires. In the jungle of words and the life in doubts afterwards, I have discoverd certain bright courses after my own heart: not to be saved; and then to portray carnal pleasures that the world denies, and we deny ourselves. Well, part of the drama of holding back and of immersing oneself is the sheer sexual set-to of marriage and our dreams. There is no contradiction between the two, but we set them to in order to avoid the perplexity, the "peril of our souls" in freedom. The problem is that we dread all inconsequential experience; our taboo is at root against unintelligible passions.

I have "selected" my works, weeded out the poetry which is not all of a tone, and composed a works that has a remote consistency. But resurrect everything: and one will discover my true book — no pleasure for aesthetes. A composite indecisive literature, attempting the rhapsodic, the austere, the mysterious, the sophisticated, the spontaneous, "higglety-pigglety" as Emory Lowenthal sez.

The host of my heros, gods and models betray an unsettled spirit. (Enter two Devils and the Clown runs up and down crying) Two Devils? What a simple distraction.

Where I am ambitious only to emulate, imitate, reconstrue, approximate, duplicate: Ezra Pound, Gertrude Stein, Joyce, Virginia Woolf, Dorothy Richardson, Wallace Stevens, D. H. Lawrence, Edith Sitwell, Cocteau, Mallarmé, Marlowe, St. John of the Cross, Yeats, Jonathan Swift, Jack Spicer, Céline, Charles Henri Ford, Rilke, Lorca, Kafka, Arp, Max Ernst, St.-John Perse, Prévert, Laura Riding, Apollinaire, Brecht, Shakespeare, Ibsen, Strindberg, Joyce Cary, Mary Butts, Freud, Dali, Spenser, Stravinsky, William Carlos Williams and John Gay.

Higglety-pigglety: Euripides and Gilbert. The Strawhat Reviewers, Goethe (of the *Autobiography* — I have never read *Faust*) and H.D.

3.

IN COMPLETE AGREEMENT ON WRITING

THE HIVE. Charlemagne, emperor of the world, sleeping in his chamber surrounded by his golden bees, the fleur de lys. Words, the royal apis. The name, immortality, a noun, prerogative of kings. And the comb of unknowing design. The hive of human being: it is this in part we work in composing. Poets, we hear languages like the murmuring of bees. Swarm in the head. Where the honey is stored. An instinct for words where, like bees dancing, in language there is a communication below the threshold of language.

There is a natural mystery in poetry. We do not understand all that we render up to understanding.

WORKING. I notice basic states, senses for language: all of them possibilities for work. Surety, "the line learnd in the hand"; inspiration, "when they seemingly arrange themselves"; confusion, "I do not seek a synthesis but a melee"; violence, "Driven by the language itself, alive with such forces, / he violates, desiring to move / the deepest sound."; intoxication, "losing so many values / just for that sound"; sight, "She hesitates upon the verge of sound. She waits upon a sounding impossibility, upon the edge of poetry." Despair, grief, anger, fear — invaluable preparations for being seized by the language to work purposes we had not contemplated.

I make poetry as other men make war or make love or make states or revolutions: to exercise my faculties at large. (*The Artist's View*, No. 5, 1953)

ROBERT CREELEY: To Define

The process of definition is the intent of the poem, or is to that sense — "Peace comes of communication." Poetry stands in no need of any sympathy, or even goodwill. One acts from bottom, the root is the purpose quite beyond any kindness.

A poetry can act on this: "A poem is energy transferred from where the poet got it (he will have some several causations), by way of the poem itself to, all the way over to, the reader." One breaks the line of aesthetics, or that outcrop of a general division of knowledge. A sense of the KINETIC impels recognition of force. Force is, and therefore stays.

The means of a poetry are, perhaps, related to Pound's sense of the *increment of association;* usage coheres value. Tradition is an aspect of what anyone is now thinking, — not what someone once thought. We make with what we have, and in this way anything is worth looking at. A tradition becomes inept when it blocks the necessary conclusion; it says we have felt nothing, it implies others have felt more.

A poetry denies its end in any *descriptive* act, I mean any act which leaves the attention outside the poem. Our anger cannot exist usefully without its objects, but a description of them is also a perpetuation. There is that confusion — one wants the thing to act on, and yet hates it. *Description* does nothing, it includes the object, — it neither hates nor loves.

If one can junk these things, of the content which relates only to denial, the negative, the impact of dissolution, — act otherwise, on other things. There is no country. Speech is an assertion of one man, by one man. "Therefore each speech having its own character the poetry it engenders will be peculiar to that speech also in its own intrinsic form." (*Nine American Poets,* 1953)

ROBERT CREELEY: Olson & Others: Some Orts for the Sports

Where writing will go to, what comes next, or the answers to any of those profoundly speculative questions bred of Saturday afternoons in comfortable surroundings, etc., — god alone knows. Where it's all come from is another such question, and a few sentences may serve as well to answer it as any more documented or descriptive account. For example, in 1950 Cid Corman, the subsequent editor of *Origin*, had a radio program in Boston called *This Is Poetry*, which by a fluke of air waves I heard one night in Littleton, N.H. The guest was Richard Wilbur, who read with such graceful accents I was filled with envious ambition to read also, although I had none of his qualifications; and some weeks later, after correspondence with Cid which that night began, I convinced him I was good enough, or he was tolerant enough, and so I read one Saturday night while I was in Boston showing chickens at the Boston Poultry Show. Literary history is like that, and this event would be altogether unnotable, were it not that a magazine which I then tried to start (with much the same motives), but could not get printed, was absorbed in the first two issues of Cid's *Origin* — and that among the contacts so contributed were Charles Olson, Paul Blackburn and Denise Levertov.

Charles Olson is central to any description of literary 'climate' dated 1958. I don't think any of those involved knew, at the time, he had written *Call Me Ishmael*; and I remember my own dumbfounded reception of that book — from a man I had assumed to be sharing my own position of unpublished hopefulness. The Olson I knew, and wrote to daily if possible, was the one whose *Y & X* had been published by Caresse Crosby's Black Sun Press, who had among other poems in manuscript a long one called *The Kingfishers*, and whose own letters were of such energy and calculation that they constituted a practical 'college' of stimulus and information. Some of this last can be seen in an article he published at that time, partly derived from letters as it happens, which he called "Projective Verse" (*Poetry New York*, No. 3, 1950). He outlines there the premise of "composition by field" (the value of which William Carlos Williams was to emphasize by reprinting it in part in his own *Autobiography*); and defines a basis for structure in the poem in terms of its '*kinetics*' ("the poem itself must, at all points, be a high energy-construct and, at all points, an energy discharge . . ."), the '*principle*' of its writing (form is never more than an extension of content), and the 'process' ("ONE PERCEPTION MUST IMMEDIATELY AND DIRECTLY LEAD TO A FURTHER PERCEPTION . . ."). He equally distinguishes between breathing and hearing, as these relate to the line: "And the line comes (I swear it) from the breath, from the breathing of the man who writes, at that moment that he writes . . ."

Some distinctions are now possible. Verse today splits in point of several emphases, and this is reasonable enough. Most familiar are those poets who have looked to a re-informing of traditional structures, at times with great ability. It is not at all a question of falling back into the same old sofa, etc., but to manage a use of that which the man back of you has given in such fashion that you will both honor him and those differences which the nature of time seems to insist upon. There are also those men, most definitive in the '30's, who extend to their writing of verse concerns which haunt them, again reasonably enough, in the other areas of their living.[1] They are in this way poets of 'content,' and their poems argue images of living to which the content of their poems points. They argue the poem as a means to recognition, a signboard as it were, not in itself a structure of 'recognition' or — better — cognition itself. Some, then, would not only not hear what Olson was saying, but would even deny, I think, the relevance of his concerns. The great preoccupation with symbology and levels of image in poetry insisted upon by contemporary criticism has also meant a further bias for this not-hearing, since Olson's emphasis is put upon prosody, not interpretation.

Those who were sympathetic, who felt as Dr. Williams did ("it is as if the whole area lifted . . ."), were those equally concerned with prosody. "Prosody," said Pound, "is the articulation of the total sound of a poem." This is an obviously difficult and

[1] Kenneth Fearing would be one man I'd think of in this connection, though that may be simply my own circumstances. Names are deceptive in any case, since they tend to develop a false chronology, granted men change. The point is that the *sociology* which the thirties develops is present in poetry also, both as methodology and sense of purpose. The method and concern is felt later in Ciardi, Shapiro, et al. It's also Weldon Kees, etc. The contrast is the early work of Rexroth, Carl Rakosi, and very certainly Zukofsky.

painstaking requirement; and, again, a division of method appears between those who make use of traditional forms, either for discipline or solution, and those who, as Olson, go "By ear . . . ," by, in effect, the complexly determined response to work literally in hand. Robert Duncan's discussion precludes mine here; I refer you to that ("Notes On Poetics Regarding Olson's *Maximus*," *Black Mountain Review*, No. 6, 1956). But, to suggest its relevance here, Duncan writes, using the image of "The coming into life of the child . . .":

> . . . that the breath-blood circulation be gaind, an *interjection!* the levels of the passions and inspiration in *phrases;* second, that focus be gaind, a *substantive*, the level of vision; and third, the complex of muscular gains that are included in taking hold and balancing, *verbs*, but more, the *movement of the language*, the *level* of the ear, the hand, and the foot. All these incorporated in *measure*.[2]

You must read, then, to know what is happening. All poets seem to suffer certain things in common, as certainly all men do: difficulties of self-support, or, if a family is involved, some means for sufficiencies in common, and the dignity any man has right to claim, granted it has never been his purpose to ask for it. We all of us live in an increasingly pinched world, pinched emotionally, pinched referentially — despite the fact the moon comes closer. 'How shall I love you? Let me count the ways' is too often a proposed calculus of possibilities; and that, alone, is no good. In despite, relationships, here as elsewhere, continue, serving a common need, for survival and growth. The issue is the poem, a single event — to which, as to the Battle of Gettysburg, or the Pan American Highway, many men may well contribute — "aperiens tibi animum . . ." Like, you dig the 85th Canto? Like — that's all. (1958; *Big Table* #4, 1960)

DENISE LEVERTOV:

I believe poets are instruments on which the power of poetry plays.

[2] Italics mine. Duncan has given, *in fine*, the steps of a poetic *grammar*.

But they are also *makers,* craftsmen: It is given to the seer to see, but it is then his responsibility to communicate what he sees, that they who cannot see may see, since we are 'members one of another.'

I believe every space and comma is a living part of the poem and has its function, just as every muscle and pore of the body has its function. And the way the lines are broken is a functioning part essential to the poem's life.

I believe content determines form, and yet that content is discovered only *in* form. Like everything living, it is a mystery. The revelation of form itself can be a deep joy; yet I think form *as means* should never obtrude, whether from intention or carelessness, between the reader and the essential force of the poem, it must be so fused with that force.

I do not believe that a violent imitation of the horrors of our times is the concern of poetry. Horrors are taken for granted. Disorder is ordinary. People in general take more and more 'in their stride' — hides grow thicker. I long for poems of an inner harmony in utter contrast to the chaos in which they exist. Insofar as poetry has a social function it is to awaken sleepers by other means than shock.

I think of Robert Duncan and Robert Creeley as the chief poets among my contemporaries. (1959)

LAWRENCE FERLINGHETTI:

. . . I am put down by Beat natives who say I cannot be beat and "committed" at the same time, like in this poem ["Tentative Description of a Dinner Given to Promote the Impeachment of President Eisenhower"], man. True, true, William Seward Burroughs said, "Only the dead and the junkie don't care — they are inscrutable." I'm neither. Man. And this is where all the tall droopy corn about the Beat Generation and its being "existentialist" is as phoney as a four-dollar piece of lettuce. Because Jean-Paul Sartre cares and has always hollered that the writer especially should be committed. *Engagement* is one of his favorite dirty words. He would give the horse laugh to the idea of Disengagement and the Art of the Beat Generation. Me too. And that Abominable Snowman of modern poetry, Allen Ginsberg, would probably say the same. Only the dead are disengaged. And the wiggy nihilism of the Beat hipster, if carried to its natural conclusion, actually means the death of the creative artist himself. While the "non-commitment" of the artist is itself a suicidal and deluded variation of this same nihilism. (Fantasy 7004, 1959)

JACK SPICER: Letter to Lorca

DEAR LORCA,

I would like to make poems out of real objects. The lemon to be a lemon that the reader could cut or squeeze or taste — a real lemon like a newspaper in a collage is a real newspaper. I would like the moon in my poems to be a real moon, one which could be suddenly covered with a cloud that has nothing to do with the poem — a moon utterly independent of images. The imagination pictures the real. I would like to point to the real, disclose it, to make a poem that has no sound in it but the pointing of a finger.

We have both tried to be independent of images (you from the start and I only when I grew old enough to tire of trying to make things connect), to make things visible rather than to make pictures of them (phantasia non imaginari). How easy it is in erotic musings or in the truer imagination of a dream to invent a beautiful boy. How difficult to take a boy in a blue bathing suit that I have watched as casually as a tree and to make him visible in a poem as a tree is visible, not as an image or a picture but as something alive — caught forever in the structure of words. Live moons, live lemons, live boys in bathing suits. The poem is a collage of the real.

But things decay, reason argues. Real things become garbage. The piece of lemon you shellac to the canvas begins to develop a mold, the newspaper tells of incredibly ancient events in forgotten slang, the boy becomes a grandfather. Yes, but the garbage of the real still reaches out into the current world making *its* objects, in turn, visible — lemon calls to lemon, newspaper to newspaper, boy to boy. As things decay they bring their equivalents into being.

Things do not connect; they correspond. That is what makes it possible for a poet to translate real objects, to bring them across language as easily as he can bring them across time. That tree you saw in Spain is a tree I could never have seen in California, that lemon has a different smell and a different taste, BUT the answer is this — every place and every time has a real object to *co-respond* with your real object — that lemon may become this lemon, or it may even become this piece of seaweed, or this particular color of gray in this ocean. One does not need to imagine that lemon; one needs to discover it.

Even these letters. They *co-respond* with something (I don't know what) that you have written (perhaps as unapparently as that lemon corresponds to this piece of seaweed) and, in turn, some future poet will write something which *co-responds* to them. That is how we dead men write to each other.

Love,

JACK

(*After Lorca,* 1957)

JACK KEROUAC:

Add alluvials to the end of your line when all is exhausted but something has to be said for some specified irrational reason, since reason can never win out, because poetry is NOT a science. The rhythm of how you decide to 'rush' yr statement determines the rhythm of the poem, whether it is a poem in verse-separated lines, or an endless one-line poem called prose . . . (with its paragraphs). So let there be no equivocation about statement, and if you think this is not hard to do, try it. You'll find that your lies are heavier than your intentions. And your confessions lighter than Heaven.

Otherwise, who wants to read?

I myself have difficulty covering up my bullshit lies. (1959)

ALLEN GINSBERG: Notes for *Howl* and Other Poems

By 1955 I wrote poetry adapted from prose seeds, journals, scratchings, arranged by phrasing or breath groups into little short-line patterns according to ideas of measure of American speech I'd picked up from W. C. Williams' imagist preoccupations. I suddenly turned aside in San Francisco, unemployment compensation leisure, to follow my romantic inspiration — Hebraic-Melvillian bardic breath. I thought I wouldn't write a *poem*, but just write what I wanted to without fear, let my imagination go, open secrecy, and scribble magic lines from my real mind — sum up my life — something I wouldn't be able to show anybody, write for my own soul's ear and a few other golden ears. So the first line of *Howl*, "I saw the best minds," etc. the whole first section typed out madly in one afternoon, a huge sad comedy of wild phrasing, meaningless images for the beauty of abstract poetry of mind running along making awkward combinations like Charlie Chaplin's walk, long saxophone-like chorus lines I knew Kerouac would hear *sound* of — taking off from his own inspired prose line really a new poetry.

I depended on the word "who" to keep the beat, a base to keep measure, return to and take off from again onto another streak of invention: "who lit cigarettes in boxcars boxcars boxcars," continuing to prophesy what I really knew despite the drear consciousness of the world: "who were visionary indian angels." Have I really been attacked for this sort of joy? So the poem got serious, I went on to what my imagination believed true to Eternity (for I'd had a beatific illumination years before during which I'd heard Blake's ancient voice & saw the universe unfold in my brain), & what my memory could reconstitute of the data of celestial experience.

But how sustain a long line in poetry (lest it lapse into prosaic)? It's natural inspiration of the moment that keeps it moving, disparate thinks put down together, shorthand notations of visual imagery, juxtapositions of hydrogen juke-box — abstract haikus sustain the mystery & put iron poetry back into the line: the last line of *Sunflower Sutra* is the extreme, one stream of single word associations, summing up. Mind is shapely, Art is shapely. Meaning Mind practiced in spontaneity invents forms in its own image & gets to Last Thoughts. Loose ghosts wailing for body try to invade the bodies of living men. I hear ghostly Academics in Limbo screeching about form.

Ideally each line of *Howl* is a single breath unit. Tho in this recording it's not pronounced so, I was exhausted at climax of 3 hour Chicago reading with Corso & Orlovsky. My breath is long — that's the Measure, one physical — mental inspiration of thought contained in the elastic of a breath. It probably bugs Williams now, but it's a natural consequence, my own heightened conversation, not cooler average-dailytalk short breath. I got to mouth more madly this way.

So these poems are a series of experiments with the formal organization of the long line. Explanations follow. I realized at the time that Whitman's form had rarely been further explored (improved on even) in the U.S. Whitman always a mountain too vast to be seen. Everybody assumes (with Pound?) (except Jeffers) that his line is a big freakish uncontrollable necessary prosaic goof. No attempt's been made to use it in the light of early XX Century organization of new speech-rhythm prosody to *build up* large organic structures.

I had an apt on Nob Hill, got high on Peyote, & saw an image of the robot skullface of Moloch in the upper stories of a big hotel glaring into my window; got high weeks later again, the Visage was still there in red smokey downtown Metropolis, I wandered down Powell Street muttering, "Moloch Moloch" all night & wrote *Howl* II nearly intact in cafeteria at foot of Drake Hotel, deep in the hellish vale. Here the long line is used as a stanza form broken within into exclamatory units punctuated by a base repetition, Moloch.

The rhythmic paradigm for Part III was conceived & half-written same day as the beginning of *Howl*, I went back later & filled it out. Part I, a lament for the Lamb in America with instances of remarkable lamblike youths; Part II names the monster of mental consciousness that preys on the Lamb; Part III a litany of affirmation of the Lamb in its glory: "O starry spangled shock of Mercy." The structure of Part III, pyramidal, with a graduated longer response to the fixed base . . . .

A lot of these forms developed out of an extreme rhapsodic wail I once heard in a madhouse. Later I wondered if short quiet lyrical poems could be written using the long line. *Cottage in Berkeley* & *Supermarket in California* (written same day) fell in place later that year. Not purposely, I simply followed my Angel in the course of compositions.

What if I just simply wrote, in long units & broken short lines, spontaneously noting prosaic realities mixed with emotional up-surges, solitaries? *Transcription of Organ Music* (sensual data), strange writing which passes from prose to poetry & back, like the mind.

What about poem with rhythmic buildup power equal to *Howl* without use of repeated base to sustain it? *The Sunflower Sutra* (composition time 20 minutes, me at desk scribbling, Kerouac at cottage door waiting for me to finish so we could go off somewhere party) did that, it surprised me, one long Who . . .

Last, the Proem to *Kaddish* (NY 1959 work) — finally, com-pletely free composition, the long line breaking up within itself into short staccato breath units — notations of one spontaneous phrase after another linked within the line by dashes mostly: the long line now perhaps a variable stanzaic unit, measuring groups of related ideas, marking them — a method of notation. Ending with a hymn in rhythm similar to the synagogue death lament. Passing into dactyllic? says Williams? Perhaps not: at least the ears hears itself in Promethian natural measure, not in mechan-ical count of accent. . . .

A word on Academies; poetry has been attacked by an ig-norant & frightened bunch of bores who don't understand how it's made, & the trouble with these creeps is they wouldn't know Poetry if it came up and buggered them in broad daylight.

A word on the Politicians: my poetry is Angelical Ravings, & has nothing to do with dull materialistic vagaries about who should shoot who. The secrets of individual imagination — which are transconceptual & non-verbal — I mean unconditioned Spirit — are not for sale to this consciousness, are of no use to this world, except perhaps to make it shut its trap & listen to the music of the Spheres. Who denies the music of the spheres denies poetry, denies man, & spits on Blake, Shelley, Christ & Buddha. Meanwhile have a ball. The universe is a new flower. America will be discovered. Who wants a war against roses will have it.

Fate tells big lies, & the gay Creator dances on his own body in Eternity. (Fantasy 7006, 1959)

JAMES SCHUYLER: Poet and Painter Overture

New York poets, except I suppose the color blind, are affected most by the floods of paint in whose crashing surf we all scramble.

Artists in any genre are of course drawn to the dominant art movement in the place where they live; in New York it is painting. Not to get mixed up in it would be a kind of blinders-on regression, like the campus dry-heads who wishfully descend tum-ti-tumming from Yeats out of Graves with a big kiss for Mother England (subject of a famous Boecklin painting: just when did the last major English poet die? not that Rossetti isn't fun . . .). The big thing happening at home is a nuisance, a publicity plot, a cabal; and please don't track the carpet. They don't even excoriate American painting; they pretend it isn't there.

Considering the painters' popular "I kissed thee ere I killed thee" attitude toward Paris, admiring, envious and spurning, and the fact (Willa Cather pointed it out a long time ago) that the best American writing is French rather than English oriented, it's not surprising that New York poets play their own variations on how Apollinaire, Reverdy, Jacob, Eluard, Breton took to the School of Paris. Americans are, really, mightily unFrench, and so criticism gets into it: John Ashbery, Barbara Guest, Frank O'Hara, myself, have been or are among the poets regularly on the staff of *Art News*. In New York the art world is a painters' world; writers and musicians are in the boat, but they don't steer.

Harold Rosenberg's Action Painting article is as much a statement for what is best about a lot of New York poetry as it is for New York painting. "It's not that, It's not that, It's not that . . ." Poets face the same challenge, and painting shows the way, or possible ways. "Writing like painting" has nothing to do with it.

For instance, a long poem like Frank O'Hara's *Second Avenue*: it's probably true to deduce that he'd read the *Cantos* and Whitman (he had); also Breton, and looked at de Koonings and Duchamp's great Dada installation at the Janis Gallery. Or to put it another way: Rrose Sélavy speaking out in Robert Motherwell's great Dada document anthology has more to do with poetry written by the poets I know than that Empress of Tapioca, The White Goddess: the Tondalayo of the Doubleday Bookshops.

Kenneth Koch writes about Jane Freilicher and her paintings; Barbara Guest is a *collagiste* and exhibits; Frank O'Hara decided to be an artist when he saw Assyrian sculpture in Boston; John Ashbery sometimes tried to emulate Léger; and so on.

Of course the father of poetry is poetry, and everybody goes to concerts when there are any: but if you try to derive a strictly literary ancestry for New York poetry, the main connection gets missed. (1959)

FRANK O'HARA:

I am mainly preoccupied with the world as I experience it, and at times when I would rather be dead the thought that I could never write another poem has so far stopped me. I think this is an ignoble attitude. I would rather die for love, but I haven't.

I don't think of fame or posterity (as Keats so grandly and genuinely did), nor do I care about clarifying experiences for anyone or bettering (other than accidentally) anyone's state or social relation, nor am I for any particular technical development in the American language simply because I find it necessary. What is happening to me, allowing for lies and exaggerations which I try to avoid, goes into my poems. I don't think my experiences are clarified or made beautiful for myself or anyone else, they are just there in whatever form I can find them. What is clear to me in my work is probably obscure to others, and vice versa. My formal "stance" is found at the crossroads where what I know and can't get meets what is left of that I know and can bear without hatred. I dislike a great deal of contemporary poetry — all of the past you read is usually quite great — but it is a useful thorn to have in one's side.

It may be that poetry makes life's nebulous events tangible to me and restores their detail; or conversely, that poetry brings forth the intangible quality of incidents which are all too concrete and circumstantial. Or each on specific occasions, or both all the time. (1959)

Philip Whalen:

This poetry is a picture or graph of a mind moving, which is a world body being here and now which is history . . . and you. Or think about the Wilson Cloud Chamber, not ideogram, not poetic beauty: bald-faced didacticism moving, as Dr. Johnson commands all poetry should, from the particular to the general. (Not that Johnson was right — nor that I am trying to inherit his mantle as a literary dictator but only the title *Doctor*, i.e. teacher, who is constantly studying.) I do not put down the academy but have assumed its function in my own person, and in the strictest sense of the word — academy — a walking grove of trees. But I cannot and will not solve any problems or answer any questions.

My life has been spent in the midst of heroic landscapes which never overwhelmed me and yet I live in a single room in the city — the room a lens focusing on a sheet of paper. Or the inside of your head. How do you like your world? (1959)

Gary Snyder:

I've just recently come to realize that the rhythms of my poems follow the rhythm of the physical work I'm doing and life I'm leading at any given time — which makes the music in my head which creates the line. Conditioned by the poetic tradition of the English language & whatever feeling I have for the sound of poems I dig in other languages. "Riprap" is really a class of poems I wrote under the influence of the geology of the Sierra Nevada and the daily trail-crew work of picking up and placing granite stones in tight cobble patterns on hard slab. "What are you doing?" I asked old Roy Marchbanks. — "Riprapping" he said. His selection of natural rocks was perfect — the result looked like dressed stone fitting to hair-edge cracks. Walking, climbing, placing with the hands. I tried writing poems of tough, simple, short words, with the complexity far beneath the surface texture. In part the line was influenced by the five- and seven-character line Chinese poems I'd been reading, which work like sharp blows on the mind.

Myths and Texts grew between 1952 and 1956. Its several rhythms are based on long days of quiet in lookout cabins; settling chokers for the Warm Springs Lumber Co. (looping cables on logs & hooking them to D8 Caterpillars — dragging and rumbling through the brush); and the songs and dances of Great Basin Indian tribes I used to hang around. The title comes from the happy collections Sapir, Boas, Swanton, and others made of American Indian folktales early in this century; it also means the two sources of human knowledge — symbols and sense-impressions. I tried to make my life as a hobo and worker, the questions of history & philosophy in my head, and the glimpses of the roots of religion I'd seen through meditation, peyote, and "secret frantic rituals" into one whole thing. As far as I'm concerned, I succeeded.

Since 1956 I've been working on a long poem I'm calling "Mountains and Rivers without End" after a Chinese sidewise scroll painting. It threatens to be like its title. Travel, the sense of journey in space that modern people have lost (it takes as long to go from Cedar Grove to the Bighorn Plateau in the Sierras as it does to cross America by train), and rise and fall of rock and water. The naked burning rocks of Oman after thirty days at sea. History and its vengeful ghosts. The dramatic structure follows a certain type of *No* play. (1959)

MICHAEL McCLURE: From a Journal

Sept. '57

The idea of "testament" is gone and the idea of book as something new — an active part of me of all my feelings and moods and my life is what I am carrying now. I have never been sure before as I am now of what I am doing, the *Hymns to St. Geryon* are more closely me than the things before. They allow for abstractions, boredom, retractions, contradictions. I am free in the forcing of what I am doing to make mistakes. I take in the language, act, object, morphology and I try to uncover all my feelings. There is my will in actions forcing the objects "chairs of my life" into the abstractions of the long poems. There are my inventions and shapes and I am a creator and speaker rather than a mimicker or portrayer of the realistic world. The *Hymns* are the real world in the sense that they are in it and part of it. As I write them I find myself growing free-er in the world moving more in it. The nervousness in my leg is there — but it is a part of my life again. I feel myself much of the time moving free-er, shifting in Bed/ walking with freedom. I am more conscious.

In the last poem "Walls do not change to pearls" I feel myself closer to describing sex. (My feelings free-er) I am stopped on the poem now I can finish or leave it. There is free will I am not obviated to carry on or not carry it on. I pause — I analyze my cessation on the poem and find it is for reasons of Pride, even dignity that I stop at the crucial moment. I find new belief in myself there. (Pride and dignity are not the words that I wanted / sounds like an excuse.) This writing in *St. Geryon* can go on into the plays that I want to write. I have found myself and I am not so influencable as I was, I am critical of writers that I respect, I feel my difference. I am close to Lawrence and Melville and I find how much I despise Williams and Pound.

> "In the cold courts of justice the dull head demands oaths, and holy writ proofs; but in the warm halls of the heart one single, untestified memory's spark shall suffice to enkindle such a blaze of evidence, that all the corners of conviction are as suddenly lighted up as a midnight city by a burning building, which on every side whirls its reddened brands."
> (Melville: *Pierre*)

Note in a depression early '58

If Olson's is poetry of the intellect and physiology, I want a writing of the Emotions, intellect and physiology. The direct emotional statement from the body (from the organs and from the energy of movements). The intellect will be the wit, discipline and truth of it — also the hanging to Science, of the known true part of the writing, that which I say I know to be true (and that also is a message).

To be clear as possible in meaning for the sake of clarity/ but not simplicity. To be direct where Olson is not and Duncan is seldom. My writing has dissolved into abstractions because I have lost in emotion and directness — and there has been my worry over the 'projective' aspect of the poem. Projective verse is natural to me to a degree below the degree that allows the language to govern me instead of vice versa. Or that I loose control of the language. (?)

Or more directly: I have lost emotional relationship to writing.

I repeat to myself: "There is no logic but sequence of feelings."

My viewpoint is ego-centric. Self-dramatization is part of a means to belief and Spirit.

The emotions push me to discoveries that afterwards I recognize intellectively to be truths. Glimpses of my physiology.

Sept. '59

I write and make no/or few changes. The prime purpose of my writing is liberation. (Self-liberation first & hopefully that of the reader.) The Bulk and its senses must be freed! A poem is as much of me as an arm. Measure, line etc. is interior and takes an outward shape, is not pre-destined or logical but immediate. I no longer have interest in the esthetic rationales of verse. The plays of John Webster, the prose of John Milton, the novels of Melville, Blake, Artaud & Lawrence. Goethe & Dante. All writing that matters to me is of the same end.

! ODEM NOT GEIST ! I write free-ing/to free the Beast Spirit; intellect (if separated, if possible for what existence it has) is a means towards aiding the felt, the feeled, through the typewriter. Real beauty is never-before-seen, is only in the world, I live in vast halls of beauty that I see as ugliness. Beauty is coiled, tortured, twisted, bright, dim, black, white, huge, minute, simple, intricate, traceried, solid, shallow. I do not see with my senses but with forms and preconceptions thru custom. I will kick in the walls and make destruction of those things the struggle to it is DARK BROWN   the struggle itself is a solid moving in an inferno, the triumph is failure! AN INFERNO! Falsehoods of logic (there is no logic but sequence!) and proportion must be destroyed. I am huge as a star! I AM A SERAPH! Hunger must be felt, love invented. Knowledge and feelings must be avowed:

> SUFFER ALL THAT MATTERS
> IS FIRE.   WHAT HURTS IS
> !CRUEL, WHAT PAINS IS AGONY!

> !

> *CHAOS   TRUTH & CHANGE*

LeRoi Jones: "How You Sound??"

"HOW YOU SOUND??" is what we recent fellows are up to. How *we* sound; our peculiar grasp on, say: a. Melican speech, b. Poetries of the world, c. Our selves (which is attitudes, logics, theories, jumbles of our lives, & all that), d. And the final . . . The Totality Of Mind: Spiritual . . . God?? (or you name it) : Social (zeitgeist) : or Heideggerian *umwelt*.

MY POETRY is whatever I think I am. (Can I be light & weightless as a sail?? Heavy & clunking like 8 black boots.) I CAN BE ANYTHING I CAN. I make a poetry with what I feel is useful & can be saved out of all the garbage of our lives. What I see, am touched by (CAN HEAR) . . . wives, gardens, jobs, cement yards where cats pee, all my interminable artifacts . . . ALL are a poetry, & nothing moves (with any grace) pried apart from these things. There cannot be closet poetry. Unless the closet be wide as God's eye.

And all that means that I *must* be completely free to do just what I want, in the poem. "All is permitted": Ivan's crucial concept. There cannot be anything I must *fit* the poem into. Everything must be made to fit into the poem. There must not be any

preconceived notion or *design* for what the poem *ought* to be.
"Who knows what a poem ought to sound like? Until it's thar."
Says Charles Olson . . . & I follow closely with that. I'm not in-
terested in writing sonnets, sestinas or anything . . . only poems.
If the poem has got to be a sonnet (unlikely tho) or whatever,
it'll certainly let me know. The only "recognizable tradition" a
poet need follow is himself . . . & with that, say, all those things
out of tradition he can use, adapt, work over, into something for
himself. To broaden his *own* voice with. (You have to start and
finish there . . . your own voice . . . how you sound.)

For me, Lorca, Williams, Pound and Charles Olson have had
the greatest influence. Eliot, earlier (rhetoric can be so lovely, for
a time . . . but only remains so for the rhetorician). And there are
so many young wizards around now doing great things that
everybody calling himself poet can learn from . . . Whalen,
Snyder, McClure, O'Hara, Loewinsohn, Wieners, Creeley, Gins-
berg &c. &c. &c.

Also, all this means that we want to go into a quantitative
verse . . . the "irregular foot" of Williams . . . the "Projective
Verse" of Olson. Accentual verse, the regular metric of rumbling
iambics, is dry as slivers of sand. Nothing happens in that frame
anymore. We can get nothing from England. And the diluted
formalism of the academy (the formal culture of the U.S.) is
anaemic & fraught with incompetence & unreality. (1959)

JOHN WIENERS: From a Journal

July 17, 1959

A poem does not have to be a major thing. Or a statement?
I am allowed to ask many things because it has been given
me the means to plunge into the depths and come up with
answers? No. Poems, which are
my salvation alone. The reader can do with them what he likes.
I feel right now even the reading of poems to an unknown
large? public is a shallow *act*, unless the reading be given for the
fact of clarity. The different *techne*

a man uses to make his salvation. That is why poetry
even tho it does deal with language is no more *holy* act
                         than, say shitting.
                                   Dis-
                         charge. Manifesting the
                                 process of
                    is it life? Or the action between this and
                                   non-action? *Lethargy vs
                                         Violence.*
For to take up arms against the void is attack, and the price of
       was
                                   is high. Millions of syllables
shed over the falls of our saliva, millions of teardrops
roll out of our eyes. Giant screams echo through the halls of our
       house
at night. We do not wish it. It is so. By the action we are en-
gaged in. Hundreds of days, months have to go by before the
spirits descend and the right word rolls out sharp and full of
                    fire air earth and water
                    off the tips of our
                         tongue. And one cannot avoid the
days. They have to parade by in all their carnage. The events of
them like images on a shield, we carry thru the streets of the town
to get a peek at the bloody hero. And is he?
                              You bet.

BIOGRAPHICAL NOTES

HELEN ADAM: "I was born in Glasgow, Scotland, December 2nd, 1909, but only lived in Glasgow for the first year of my life, educated in Nairnshire, and Edinburgh University. Worked as a journalist in Edinburgh and London. Came to America with my mother and sister in 1939. Worked summers in the land army during the war, and in various business jobs in New York. We moved to the West in 1949, living in Reno and Oakland, and to San Francisco in 1953."

BROTHER ANTONINUS (William Everson): "Was born in 1912 in Sacramento, Calif., and grew up in the town of Selma. During the war he served as a conscientious objector and in 1948 his privately published poems were collected and issued by New Directions under the title of *The Residual Years,* leading to a Guggenheim Fellowship in 1949. That same year he entered the Catholic Church and soon began a term with the Catholic Worker Movement, leaving it in 1951 to enter the Dominican Order as a *donatus,* or lay brother without vows. After several years of monastic withdrawal he re-emerged in 1957 in the *Evergreen Review* as a member of the San Francisco Renaissance."

JOHN ASHBERY: "Born in Rochester, N.Y., July 28, 1927; brought up in Sodus, N.Y.; went to Deerfield and Harvard (BA, 1949); then Columbia (MA, 1951); worked in publishing 1951-55; Fulbright to France in 1955, renewed in 1956. Am at present in France and writing a book on Raymond Roussel. Have written plays: *The Heroes* (1950) put on by the Living Theater (1952) and the Artists' Theater (1953); *The Compromise* (1955) put on by Poets' Theater in Cambridge in 1956. Am an editorial associate with *Art News.*"

427

PAUL BLACKBURN: "Born in St. Albans, Vermont, November 24, 1926. Attended NYU and the University of Wisconsin. BA from Wisconsin, June 1950. Fulbright scholar, University of Toulouse 1954-55. Lecteur americain, University of Toulouse, 1955-56; followed courses in Provençal at both Wisconsin and Toulouse. Lived in Spain various periods from 1954 through 1957. Poet, translator, editor."

ROBIN BLASER: "Born in 1925. Tied to universities from 1943-59: Northwestern, College of Idaho, Berkeley, California as a student; Harvard as a librarian from 1955-1959. Now free and hoping to remain that way. But it's doubtful. Money!"

EBBE BORREGAARD: "Born in 1933 and grew up on Long Island. He attended school in Vermont, and served in the army. He has been in California since 1955."

BRUCE BOYD: "Born San Francisco, 1928. Have lived there, in Los Angeles & in Berkeley. Now living in San Francisco, intending to go to Japan eventually."

RAY BREMSER: "Born Jersey City 1934, educated at Bordentown Reformatory. I dug Billy Holiday at 15, & Wayne Shorter at 25. Best poets alive are me, Ginsberg, Jones, Kerouac, Orlovsky & Corso. Have read at Vassar, Princeton, Lehigh, etc."

JAMES BROUGHTON was born in Modesto, California in 1913. He has produced five poetic experimental films: *Mother's Day, Loony Tom, Adventures of Jimmy, Four in the Afternoon,* and *The Pleasure Garden.* He is also active in the theatre, having written several plays and two musical revues. He makes his home in San Francisco.

PAUL CARROLL: "I was born in 1927 in Chicago to an Irish emigrant father, who made several million in Chicago banking & real estate, and to a mother who came from Austrian peasants. University of Chicago (MA 1952). Was poetry editor of *Chicago Review*; now editor of *Big Table*."

GREGORY CORSO: "Born by young Italian parents, father 17 mother 16, born in New York City Greenwich Village 190 Bleecker, mother year after me left not-too-bright-father and went back to Italy, thus I entered life of orphanage and four foster parents and at 11 father remarried and took me back but all was wrong because two years later I ran away and caught sent away again and sent away to boys home for two years and let out and went back home and ran away again and sent to Bellevue for observation where I spent 3 frightening sad months with mad old men who peed in other sad old men's mouths, and left and went back home and knew more than father and step-mother did about woe and plight of man at age of 13 so ran away again and for good and did something really big and wrong and was sent to prison for three years at age of 17, from 13 to 17 I lived with Irish on 99th and Lex, with Italians on 105th and 3rd, with two runaway Texans on 43rd, etc, until 17th year when did steal and get three years in Clinton Prison where an old man handed me *Karamatsov, Les Misérables, Red and Black*, and thus I learned, and was free to think and feel and write, because when I wanted to write before, when I used to tell my father that I want very much to write, he used to say, a poet-writer aint got no place in this world. But prison was different, the "poet-writer" had a place, before prison only went to sixth grade. Came out of prison loving my fellow man because all the men I met there were proud and sad and beautiful and lost, lost. I must also say that the most cruel thing that did happen to me in my youth was when I was 12 at the boys home. I went there because I stole a radio and sold it to a dealer and the dealer was taken to court and I had to appear as witness so they took me from good boys home to TOMBS at the age of 12! For five months I stayed there, no air, no milk, and the majority were black and they hated the white and they abused me terribly, and I was indeed like an angel then because when they stole my food and beat me up and threw pee in my cell, I, the next day would come out and tell them my beautiful dream about a floating girl who landed before a deep pit and just stared.

I say this to you because I think it is the first time I have ever felt the horror of that 12 year old gregory. I want to fight it now, I couldn't then, because I was true then, somehow, along the way, I lost that gregory.

Came out 20 well read and in love with Chatterton, Marlowe and Shelley, went home, stayed two days, left family forever, but returned at night to beg their forgiveness and retrieve my stamp collection. Got mad job in Garment District; lived in Village and one night 1950 in a dark empty bar sitting with my prison poems I was graced with a deep-eyed apparition: Allen Ginsberg. Through him I first learned about contemporary poesy, and how to handle myself in an uninstitutional society, as I was very much the institutional being. Beyond the great excited new joyous talks we had about poetry, he was first gentle person and dear friend to me. Quit job later and lived in Village with kind girl until 1952 when I went to Los Angeles and got, by fluke, good job on Los Angeles *Examiner*, cub reporting once a week, rest of week working in file-morgue. Left 7 months later to ship out on Norwegian line to South America and Africa and did. Went back to Village, did nothing but get drunk and sleep on rooftops till 1954 when beautiful now dead Violet Lang brought me to Harvard where I wrote and wrote and met lots of wild young brilliant people who were talking about Hegel and Kierkegaard. Had *Vestal Lady* published there by contributions from fifty or more students from Radcliffe and Harvard. *Harvard Advocate* first to publish me. Then in 1956 went to S.F. and there rejoined Allen, and Ferl asked for book of mine, *Gasoline*, stayed in S.F. five months, gave poetry reading with Allen, then we took off to Mexico. Wrote most of *Gasoline* there, and now Paris." (1957)

ROBERT CREELEY: "I was born in Massachusetts, May 21, 1926, and raised there mainly. I went to Holderness School, Plymouth, N.H., and after that to Harvard, which I left in 1944, to go in the American Field Service, where I served in India and Burma until 1945, when I returned to Harvard. I left college in 1947, a half-year short of a degree, having married, etc. I lived then in Littleton, N.H. for about three years, after which we went to France, where we lived near Aix-en-Provence. After about a year and a half there, we moved to Banalbufar, Mallorca, Spain, where I started the Divers Press. I previously was an associate editor for Rainer Gerhardt's *Fragmente* (Freiberg im Breisgau, Germany), and also had association with Katue Kitasono's *Vou* (Tokyo, Japan). In 1954 I went to Black Mountain College, Black Mountain, N.C. at the invitation of Charles Olson and the faculty to teach writing. I had just begun editing the *Black Mountain Review* for the same college. I taught there for the spring term, then left, returning again the summer of 1955 to teach until January 1956. After that I lived in Taos and then San Francisco for short periods, returning to New Mexico in the fall of 1956 to teach at a boys' school in Albuquerque. Having secured an M.A. from the University of New Mexico in 1959, I took a job teaching on a coffee *finca* in Guatemala where I presently live."

EDWARD DORN: "In 1929 I was born in the Prairie town of Villa Grove, Illinois. I was reared more or less alternately between the factory towns of Michigan and the vicinity of my birthplace. I was Educated at the University of Illinois, and somewhat corrected at Black Mountain College. At present I somehow manage to live in Santa Fe."

KIRBY DOYLE: "Born November 27, 1932 in San Francisco. Was a juvenile delinquent for the first 16 years. Am well acquainted with the insides of various police stations and other minor prisons.

At the age of 16 I left home to join the army to hear the guns go boom and find out about the world. I heard the guns and figured the world was a spooky place. Did graduate work at San Francisco State College, sailed in the merchant marine and rode a motorcycle in the darkly night. Was married, have two children and am at present living in New York working on poetry and a novel under the dubious security of unemployment checks."

RICHARD DUERDEN: "Born July 14, 1927 in Utah. The Blood, English & French. Raised in Bay Area: Goat Island, Oakland, S.F. Merchant Marine, Marine Corps, University California 3½ yrs, no degree. I've been writing since; living by clerking, surveying, gardening etc. We — my wife, son & myself — are living in S.F."

ROBERT DUNCAN: "Born January 7, 1919, in Oakland, California. I have had two teachers in my lifetime who belong in a biography of my existence as poet: in high school, Edna Keough, who brought me to the vocation of writing as at once demanding and in the same making possible intensity and depth of feeling. She saw poetry not as a cultural commodity or an exercise to improve sensibility, but as a vital process of the spirit. Years later, there was Ernst Kantorowicz, whose genius and art in history brought me to a new vision of the creative spirit and the world of forms in which that spirit is manifest. Robin Blaser, Jack Spicer, and I, as poets, are all variously students of Kantorowicz and share through his teaching the sense of creative ground in history that is also in poetry, the concept that to form is to transform, is a magic then, and that a metaphor is not a literary device but an actual meaning arising from, operating in, and leading us to realize the co-inherence of being in being, that we perceive forms because there are correspondences.

There have been many friends and associations in my life as a poet. Among these, the following seem important today as having their share in shaping or releasing my concept of what poetry or the process of making is. My history is for me in part a history of contemporaries. Earliest, from 1938, Mary Fabilli (though she has disowned her writing from those years [1938-50]) whose sensuality, humor, daring and simplicity, her sense of fabulous being projected as Aurora Bligh, I keep as a living example. Then, Sanders Russell, with whom I edited *The Experimental Review* (1940-41). 'Awareness' and 'states of consciousness' were for him the essence of poetry; and his own work realized through evocative images and meditative landscapes an immediate correspondence between inner being and outer world, a metaphysical aura, that remains for me a sign of the poem. The poem was a field of fantastic life and the poem was an art that involved intensities of the real.

In the period between 1946 and 1950 when I was living in Berkeley, Jack Spicer (who was some six years younger than I was) came to be mentor, censor and peer. He taught the recognition of disgust as a key to the dramatic transformation of sensuality in the poem so that opulence of feeling became disturbed and longing appeared. As censor, Spicer has always demanded obedience to the poem itself as reality and despised as an evil whatever in verse he felt to be worldly-wise or profitable. Through early years of common exploration he and I share certain methods in poetry that have to do with the art as "magic": drawing the sorts, evoking of and from the cult or care of powers in the poem, cultivating the metaphorical ground in life, taking and, in this, testing what we believed to be "poetry" as directive or key from reality in the sense of a lasting doctrine. With Jack Spicer I learned that the poem that might be fantastic life, that might be insight into the real, was a rite. The poem was a ritual referring to divine orders.

Since 1951 my work has been associated in my mind with a larger work that appeared in the writing of Charles Olson, Denise Levertov, and Robert Creeley. In 1948 with *The Venice Poem* I had turned from the concept of a dramatic form to a concept of musical form in poetry. Spicer never accepted the last movement of *The Venice Poem*; he mistrusted the genuineness of the birth of the baby into which the coda of the poem moves. In the period that followed he was further alienated by my imitations of Gertrude Stein as I set about questioning the whole basis of an unbroken continuum in poetic language and tried to force a new sense of interrupted movement. Between 1948 and 1952 when I first saw what I shared in the work appearing in *Origin*, I worked in isolation from the sense of contemporaries, turning to the genius of older artists for my clues. In 1950 the creative generation of Stravinsky, Frank Lloyd Wright, Ezra Pound and Bonnard presented a challenge in their contemporary work that my peers did not present. *The Pisan Cantos*, and the first three volumes of *Paterson*, gave us measure. Satie, Stravinsky and Schönberg went further in the articulation of time than poetry was prepared to go. And in 1950 there was the new painting in San Francisco where I found my peers among painters — Brock Brockway, Lynne Brown, Jess Collins, Harry Jacobs and Lili Fenichel, and their teachers, Still, Hassel Smith, Corbett and Bischoff — who displayed new organizations allowing for discontinuities in space, for more vitality then (variety of impulse) than I had in my work in poetry.

What released my sense of a new generation in poetry was first a poem (*The Shifting* by Denise Levertov) in *Origin* VI, 1952; then in 1954 thru *The Gold Diggers* a grasp of the art of Robert Creeley, where such minute attentions and cares moved in the line; and third, but from the first, the break-thru to a meaningful reading of Olson's *Maximus*, from which his *Projective Verse* and *In Cold Hell In Thicket* took on new meaning: that, for one thing, the task in poetry could be promethean. In Whitman's words: "The theme is creative and has vista." Here biography passes into the living present that has no summary. My convictions lie here, that these are at work where I would work. And since 1957 with his *After Lorca*, Spicer has taken his place again among my primaries.

That is the story of the romance of forms. It involves for all of us numinous powers, quests and workings of the spirit, apprehensions of our share in history, reverence for our "ancestors" in spirit. Yes, I should name them, the poets that have been my Masters, for they are not everywhere revered. Indeed, in academic circles reverence is thought of as a vice not a virtue. The sources of my *virtus* lie among those immediately preceding me in Stein, Lawrence, Pound, H.D., William Carlos Williams, Marianne Moore, Stevens, and Edith Sitwell. They are all problematic, arent they? And the two *sure* things — Frost and Eliot — are not there.

But then, my life has come round to dwell in the problematic, to seek those forms that allow for the most various feelings in one, so that a book is more than a poem, and a life-work is more than a book, yet they have no other instance than a word. A multiphasic experience sought a multiphasic form. It was Charles Olson who brought me to read Whitehead, where I found principles that paralleled those of the art I longed for: that 'we may not neglect the multifariousness of the world — the fairies dance and Christ is nailed to the cross' towards fullness of feeling. And I found too the philosophic expression of what we were beginning to realize in the art of the poem — that wholeness must be ever-present in the part: 'The communion of saints is a great and inspiring assemblage,' Whitehead wrote, 'but it has only one possible hall of meeting, and that is, the present; and the mere lapse of time through which any particular group of saints must travel to reach that meeting-place, makes very little difference.'

Since 1951 the painter Jess Collins has been my constant companion in life. He was one of those painters who awakened me to new possibilities of discontinuous form in spatial composition; and in these last years his work like mine has sought to be a ground for what I have called the Romance, for the life of the spirit that involves fairies and Christs, saints and the present. This was once called the Imagination. With Jess Collins there is one more, the latest of these teachers and companions — but this was later, in 1954 — Helen Adam, who opened the door to the full heritage of the forbidden romantics. Her ballads were the missing link to the tradition. How troublesome at first they were! They fascinated; they seemed entirely anachronistic. There was the mere lapse of time through which they had traveled. They were powerful; they should have been *wrong*. They were entirely concerned with event, with marvelous event; nowhere was the language shaded to hint at the poet's sensibility. In grasping the inspiration of Helen Adam, in admitting her genius, I was able to shake off at last the modern proprieties — originality, style, currency of language, sensibility and integrity. I have a great appetite for approval from whatever source, and only the example of this poet who cares nothing for opinions but all for the life of the imagination, for the marvellous that is the grain of living poetry, saves me at times. And Helen Adam was right, passions may have voice in ballads and orders appear in fairy tales that were otherwise mute or garbled.

These are the threads. And the weaving now of the design is so close, so immediate and so intertwined, with so many undiscovered threads, that I must trust the figures as they emerge, have faith that there is the wholeness of form (have the constant feeling of present form then). There is a wholeness of what we are that we will never know; we are always, as the line or the phrase or the word is, the moment of that wholeness — an event; but it, the wholeness of what we are, goes back into an obscurity and extends to and into an obscurity. The obscurity is part too of the work, of the form, if it be whole." (1959)

LARRY EIGNER: "Born 1927 in Swampscott, Mass. (out of the nearby hospital in Lynn); still living there, where after public school I took correspondence courses from U of Chicago. I'm a 'shut-in,' partly. In 1949, a couple of months after finishing up the last course, I bumped into Cid Corman reading Yeats, on the radio, in his first program, I gather, from Boston. I disagreed with his non-declamatory way of reciting, and wrote him so. This began a correspondence in which I got introduced to things, and the ice broke considerably."

LAWRENCE FERLINGHETTI: "Probably was born in New York about 1919 or thereafter. He seems to have been transported into France in swaddling clothes, saw the white mountains of Alsace from a balcony, and returned to the States sometime, years later, to distinguish himself in the upper grades by outstanding achievement in the art of flatulence. After that the record is none too clear. It seems he returned to France during World War II and had some underhand connection with the Free French and the Norwegian Underground. After the War he may have written two unpublishable novels and a doctoral thesis at the Sorbonne which should have been titled Histoire du pissoir dans la poésie moderne. It also seems fairly certain that he reached San Francisco overland about 1951, built a bookstore, and began to publish the Pocket Poets Series."

EDWARD FIELD: "I was born June 7, 1924, in Brooklyn, N.Y. and grew up in Lynbrook, L.I., N.Y. After high school I enlisted in the U.S. Army where I started to write poetry. I became an aviation cadet and was graduated Navigator and 2nd Lieutenant. I flew on 27 combat missions over Germany. After the war I went to New York University for a few years on the G.I. Bill and then left for Europe where I lived for a year and a half. There I met the poet, Robert Friend, who taught me technique of poetry. It was in this period that I published my first poems, in *Botteghe Oscure*. When I came back from Europe I worked at different jobs, warehouse, art reproduction, machinist, and finally clerk-typist. I started acting five years ago in an amateur group and then went on to study with the great Vera Soloviova of the Moscow Art Theatre. The last few summers I have been leading man in summer theatres. I am trying to make the New York theatre scene."

ALLEN GINSBERG: "Born June 3, 1926, the son of Naomi Ginsberg, Russian emigre, and Louis Ginsberg, lyric poet and school-teacher, in Paterson, New Jersey. High School in Paterson till 17, Columbia College, merchant marine, Texas and Denver, copyboy, Times Square, amigos in jail, dishwashing, book reviews, Mexico City, market research, Satori in Harlem, Yucatan & Chiapas 1954, West Coast Howl 1955, Arctic Sea Trip & then Tangier,

Venice, Amsterdam, Paris, London, readings Oxford Harvard Columbia Chicago, New York Kaddish 1959, returned to SF & made record to leave behind and fade awhile in Orient."

MADELINE GLEASON was born in North Dakota in 1913. In 1935 she came to San Francisco where she founded the S.F. Poetry Guild, has shown several exhibitions of her paintings, and has had her two plays, *Three Voices* and *Why in the World*, produced recently. In 1959-60 she conducted the master workshop in poetry for the Poetry Center of S. F. State College.

BARBARA GUEST: "Born — North Carolina, 1923. Lived in California from 1933. Colleges: U.C.L.A., graduated Univ. of Calif. at Berkeley. Spent nine months in Europe last year (1958). Resident — New York City."

LEROI JONES: "Born 7 October 1934, Newark, New Jersey. Rutgers University, Howard University, Columbia University, New School for Social Research (M.A. German Lit.). Canada-Mexico, 1953. USAirForce Oct 1954 — Jan 1957 (aerial-climatographer). Was stationed for two & one half yrs in Puerto Rico 1954-57 with intervening trips to Europe, Africa, Middle East. Editor *Yūgen* magazine, Totem press."

JACK KEROUAC (b. 1922): "After my brother died, when I was four, they tell me I began to sit motionlessly in the parlor, pale and thin, and after a few months of sorrow began to play the old Victrola and act out movies to the music. Some of these movies developed into long serial sagas, 'continued next week,' leading sometimes to the point where I tied myself with rope in the grass and kids coming home from school thought I was crazy. My brother had taught me how to draw so at the age of 8 I began to produce comic strips of my own: 'Kuku and Koko at the Earth's Core,' (the first, rudely drawn) on to highly developed sagas like 'The Eighth Sea.' A sick little boy in Nashua N.H. heard of these and wanted to borrow them. I never saw them again. At the age of 11 I wrote whole little novels in nickel notebooks, also magazines (in imitation of *Liberty Magazine*) and kept extensive horse racing newspapers going. The first 'serious' writing took place after I read about Jack London at the age of 17. Like Jack, I began to paste up 'long words' on my bedroom wall in order to memorize them perfectly. At 18 I read Hemingway and Saroyan and began writing little terse short stories in that general style. Then I read Tom Wolfe and began writing in the rolling style. Then I read Joyce and wrote a whole juvenile novel like *Ulysses* called 'Vanity of Duluoz.' Then came Dostoevsky. Finally I entered a romantic phase with Rimbaud and Blake which I called my 'self-ultimacy' period, burning what I wrote in order to be 'Self-ultimate.' At the age of 24 I was groomed for the Western idealistic concept of letters from reading Goethe's *Dichtung und Wahrheit*. The discovery of a style of my own based on spontaneous get-with-it, came after reading the marvelous free narrative letters of Neal Cassady, a great writer who happens also to be the Dean Moriarty of *On the Road*. I also learned a lot about unrepressed wordslinging from young Allen Ginsberg and William Seward Burroughs."

KENNETH KOCH: "I was born in Cincinnati, Ohio, in 1925. I began writing poetry in 1930 but I don't think I wrote anything very good till 1942, when I read dos Passos and started writing 'stream of consciousness.' In 1943 I went in the army for three years — I was a rifleman in the Pacific; after that I went to Harvard and then to Columbia. I've spent three years in Europe, mostly in France and Italy. My first year in France had a huge effect on my poetry — the only thing comparable to it has been the influence of John Ashbery & Frank O'Hara; since I didn't read French very well but managed to be very excited by French poetry anyway, I began to try to get the same incomprehensible excitement into my own work. It wasn't a deliberate attempt to be obscure (I hate obscurity) but to recreate an excitement I had felt. My poetry was very much like a foreign language for about a year and a half after that. Then it became, under the influence of some rather demanding personal experiences and some strange substance in the air, more 'realistic.' I live in New York. Last year Larry Rivers and I tried to kill poetry-and-jazz by parodying it; our first session at the Five Spot, however, turned out to be so enjoyable (for us, at least) that we repeated the experience several times. I don't think we killed it. I write in the afternoon."

PHILIP LAMANTIA: "Born 1927 in San Francisco. Lived in New York City, Mexico, Europe and North Africa. Hailed by André Breton as an authentic surrealist poet; first appearances in *View*, 1943-45; broke with surrealism by 1946. Since then mostly underground, and traveling."

DENISE LEVERTOV: "My mother was descended from the Welsh tailor and mystic Angel Jones of Mold, my father from the noted Hasid, Schneour Zalman (d. 1831), 'the Rav of Northern White Russia.' My father had experienced conversion to Christianity as a student at Königsberg in the 1890s. His lifelong hope was towards the unification of Judaism and Christianity. He was a priest of the Anglican Church (having settled in England not long before I was born), author of a Life of St. Paul in Hebrew, part translator of *The Zohar*, etc.

I was born in October 1923 at Ilford, Essex. I did lessons at home, and never attended any school or college, except for some years at a ballet school. However, we had a house full of books and everyone in the family engaged in some literary activity. Jewish booksellers, German theologians, Russian priests from Paris, and Viennese opera singers, visited the house; and perhaps my earliest memory is of being dandled by the ill-fated son of Theodor Herzl, the great Zionist.

During the war I received partial training and lots of experience as a (civilian) nurse. A different world! I was in London during all but a few of the airraids but it does not seem to have been such a memorable experience as one might expect.

In 1947 I met my husband in Geneva. We first lived in Paris, where I had been working earlier that year, and in Florence (on the G.I. Bill) but settled in New York at the end of 1948. Our son was born the next year. My husband had known Robert Creeley at Harvard, and through our friendship with him we later came to know a number of people connected with Black Mountain College, but never visited it. Cid Corman was the first U.S. editor to give a place to my poems (Charles Wrey Gardiner had first published my work in England). Marrying an American and coming to live here while still young was very stimulating to me as a writer for it necessitated the finding of new rhythms in which to write, in accordance with new rhythms of life and speech. My reading of William Carlos Williams and Wallace Stevens, which began in Paris in 1948; of Olson's essay, 'Projective Verse'; conversations and correspondence with Robert Duncan; a renewed interest through Buber in the Hasidic ideas with which I was dimly acquainted as a child; the thoughts and shared experiences of my husband; an introduction to some of the concepts of Jung; the friendship of certain painters such as Albert Kresch — have all been influential and continue to be so.

I feel the stylistic influence of William Carlos Williams, while perhaps too evident in my work of a few years ago, was a very necessary and healthful one, without which I could not have developed from a British Romantic with almost Victorian background to an American poet of any vitality."

RON LOEWINSOHN: "Born 15 December, 1937, in the Philippines. First came to U.S. in 1945 & lived in Los Angeles & the Bronx before settling with parents in San Francisco. Graduated from high school there in 1955 & spent the following 2 years travelling around the country. Married in 1957; first son born January, 1958. Now employed as a lithographer & have settled permanently in the S.F. Bay Area."

EDWARD MARSHALL: "Born in Chichester, N.H., 1932. Basic 3 R's in Concord, N.H., then University of N.H. and New England College, Henniker, N.H. Boston episode: 1953-56. Then under influence of Black Mountain and Boston poets. New York since 1956. Presently at Columbia, studying religion and culture."

MICHAEL MCCLURE was born in the Midwest in 1932, and he attended schools in the Midwest, the Southwest and in San Francisco, where he has lived since 1953. He is married and has a daughter.

DAVID MELTZER: "Born 1937, Rochester, New York. Lived in Brooklyn until I was 13. Moved to Long Island for an eventful year of family chaos. At 14 left for the West & stayed in L.A. for 6 formative years in which I met Wallace Berman & Robert Alexander, who were instrumental in turning me on to the fantastic possibilities of art & the self. Moved to San Francisco in 1957, and married in 1958. Spent many months reading at The Cellar with jazz. I no longer believe in the poet as a public target.

I have decided to work my way thru poetry & find my voice & the stance I must take in order to continue my journey. Poetry is NOT my life. It is an essential PART of my life."

FRANK O'HARA: "Born in Baltimore, Maryland, 1926; grew up in New England; Navy 1944-46; Harvard 1946-50 (AB); U. of Michigan 1950-51 (MA and Hopwood Award for poetry); in New York since 1951, worked for *Art News* and The Museum of Modern Art."

CHARLES OLSON was born December 27, 1910 at Worcester, Mass. "Uneducated" at Wesleyan, Yale and Harvard. Taught at Clark, at Harvard (1936-1939) and at Black Mountain College, where he was instructor and rector, 1951-1956. His first publication was the essay, "Lear and Moby Dick," in *Twice-a-Year*, 1938. His first poem was published in 1945. Olson has been the recipient of two Guggenheim fellowships, and in 1952 he received a grant from the Wenner-Gren Foundation to study Mayan hieroglyphics in Yucatan. In recent years he has returned to his home town of Gloucester where he is writing his *Maximus* poems.

JOEL OPPENHEIMER: "Born 1930, Yonkers, N.Y. Educated public schools Yonkers, N.Y. 1935-47. Cornell Univ., School of Engineering, 1947-48. Univ. of Chicago, The College, 1948-49. Black Mountain College, 1950-53. No degrees. Born for the Depression, but too young to remember any suffering. Too young for WW II — in school and 4F during Korean. Consequently, having missed the 3 major social calamities of my time, I am always feeling just a little guilty. Now living in NYC."

PETER ORLOVSKY: "My biography was born July 1933. Grew up with dirty feet & giggles. Cant stand dust so pick my nose. Trouble in school: always thinking dreaming sad mistry problems. Quit high school in middle of last term & got lost working in Mental hospital old man's bed slopy ward. Love pretzles & cant remember dreams anymore. Will somebody please buy me mountain with a cave up there. I dont speack any more. Wanted to be a farmer went to high school for that & worked hard, hard, I tell you, very hard, you'd be amazed. Did weight lifting with bus stops. Got to enjoy burnt bacon with mothers help. Stare at my feet to much & need to undue paroniac suden clowds. Enjoy mopping floors, cleaning up cat vommit. Enjoy swinning underwater. I want the moon for fun. Getting to enjoy blank mind state, especially in tub. This summer got to like flies tickleing nose & face. I demand piss be sold on the market, it would help people to get to know eachother. I.Q. 90 in school, now specialized I.Q. is thousands."

STUART Z. PERKOFF was born in St. Louis in 1930, and educated in the Midwest. He left home at 17 and traveled to New York, later moving to California, where he has been living, chiefly in Venice West, since 1950. In recent years he has also been painting and sculpturing.

JAMES SCHUYLER: "Born 1923 in Chicago, Illinois, grew up in Washington, D.C., Western New York and West Virginia, where he attended Bethany College, an attractive group of buildings on a small, steep hill. For several years he lived in Italy. He is the author of a novel, *Alfred and Guinevere*, two way-off Broadway plays, *Presenting Jane* and *Shopping and Waiting*, *A Picnic Cantata* (with Paul Bowles) and a book of poems, *Salute*. He is on the staff of The Museum of Modern Art."

GARY SNYDER: "I was born 1930 in San Francisco & raised up on a feeble sort of farm just north of Seattle. Reed College very kindly scholarshipped me & I graduated from there in 1951, majoring in mythology. I studied linguistics one term at Indiana University, & after that sort of bummed around working at logging & forestry work alternate with classical Chinese study at Berkeley up til 1956 when I came to Japan to study the formal Zen training. I was in Japan from May 1956 to August 1957; working on a tanker until April 1958 visiting Mediterranean & Pacific oil ports; in San Francisco until January 1959, when I returned to Japan."

GILBERT SORRENTINO: "Born 1929, New York City, raised in same city, attended N.Y. public schools, many jobs. Brooklyn College 1949-1951, U.S. Army 1951-1953, Brooklyn College 1955-1956. Did not graduate. Married, father of 2 children, live in Brooklyn. Began *Neon* in 1956 as mimeo sheet, it still happily continues. Three great literary markers are Pound, who taught me that verse is the highest of arts and gave me the sense of tradition, Williams, who showed me that our language can produce it, and Creeley, who demonstrated that the attack need not be head on."

JACK SPICER: "does not like his life written down. He was born in Hollywood in 1925. Anyone interested in further information should contact him at THE PLACE, 1546 Grant Avenue, San Francisco."

LEW WELCH: "Born August 16, 1926. High school track star and pool hustler. Army amnesia. Wake-up at College of the Pacific and Reed (where I roomed with Phil Whalen and Gary Snyder) via Gertrude Stein and fine teachers. Importantly influenced by meeting with W. C. Williams at Reed and, later, at his N. J. home. Unpublished book on Stein: Reed thesis.

Acedia in New York. Walden in Florida. Graduate study at Univ. of Chicago — literature and structural linguistics. Crack up, including psychoanalysis and advertising writing. Am preparing a cabin in Oregon which will be my permanent, rent-free, base far into the foreseeable future."

PHILIP WHALEN: "Born Portland, Oregon, October 20, 1923. US Army Air Force 1943-46. Reed College, Bachelor of Arts (Literature & Languages) 1951."

JOHN WIENERS: "Born on January 6, 1934. I graduated from Boston College in June of 1954, and attended Black Mountain for the spring of 1955 and the summer of 1956. In between I worked in the Lamont Library at Harvard, until the day that *Measure* #1 arrived in Boston, and then they fired me. I first met Charles Olson on the night of Hurricane Hazel, September 11, 1954, when I 'accidentally' heard him read his verse at the Charles St. Meeting House. They passed out complimentary copies of the *Black Mountain Review* #1, and I aint been able to forget."

JONATHAN C. WILLIAMS: "Born March 8, 1929, Asheville, North Carolina. Educated at St. Albans School, Princeton University, Atelier 17 (S.W. Hayter), Phillips Memorial Gallery (Karl Knaths), Institute of Design (Chicago), and Black Mountain College. Began Jargon Books in San Francisco, 1951. Guggenheim Fellowship in poetry, 1957-58. Live in Highlands, North Carolina."

SHORT BIBLIOGRAPHY

Legend: [b] indicates broadsheets, [d] drama, [f] fiction, [p] prose essay, [s] movie script, [t] translation.

I. BOOKS AND BROADSHEETS

Helen Adam: *The Queen o' Crow Castle* (SF: White Rabbit, 1958)

Brother Antoninus (William Everson): *The Residual Years* (NY: New Directions, 1948); *The Crooked Lines of God, Poems 1949-1954* (Detroit: University of Detroit, 1959)

John Ashbery: *Turandot and Other Poems* (NY: Tibor de Nagy, 1953); *Some Trees* (New Haven: Yale University, 1956); *The Heroes* [d], in Herbert Machiz, ed.: *Artists' Theatre: Four Plays* (NY: Grove, 1960)

Paul Blackburn: *Proensa* [t] (Mallorca: Divers, 1953); *The Dissolving Fabric* (Mallorca: Divers, 1955); *Brooklyn-Manhattan Transit* (NY: Totem, 1960)

Ebbe Borregaard: *The Wapitis* (SF: White Rabbit, 1958)

James Broughton: *The Playground* (SF: Centaur, 1949); *Musical Chairs* (SF: Centaur, 1950); *The Right Playmate* (NY: Farrar, Straus, 1952); *An Almanac for Amorists* (Paris: Olympia, 1955); *True and False Unicorn* (NY: Grove, 1957)

Gregory Corso: *The Vestal Lady on Brattle, and Other Poems* (Cambridge: Richard Brukenfeld, 1955); *Gasoline* (SF: City Lights, 1958); *Bomb* [b] (SF: City Lights, 1958); *The Happy Birthday of Death* (NY: New Directions, 1960); *American Express* [f] (Paris: Olympia, 1961)

Robert Creeley: *Le Fou* (Columbus: Golden Goose, 1952); *The Immoral Proposition* (Highlands, N.C.: Jargon, 1953); *The Kind of Act of* (Mallorca: Divers, 1953); *The Gold Diggers* [f] (Mallorca: Divers, 1954); *All That Is Lovely in Men* (Highlands, N.C.: Jargon, 1955); *If You* (SF: Porpoise, 1956); *The Whip* (Worcester, Engl.: Migrant, 1957); *A Form of Women* (NY: Jargon / Corinth, 1959)

Edward Dorn: *What I See in the Maximus Poems* (Ventura: Migrant, 1960); *The Newly Fallen* (NY: Totem, 1961)

Robert Duncan: *Heavenly City, Earthly City* (Berkeley: Bern Porter, 1947); *Poems 1948-49* (Berkeley: Berkeley Miscellany Editions,

1949); *Medieval Scenes* (SF: Centaur, 1950); *Song of the Bor-
derguard* [b] (Black Mountain, N.C.: Black Mountain College,
1952); *Caesar's Gate* (poems 1949-50) (Mallorca: Divers, 1955);
Letters: Poems 1953-56 (Highlands, N.C.: Jargon, 1958); *Se-
lected Poems* (1942-50) (SF: City Lights, 1959); *Faust Foutu*
[d] (Stinson Beach, Calif.: Enkidu Surrogate, 1960); *The
Opening of the Field* (NY: Grove, 1960)

Larry Eigner: *From the Sustaining Air* (Mallorca: Divers, 1953);
On My Eyes (Highlands, N.C.: Jargon, 1960)

Lawrence Ferlinghetti: *Pictures of the Gone World* (SF: City Lights,
1955); *A Coney Island of the Mind* (NY: New Directions, 1958);
Selections from Paroles by Jacques Prévert [t] (SF: City Lights,
1958); *Tentative Description of a Dinner Given to Promote the
Impeachment of President Eisenhower* [b] (SF: Golden Moun-
tain, 1958); *Her* [f] (NY: New Directions, 1960)*

Edward Field: *Stand Up, Friend, With Me* (NY: Grove, 1963)

Allen Ginsberg: *Howl and Other Poems* (SF: City Lights, 1956);
Empty Mirror (poems 1948-51) (NY: Totem, 1960)*; *Kaddish —
Poems 1958-1960* (SF: City Lights, 1961)

Madeline Gleason: *Poems 1944* (SF: Grabhorn, 1945); *The Meta-
physical Needle* (SF: Centaur, 1949)

Barbara Guest: *The Location of Things* (NY: Tibor, 1960)

Jack Kerouac: *The Town and the City* [f] (NY: Harcourt, Brace,
1950); *On the Road* [f] (NY: Viking, 1957); *The Subterraneans*
[f] (NY: Grove, 1958); *The Dharma Bums* [f] (NY: Viking,
1958); *Doctor Sax* [f] (NY: Grove, 1959); *Maggie Cassidy* [f]
(NY: Avon, 1959); *Mexico City Blues* (NY: Grove, 1959); *Vi-
sions of Cody* [f] (NY: New Directions, 1959); *The Scripture of
the Golden Eternity* [p] (NY: Totem/Corinth, 1960); *Lone-
some Traveler* [f] (NY: McGraw-Hill, 1960); *Rimbaud* [b]
(SF: City Lights, 1960); *Tristessa* [f] (NY: Avon, 1960);
Book of Dreams [f] (SF: City Lights, 1961); *Pull My Daisy*
[s] NY: Grove, 1961); *Visions of Gerard* [f] (NY: Farrar,
Straus, 1963)

Kenneth Koch: *Poems* (NY: Tibor de Nagy, 1953); *KO, or A Season
on Earth* (NY: Grove, 1959); *Permanently* (NY: Tiber, 1960)*

Philip Lamantia: *Erotic Poems* (SF: Bern Porter, 1946); *Ekstasis* (SF:
Auerhahn, 1959); *Narcotica* (SF: Auerhahn, 1959)

Denise Levertov: *The Double Image* (London: Cresset, 1946); *Here
and Now* (SF: City Lights, 1957); *5 Poems* (SF: White Rabbit,

1958); *Overland to the Islands* (Highlands, N.C.: Jargon, 1958);
With Eyes at the Back of Our Heads (NY: New Directions, 1959)

Ron Loewinsohn: *Watermelons* (NY: Totem, 1959)

Michael McClure: *Passage* (Big Sur, Calif.: Jargon, 1956); *Peyote Poem* [pt. 1] [b] (SF: Semina, 1958); *For Artaud* (NY: Totem, 1959); *Hymns to St. Geryon and Other Poems* (SF: Auerhahn, 1959); *The New Book / A Book of Torture* (NY: Grove, 1961); *Dark Brown* (SF: Auerhahn, 1961)

David Meltzer: *Ragas* (SF: Discovery, 1959)

Frank O'Hara: *A City Winter and Other Poems* (NY: Tibor de Nagy, 1952); *Meditations in an Emergency* (NY: Grove, 1957); *Jackson Pollock* [p] (NY: Braziller, 1959); *Second Avenue* (NY: Totem / Corinth, 1960); *Try! Try!* [d], in Herbert Machiz, ed.: *Artists' Theatre: Four Plays* (NY: Grove, 1960)

Charles Olson: *Call Me Ishmael* [p] (NY: Reynal & Hitchcock, 1947; Grove, 1958); *Y & X* (Washington: Black Sun, 1950); *Letter for Melville, 1951* [b] (Black Mountain, N.C.: Black Mountain College, 1951); *Apollonius of Tyana* [p] (Black Mountain, N.C.: Black Mountain College, 1951; *Origin* No. 6, 1952); *This* [b] (Black Mountain, N.C.: Black Mountain College, 1952); *In Cold Hell in Thicket* (Dorchester, Mass.: Origin, 1953 [*Origin* No. 8]); *The Maximus Poems 1-10* (Highlands, N.C.: Jargon, 1953); *Mayan Letters* [p] (Mallorca: Divers, 1953); *Anecdotes of the Late War* [b] (Highlands, N.C.: Jargon, 1955); *The Maximus Poems 11-22* (Highlands, N.C.: Jargon, 1956); *O'Ryan* (SF: White Rabbit, 1958); *Projective Verse* [p] (NY: Totem, 1959); *The Maximus Poems* (NY: Jargon/Corinth, 1960); *The Distances* (NY: Grove, 1960)

Joel Oppenheimer: *The Dutiful Son* (Highlands, N.C.: Jargon, 1957)

Stuart Z. Perkoff: *The Suicide Room* (Highlands, N.C.: Jargon, 1956)

James Schuyler: *Alfred and Guinevere* [f] (NY: Harcourt, Brace, 1957)

Gary Snyder: *Riprap* (Ashland, Mass.: Origin, 1959); *Myths & Texts* (NY: Totem / Corinth, 1960)

Gilbert Sorrentino: *The Darkness Surrounds Us* (Highlands, N.C.: Jargon, 1960)

Jack Spicer: *After Lorca* (SF: White Rabbit, 1957); *Billy the Kid* (Stinson Beach, Calif.: Enkidu Surrogate, 1959)

Lew Welch: Wobbly Rock (SF: Auerhahn, 1960)

Philip Whalen: *Self-portrait, from Another Direction* [b] (SF: Auer-
    hahn, 1959); *Like I Say* (NY: Totem, 1960) ; *Memoirs of an
    Interglacial Age* (SF: Auerhahn, 1960)

John Wieners: *The Hotel Wentley Poems* (SF: Auerhahn, 1958)

Jonathan Williams: *Red / Gray* (Highlands, N.C.: Jargon, 1952);
    Four Stoppages (Highlands, N.C.: Jargon, 1953); *The Empire
    Finals at Verona* (poems 1956-57) (Highlands, N.C.: Jargon,
    1959)

II. ANTHOLOGIES, ETC.

Daisy Aldan, ed.: *A New Folder. Americans: Poems and Drawings*
    (NY: Folder, 1959)

Robert Cooper, ed.: *Nine American Poets* (Liverpool: Heron, 1953)

Frederick Eckman: *Cobras and Cockle Shells: Modes in Recent Poetry*
    [p] (Flushing: Vagrom, 1958)

LeRoi Jones, ed.: *Jan 1st 1959: Fidel Castro* (NY: Totem, 1959)

Jonathan Williams, ed.: *Jargon 31: 14 Poets, 1 Artist* (NY: Jargon,
    1958)

Index to Little Magazines: 1948-52, ed. by Harriet Colgrove & others;
    1953-59, ed. by Eugene P. Sheehy and Kenneth A. Lohf (Den-
    ver: Alan Swallow)

III. RECORDINGS

Lawrence Ferlinghetti & Kenneth Rexroth: *Poetry Readings in the
    Cellar,* with the Cellar Jazz Quintet, Fantasy 7002 (1957); *Ten-
    tative Description of a Dinner Given To Promote the Impeach-
    ment of President Eisenhower and Other Poems* by Lawrence
    Ferlinghetti, Fantasy 7004 (1958)

Allen Ginsberg reads Howl and Other Poems, Fantasy 7006 (1959)

Jazz Canto, Vol. I: An Anthology of Jazz & Poetry, World Pacific
    WP-1244 (1958) [includes readings of poems by Ferlinghetti and
    Whalen]

Jack Kerouac & Steve Allen: *Poetry for the Beat Generation,* Hanover
    HML 5000 (1959); *Readings by Jack Kerouac on the Beat Gen-
    eration,* Verve MG V-15005 (1959); Jack Kerouac: *Blues and
    Haikus,* featuring Al Cohn and Zoot Sims, Hanover HM 5006
    (1959)

IV. CHIEF PERIODICALS

The Ark: Sanders Russell, ed. (1947); *Ark II / Moby I*: Michael Mc-
Clure & James Harmon, ed's. (1956); *Ark III*: James Harmon, ed.
(1957), San Francisco

Beatitude: (1959-61), San Francisco

Big Table: Paul Carroll, ed. [Irving Rosenthal, ed. of No. 1] (1959 –),
Chicago.

Black Mountain Review: Robert Creeley, ed. (1954-57), Black
Mountain College, Black Mountain, N.C.

Chicago Review: Irving Rosenthal, ed. (Vol. XI, No. 4; Vol. XII, No's.
1-3, 1958), Chicago

Contact: Raymond Souster, ed. (1952-54), Toronto

Evergreen Review: Barney Rosset, ed. [Donald Allen, co-editor of No's.
1-8] (1957 –), New York

Folder: Daisy Aldan & Richard Miller, ed's. (1953-56), New York

Foot: Richard Duerden, ed. (1959), San Francisco

Four Winds: Vincent Ferrini, ed. (1952-53), Gloucester

Fragmente: Rainer M. Gerhardt, ed. (1951-52), Freiburg im Breisgau

Goad: Horace Schwartz, ed. (1951-53), Columbus & Sausalito

Golden Goose: Richard Wirtz Emerson & Frederick Eckman, ed's.
(1948-54), Columbus

i.e., The Cambridge Review: Leo Raditsa & Angus Fletcher, ed's.
(1954-56), Cambridge

Jabberwock 1959: Alex Neish, ed. (1959), Edinburgh

Measure: John Wieners, ed. (1957-58), Boston

Montevallo Review: Robert Payne, ed. (1950-53), Montevallo, Ala.

New Directions Annuals: James Laughlin, ed. (1936 –), New York

Origin: Cid Corman, ed. (1951-57, 1961-), Ashland, Mass.

Poetry: Karl Shapiro, ed. (1950-55); Henry Rago, ed. (1955 –), Chi-
cago

Yūgen: LeRoi Jones, ed. (1958 –), New York

ALSO OF VALUE:

Artisan (1953-55, Liverpool), *Berkeley Bussei* (1955-58, Berkeley),
Berkeley Miscellany (1947, Berkeley), *Botteghe Oscure* (1949 –,
Rome), *Circle* (1944-48, Berkeley), *The Fifties* (1958 –, Pine Island,
Minn.), *Four Pages* (1948, Galveston), *Hearse* (1958 –, Eureka,
Calif.), *The Naked Ear* (1956-59, Ranches of Taos, N.M.), *Neon*
(1956 –, Brooklyn), *Poetry New York* (1949-51, New York), *Pros-*

pect (1959 –, Cambridge, Engl.), *Quarterly Review of Literature* (1943 –, Annandale-on-Hudson, N.Y.), *Semicolon* (1954-57, New York), *Sparrow* (1954 –, Flushing), *The White Dove Review* (1959 –, Tulsa)

V. ADDRESSES OF PUBLISHERS:
Auerhahn Press, 1334 Franklin St., San Francisco 9, Calif.
City Lights Books, 261 Columbus Ave., San Francisco 11, Calif.
Corinth Books, Inc., 32 West 8th St., New York 11, N.Y.
Discovery Books, 241 Columbus Ave., San Francisco 11, Calif.
Enkidu Surrogate, 3735 20th St., San Francisco 10, Calif.
Folder Editions, 325 East 57th St., New York 22, N. Y.
Golden Mountain Press, 539 Vallejo St., San Francisco 11, Calif.
Grove Press, Inc., 80 University Place, New York 3, N.Y.
Jargon Books: Jonathan Williams, Highlands, N.C.
Migrant Press, 1199 Church St., Ventura, Calif. (or, 2 Camp Hill
    Road, Worcester, Engl.)
New Directions, 333 Sixth Avenue, New York 14, N.Y.
Origin Press, 214 Main St., Ashland, Mass.
Tibor de Nagy Editions, 149 East 72nd St., New York 21, N. Y.
Totem Press, 402 West 20th St., New York 11, N.Y.
Vagrom Press, P.O. Box 25, Flushing 52, N.Y.

INDEX OF AUTHORS

453